Light, Shadow & Skin Tone

The Complete Guide to Shooting Black & White Glamour Photography Digitally and on Film

Bill Lemon

Light, Shadow & Skin Tone: The Complete Guide To Shooting Black & White Glamour Photography Both Digitally And On Film

BILL LEMON

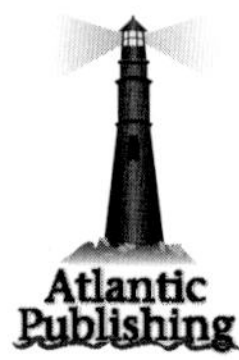

Published by Atlantic Publishing Group, Inc.
1405 SW 6th Avenue • Ocala, Florida 34471 • 800-814-1132 • 352-622-1875–Fax
Web site: www.atlantic-pub.com • E-mail: sales@atlantic-pub.com
SAN Number: 268-1250 • Member American Library Association

ISBN-13: 978-1-60138-390-7 • ISBN-10: 1-60138-390-8

Library of Congress Cataloging-in-Publication Data
Lemon, Bill.
Light, shadow & skin tone : the complete guide to shooting black & white glamour photography both digitally and on film / by Bill Lemon.
p. cm.
Includes bibliographical references.
ISBN-13: 978-1-60138-390-7 (alk. paper)
ISBN-10: 1-60138-390-8 (alk. paper)
1. Glamour photography. 2. Black-and-white photography. I. Title. II. Title: Light, shadow, and skin tone.
TR678.L459 2009
778.3--dc22

2009038451

10 9 8 7 6 5 4 3 2

COVER & INTERIOR DESIGN: Meg Buchner • megadesn@mchsi.com

Printed in the United States.

Acknowledgments

If it came down to it, I could write a book by itself thanking all the people who have helped me achieve what I have over the years. To start with, my two daughters and my five grand kids: Logan, Sean, Andersen, Kayla, and little Patrick.

To name some of my closest friends who have been there to help me when I needed them: Spencer, Arthur, Erik, Dutch, Lyn, and Ernie. Also, thank you to my attorney, Dale Reicheneder, for his consultation on past and present publications.

And a big thank you goes out to all the photographers who have taken my workshops over the years. I've met some wonderful people through the workshops, people who come back year after year and take more than one workshop a year. Hopefully I'm doing something right!

And to all the models I've photographed over the years; with all your hard work and patience, you have helped me create some wonderful images. You'll see some of these in this book.

To Doug Brown and Meg Buchner of Atlantic Publishing, thank you for your enthusiasm in publishing this book. A big thanks to Meg for the layout of this book.

Again, thanks to all of you.

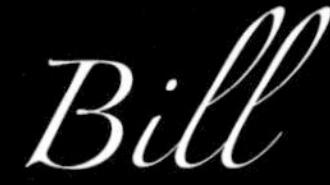

Foreword

Bill Lemon has done it again: He has created his fifth book on photography that celebrates the female form. Bill has the ability to see his subjects and bring out their best. He sees models' finer points, and combines this with his ability to use light to create spectacular images. I've known this photographer for about 15 years, and his talent and eye amaze me.

Many years ago, my father told me to look for people in life who have achieved success and who understand perfection. He told me to mimic those people. Mimicking a lighting style or great pose is, to me, the highest form of flattery. You cannot copyright a pose or lighting style, so learn from the best — and Bill Lemon is one of them.

In order to employ his lighting and posing techniques, women are the architecture for his art. His tool is his camera. The images in this book illustrate a photographer who loves — perhaps adores — women. They are his obsession and passion in life. Viewing the images of women in this book awakens our senses to beauty and form, as Bill has the ability to project class, beauty, and art in his photography. He understands the finer points of posing and creates a documentary of true beauty in his books.

You will learn from a photography genius in Bill Lemon's latest book.

Art Ketchum, Art Ketchum Studios
Author of *Painting the Body Beautiful: A Showcase of Expert Body Painting*

Introduction

I am known for my distinctive type of glamour photography, which is typically of female models in unique settings. I specialize in capturing the beauty of nature along with the beauty of the female form. To do this, I often utilize natural light both in the studio and outdoors.

In this book, you will read about my photography philosophy and see my methods through visual examples. You will learn what elements make a successful black and white photo, and see ways to effectively convert digital color images to black and white.

Who Should Read This Book

This book is for photographers who have an understanding of photography and photographic terms. Of course, anyone can simply enjoy the images. However, in order to learn to emulate my style, you need to already know how to use a camera, light meter, and supplemental lighting.

How To Use This Book

I believe in teaching through example — you know the old saying, "a picture is worth a thousand words." This book is a collection of my images, some shot on film and some shot digitally. Each image has a description about what makes the image work or what makes it unique. I include technical specifications for each image to use as a starting point for you to recreate a similar type of image. I also point out the strengths and weaknesses of the photo, or ways the photo could have been changed or improved.

Before reviewing the images, I strongly suggest you read the following section. All photographers work in different ways. Here are my primary methods of shooting, as well as general tips for models, lighting, and software.

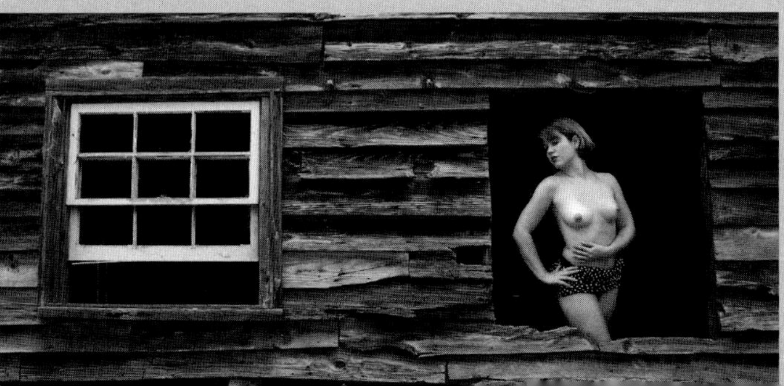

Bill Lemon's Photography Methods

Shooting By F-Stop

A good glamour photograph is more than just a beautiful model. It is a combination of lighting and composition. When setting up a glamour photo session, I begin by surveying the entire location, either in studio or outdoors. I determine how I want to showcase the model. Will she be interacting with elements, such as outdoors under a waterfall? If so, the background needs to be clear. Do I want the focus to be on the model and make the background elements more a blurred pattern? Every situation is different, especially outdoors. I tend to concentrate more on F-stops than shutters speeds. Shutter speeds will always vary, based on the type and amount of light. The F-stop determines the type of image that will result, because it regulates the distance from focus point A to Z.

Most of my photos have an F-stop value from 5.6 to 8.0. This creates a pleasing composition where the background has definition. Regulating the F-stop can change the depth of field.

Using a Light Meter

I always use a separate, hand-held light meter. A good light meter can be as important as, if not more than, your camera. This provides an accurate reading that you can use to set the histogram within your camera. I personally like the line of Sekonic® light meters. Many fit in the palm of your hand, measure all different types of lighting, and can process and provide results for incandescent and strobe lighting. What a light meter ultimately allows you to do is get an accurate, precise camera setting that will make post production easier.

Do not rely on the image in the LCD screen of your digital camera. It isn't accurate. If you do not have a light meter, or want to double-check your light, the histogram can be useful. The histogram graph will show you how the light is distributed in your picture. There should not be large spikes on either the left or right side of the histogram, as then your image will be either under- or over-exposed.

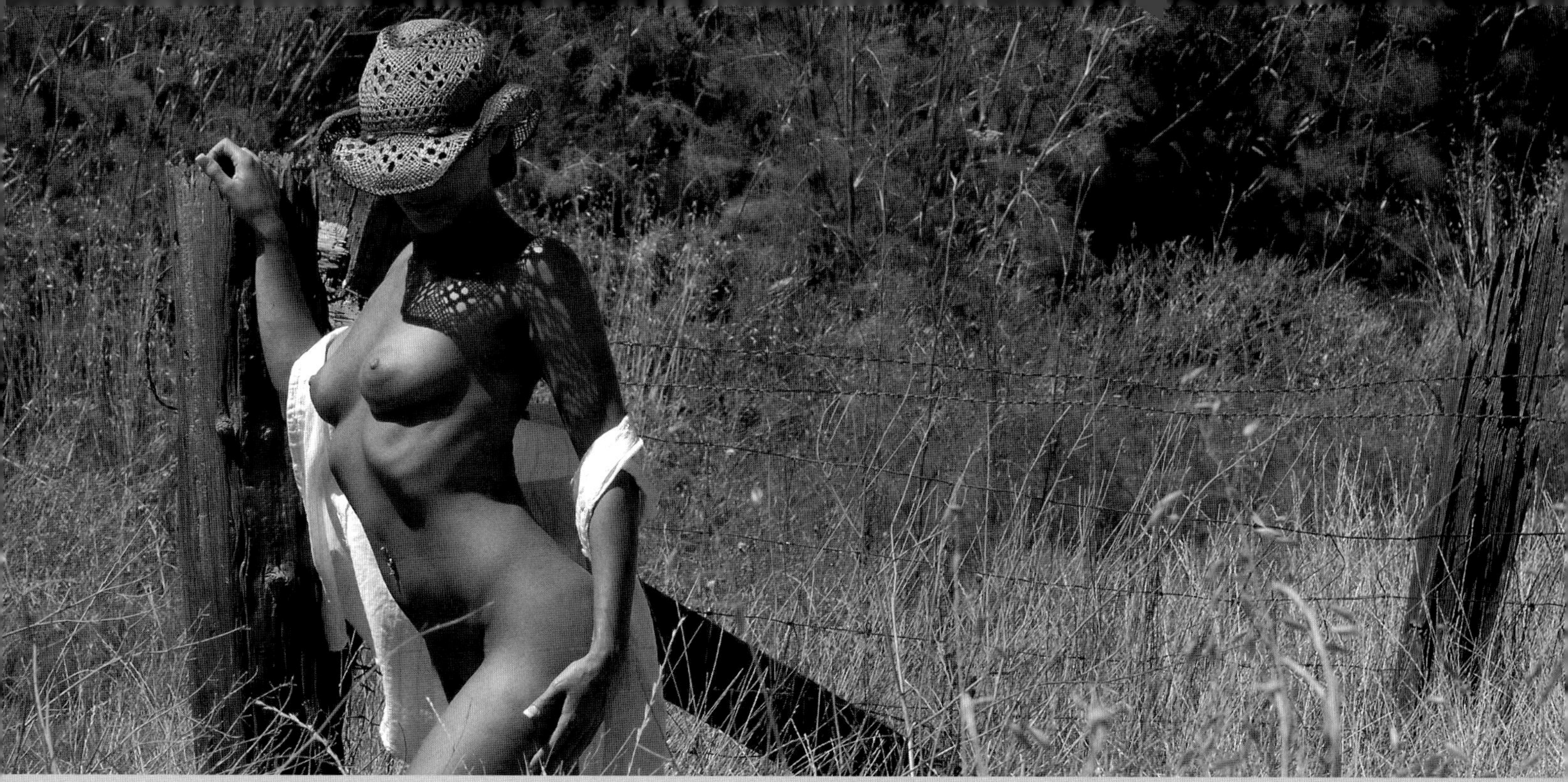

Black and White Photography

Black and white photography is a classic type of photography. It reduces photos to their most basic elements of patterns of light and dark. It is simple yet sophisticated. Black is black, white is white, and everything else is a shade of gray.

Shooting black and white glamour photography has advantages and disadvantages. It can soften and smooth skin tones. It can enhance drama in an image and emphasize composition. Creating effective black and white photos can be challenging. The world is in vibrant color and the photographer has to mentally block out the distraction of color and look for contrast and tone. When you are shooting with a digital camera, you may find that a gorgeous color image does not convert well to black and white at all (see the examples in the color insert section of this book).

There are two fundamental elements for creating successful black and white images: contrast and texture. You will notice that I mention them again and again in this book to reinforce why an image works.

Shooting with Film

Film is a classic. Different films have different effects: some have different mid tones, some have blacker blacks, some have more grain. Working with film requires more skill and precision as a photographer. It's a good idea to shoot a Polaroid first to get an impression of how the image will work. It is possible to do some correcting of exposure and other problems in the darkroom, but not as much as you can do digitally.

You will see a number of images in this book shot with film. I believe a good photographer should be able to work with both film and digital images and the results should be almost the same.

Disadvantages of Film

I find that film has one major disadvantage: cost. I shoot more conservatively when working with film and will limit my number of exposures. I also take a limited number of rolls of film along when working on location, so I am less willing to take chances with lighting, location, or poses.

Shooting Digitally

The world has moved into the digital age and so has photography. Almost all the images I shoot now have been taken digitally. I primarily use a Nikon D300.

Advantages of Shooting Digitally

Digital cameras have a number of advantages. The histogram assists with exposures by showing light distribution. Digital photography is much more flexible. You immediately see a screen capture of your image and are able to fix small details, such as hand placement. You are no longer limited by how many rolls of film you have, and you can shoot an almost unlimited number of poses or try a different location when shooting outdoors.

You are able to shoot in a number of formats including TIF, RAW, and JPG. I shoot 98 percent of the images I capture in Fine JPEG, due to storage. While raw format provides much greater flexibility in correcting poorly exposed images or mixed lighting images, it takes a vast amount of space to store such images. They are significantly larger on the camera than a Fine JPEG image, and when they are transferred to your computer, they will require a second transfer to either TIF or PSD format, and then again to JPEG, requiring a large collection of images that take up even more space, a costly and space-consuming option.

Exposures When Shooting Black and White Digital Photography

Black and white exposure is much different than color. As long as you do not over-expose an image, which causes you to lose detail, you can correct exposure problems with editing software.

Editing Software

There are many software programs available for viewing, editing, and retouching your digital photos. I use Adobe Photoshop® CS4 with Nik Software's Complete Collection Ultimate Edition. These are Photoshop plug-ins, which include Dfine® 2.0, Viveza™, Color Efex Pro™ 3.0, Silver Efex Pro™, and Sharpener Pro™ 3.0. You can read more about the product line and download 15-day trial software at **www.niksoftware.com**. If you are interested in purchasing any of the Nik plug-ins, use the promotional code BLEMON and receive a 15 percent discount.

Silver Efex Pro™ is especially effective for converting color images to black and white. It has a comprehensive collection of black and white film types, such as Agfa AP X Pro, Kodak™ 100 T-Max Pro, Fuji™ Neopan Acros 100 and Kodak™ Plus X, just to name a few. You simply select the type of film you want to emulate and apply it to your image.

There are also a number of presets in Silver Efex Pro™ where you can quickly correct exposure, change contrast, use sepia toning, and more. These are good starting points for image conversion. You can also create your own presets. For more details on Silver Efex Pro™, as well as screen shots on some of my favorite methods within the software, turn to the color conversion section in the center of this book.

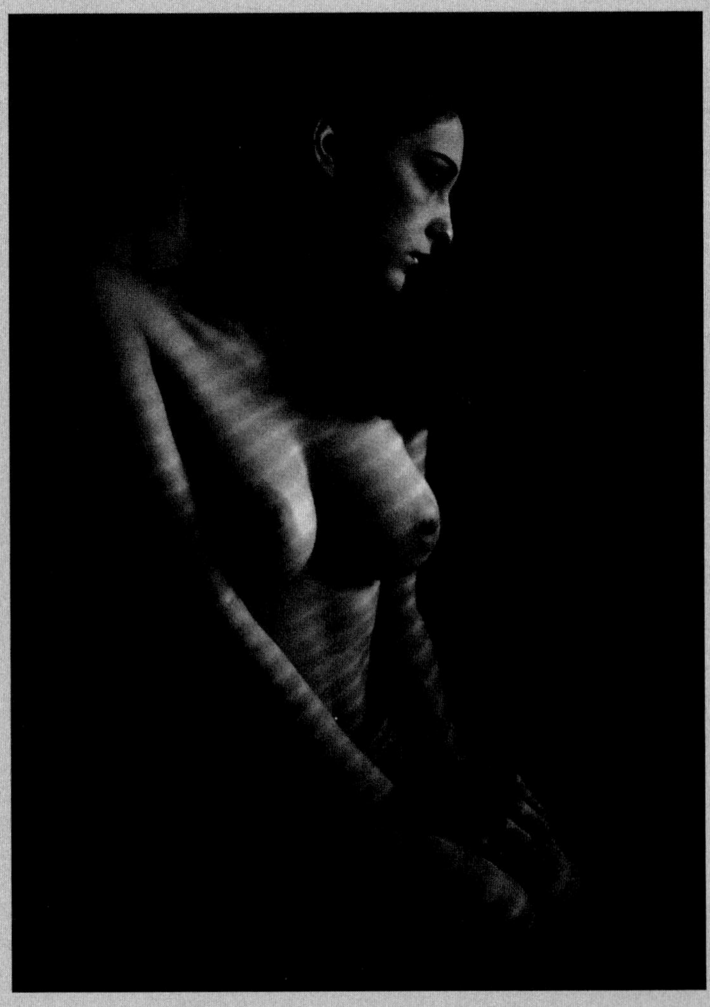

Models

Finding Models

In order to find models, I suggest the following Web sites:

- **www.onemodelplace.com**
- **www.modelmayhem.com**
- **www.modelbrigade.com**

When contacting a model, you should maintain a professional demeanor at all times. It is very helpful if you have an established presence on the above sites or have your own Web site and portfolio for a model to view. My Web sites are: **www.billlemon.com**, **www.billlemonworkshops.com**, and **www.fashionglamourphotography.com**. I also maintain a Facebook® page and models contact me there as well.

Communicating with a Model Before Shooting

Being able to effectively communicate with a model is one of the most important things you can do in creating quality images. It allows you to detect the personality and energy in a model as well as the willingness to go that extra mile in creating a good image. I insist on talking with every model on the phone before the shoot. Often, they are content to communicate via e-mail, but I want to hear their voices and for them to hear mine. This is helpful in communicating and getting to know each other better before the shoot begins.

There are certain things I like to ensure before a shoot even begins. What is the goal of the image? What are we trying to accomplish? Is there a particular look or style we are trying to emulate? If we can decide these things early on, the model will know what clothing she needs and how to prepare before a shoot even begins.

Communicating with a Model While Shooting

During the shoot, I like to continually talk to the model so I can tell her exactly what I want her to do. Some models are extremely good at what they do, and will only require a little fine-tuning on the photographer's part. It is important to communicate and make these adjustments, but it is equally important to always maintain a friendly rapport, being polite and positive the entire time. It will cut down on shooting and post-production time, producing better images in the process.

Things to Watch For with Models

Here are three critical things to watch for when a model is posing: eyes, hands, and leg position.

Eyes. Often, I see images with the head turned too far while still looking at the camera, which shows too much white in the eye. If the head is turned to the side, have the model look away from the camera to reduce the chance of bad eye placement within the shot.

Hands. Look for hand placement. If the model's fingers are wide open, they will look more like an open claw than the soft, flowing female hand that you are trying to capture.

Legs. For standing poses, if the model bends her leg, it should be the leg closest to the camera. This creates the nice S-curve that can truly accentuate the shape of the model's body.

Another important factor to be aware of is the model's position within the composition. Avoid horizontal lines that might appear in the background and cut through important lines of her body, such as neck, eyes, or upper torso. This can break apart the body and result in an uneven shot with awkward cuts. Include arms in your list of possible cutting points to watch. Often in images, I see arms hidden behind door jambs, looking as though they have been cut off at the shoulder. This is exactly the kind of division in the composition you must avoid.

Hair Color and Models

Models come in all shapes and sizes. You need to build your shoot around the model you are working with. In black and white photography, skin tone and hair color are key factors because you need contrast for an effective black and white photo.

If you are working with a dark-haired model and you want her to separate from the background, you need to place her against a light-colored background. The opposite is true for a light-haired model.

You can also get dramatic effects by placing a dark-haired model against a dark background. This works best if she has fair skin for contrast. Her hair will blend into the background and cause the skin to really stand out. Below are two examples of models shot in the same setting, one with dark hair and one with light.

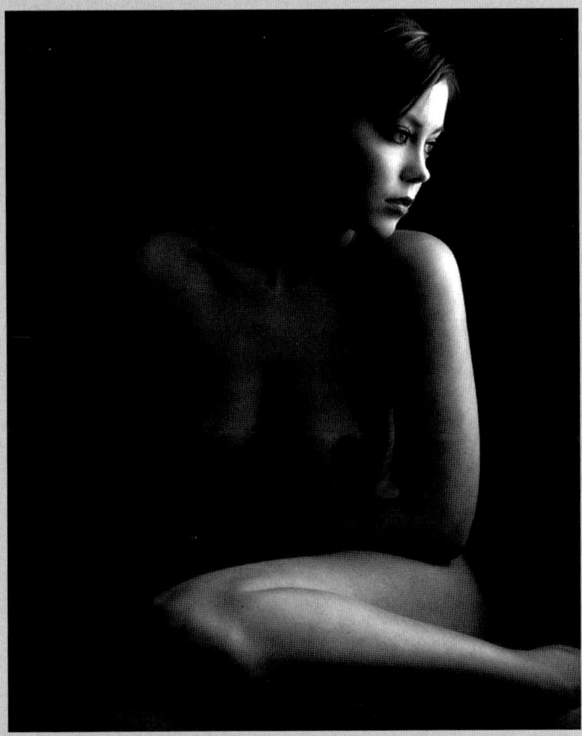

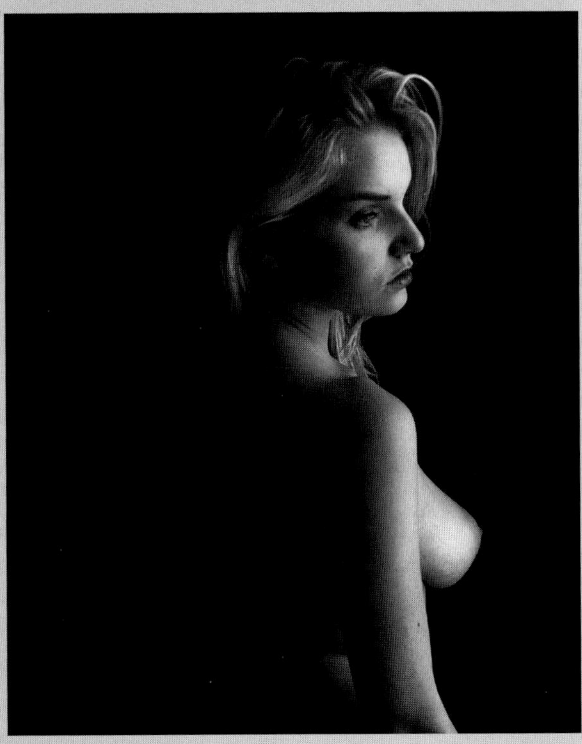

Shooting In Studio

Shooting black and white images in a studio can be easier than outdoors because you have more control over your lighting and contrast. You can work with a black background and a nude model and have her hair and skin tone provide the contrast, as in the images at left.

You can have both white and black in the background and have the model be the only shades of gray. The variations are endless. You can see many examples of studio set-ups and poses throughout this book. I tend to keep my studio set-ups simple with more emphasis on contrast, the sensuality and beauty of the female form, and the impact of dramatic lighting.

Shooting Outdoors

When shooting outdoor black and white photography, you want to look for two things: contrast and texture.

Contrast

An effective setting will have many areas of contrast — places that are both dark and very light. Look for settings that have deep shadows and patches of bright sunlight. Remember to look at the tones in an area and think about how they will translate to black and white. A bright yellow flower will convert to a light gray. A deep blue cloudless sky may be a gorgeous background for a tan or darker skinned model in the color image but provide very little separation in black and white. Often a blue sky with large, white cumulus clouds provides better contrast.

Be aware that you can add contrast to an image simply by what the model is wearing or holding. I always have an article of solid white clothing and an article of solid black clothing for this purpose. Pages 56 and 57 include examples where using clothing adds contrast to a photo.

Texture

Texture can be found everywhere outdoors. Trees, grass, bushes, and foliage are all wonderfully textured backdrops. I look for locations that have multiple levels of texture, or sharply contrasting textures. In black and white, these will translate to patterns of gray. The more textured the background, the better it sets off the smooth, delicate skin of the model. A textured background can be as simple as a field of grass. It still has wonderful texture, as demonstrated in the image below.

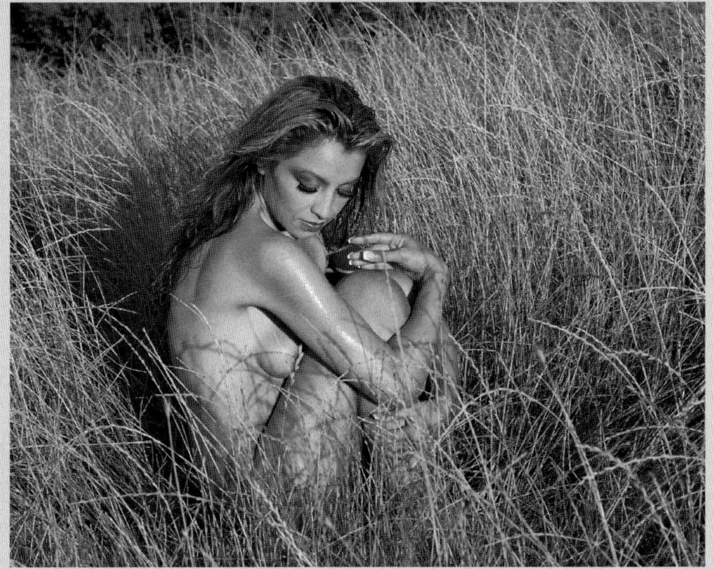

The Beauty of Nature

I like to create images that compare and contrast the beauty of nature with the beauty of the female form. To do this, I will often encompass more of the landscape in the frame, making the model less of a focal point and more of a contrasting element. See pages 16, 17, and 110 for examples of this.

Contrasting Elements

When working outdoors, look for beauty in unexpected places. I have shot some amazing images in rusted-out old cars, on top of tractors, and in concrete drain pipes. Placing a beautiful model in an area that is hard, rough, or masculine immediately creates contrasting elements in a composition.

Be Natural

My photos have a signature look and part of that is taking advantage of natural beauty in models, location, and lighting. I encourage you to work on developing your artistic eye and to take advantage of the world around you for your glamour photography.

Lighting

To me, lighting is the most important element in photography, whether outdoors or in a studio. I treat the sun as just another light source and work to take advantage of natural light whenever possible. I enjoy natural light because it is always a challenge and never the same. Light changes based on the location, time of day and season of the year. There are no equations or set rules for working with natural light; you have to be flexible and work with the given conditions. That being said, I do have some general pointers.

- **Be aware of the sun's location.** Know where the sun rises and sets in your area and how the season will affect the light. Sunset and sunrise are at different times every day of the year.
- **Sunlight is directional.** The sun is at its highest point in the sky at noon. Mid-afternoon light is very bright. It can cast harsh shadows on a model's face, so I often have a model tip her head back, look up, and close her eyes in mid-afternoon sun. Mid-afternoon sun can also create the most dramatic shadow areas in patches of trees or other foliage.
- **Time of day.** Sunrise and sunset are beautiful times for outdoor glamour photography. The light is very soft, directional, and diffused. Dusk is my favorite time of the day to shoot.
- **The weather affects the light.** This may sound like an obvious statement, but there are so many weather factors that influence light. An overcast day can give very even lighting. This can cause dull, flat images without highlights. Smoke, fog, or mist in the air will act as a filter that gently diffuses the light. Clouds can not only create interesting backgrounds in the sky; they can break up light and make it patchy.

I use supplemental lighting outdoors. Flash fill can be very effective and I have detailed how it is used on a number of images throughout the book. On the following page, you will find diagrams of three of my most common ways to use supplemental lighting outdoors.

FIGURE 1

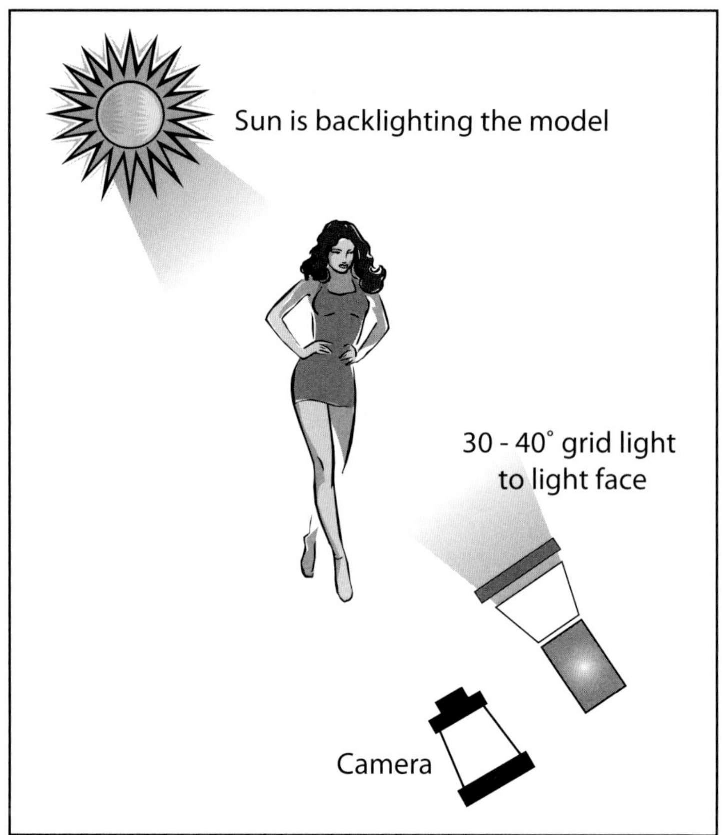

FIGURE 2

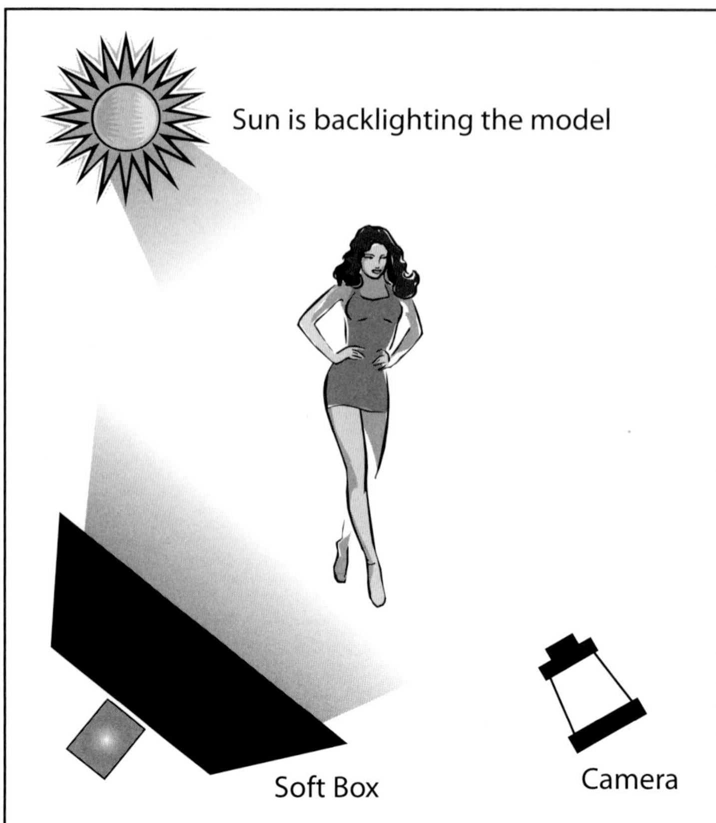

FIGURE 3

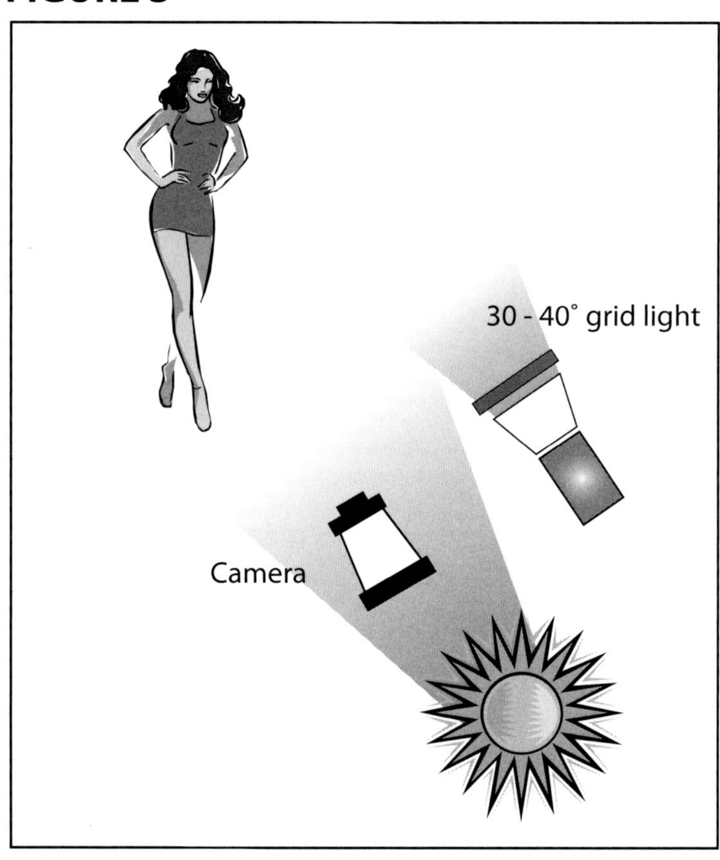

In these examples, the sunlight would be directional (not directly overhead). These lighting set-ups would work best in the morning or late afternoon to mid-evening.

Figure 1

In this diagram the sun is backlighting the model. I use a 30- 40° grid as fill light for the model. This softens and diffuses the light.

Figure 2

In Figure 2, the sun is also backlighting the model. I add a large soft box to soften and fill to the image. Depending on the placement of the light, to shadowing to the opposite side of the model.

Figure 3

In this diagram the sun is behind the camera, which creates even lighting on the body. By adding a 30- 40° grid, the light on the face is strengthened.

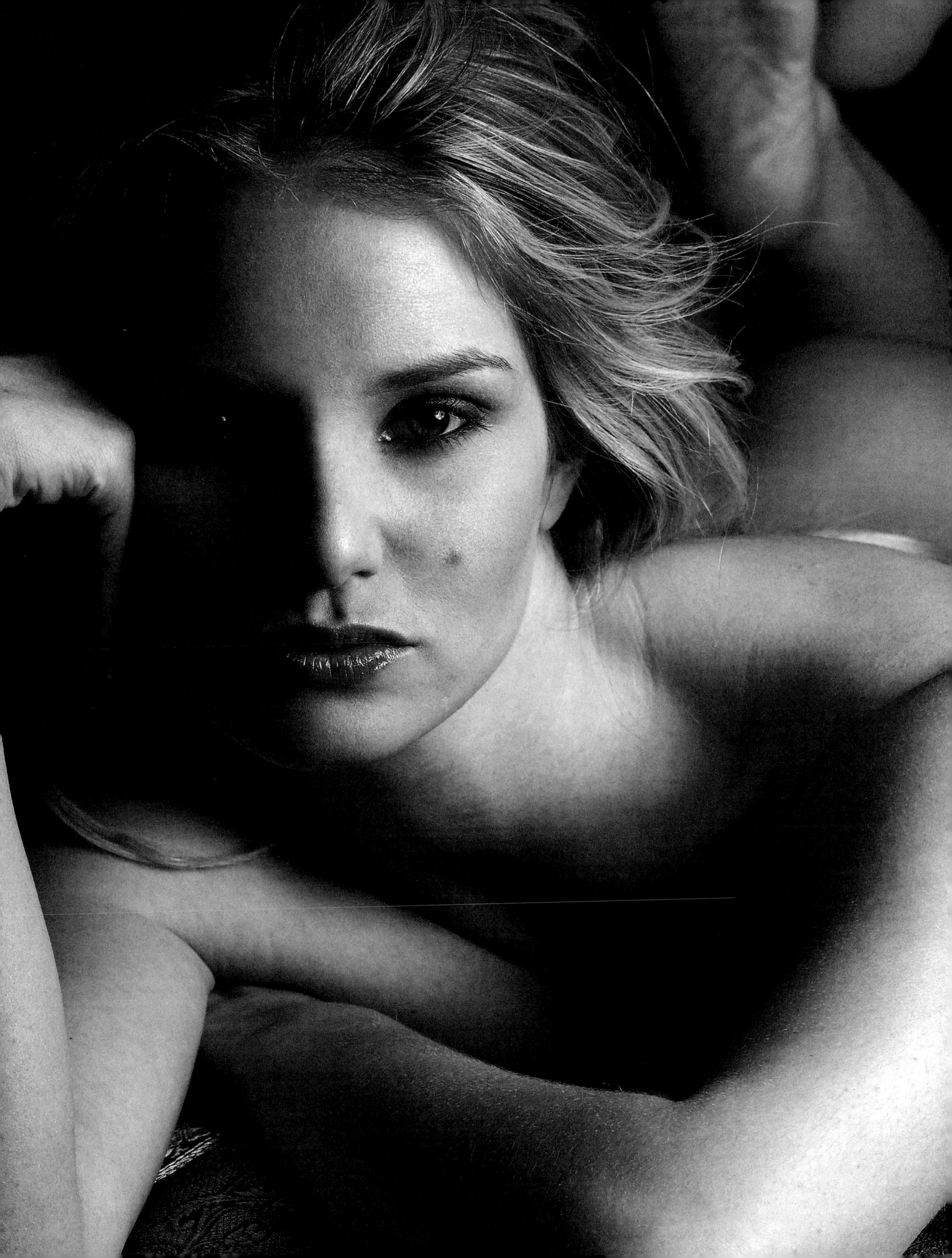

Shadows

The image on the preceding page is a classic example of simple, yet striking, black and white photography. Shot in my Novato studio, this image utilizes soft, early morning light as well as flash fill. The right side of the model's face is in shadow, emphasizing the beautiful angles of her face as well as the fullness of her lips. The shadows also enhance the model's skin by adding depth.

Pose

To create a sensual, almost sassy image, the right pose is crucial. This pose is casual, comfortable, and relaxed. The right hand by her face adds contrast to the upper left section of the image. The model is also making eye contact with the camera, and her serenely confident expression lends to the overall feeling of sensuality.

Camera: Nikon D200

Lens: Nikon 70-300VR

Shutter Speed: 125th Second

F-Stop: 10.0

Mode: Digital color conversion

Model: Liz

hint

Be aware of the model's clothing and how it impacts the image. In this image, the edge of the model's panty line can be seen at the top of her shoulder. The effect here is minimal, but it could be removed in Photoshop®.

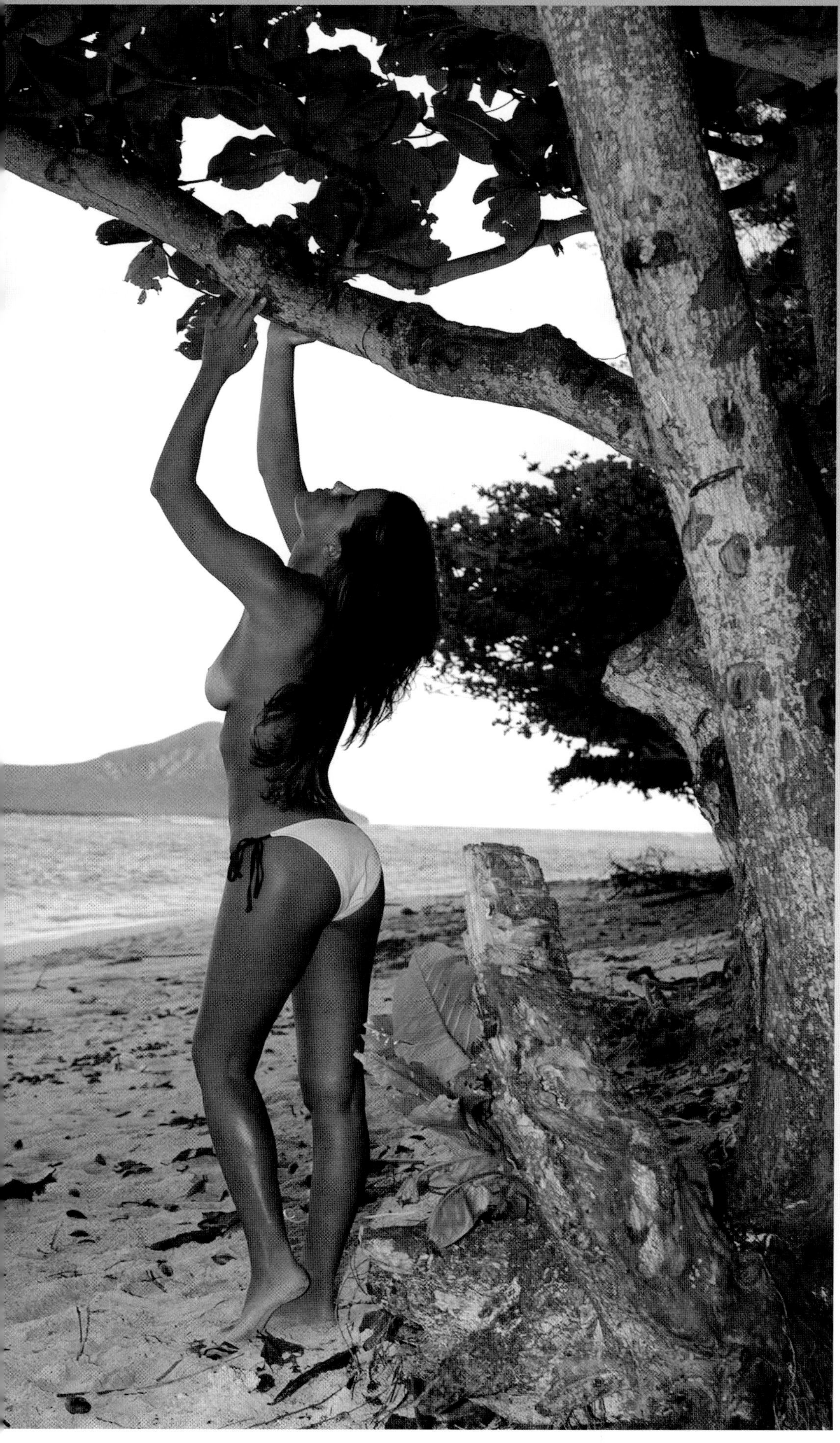

Location

Shot in Hawaii, the scenic location adds to the beauty of this image. However, a tropical landscape is not necessary to create a stunning photo. This image is effective because of the multitude of textures found in the vegetation, sand, tree bark, and water. The tree frames the image and serves as a prop for the model.

Pose

Having the model reach up and grasp the tree creates sensual angles with her arms and lifts her breasts. Her bent leg also adds curves and dimension to the pose.

Contrast

Contrast is always critical in black and white photography. Note how the model's darker skin tone and dark hair is framed by the light background. Her bikini bottoms also add another area of lightness to the photo and give separation to the image.

Camera: Nikon D100

Lens: Tamron 28/75

Shutter Speed: 180th Second

F-Stop: 7.5

Mode: Digital color conversion

Model: Karen

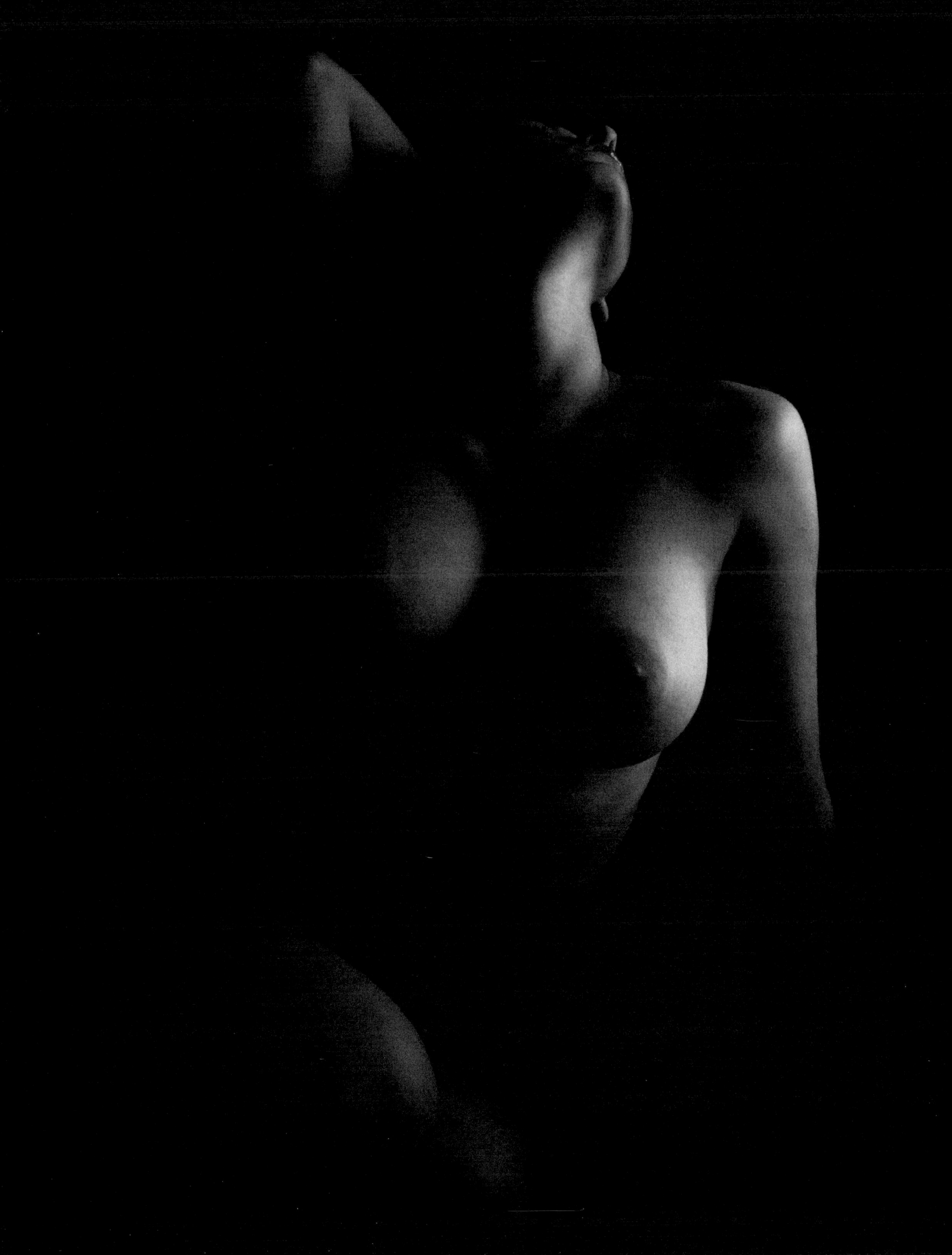

Lighting

The image at left was shot in my Novato studio with only the early morning eastern light from a window. It creates soft, directional light across the right side of the model's body. Don't be afraid to experiment using natural window light indoors; it can bring spectacular results.

Black

There is nothing more dramatic in black and white photography than the effective use of black. A rich, solid black background allows the photographer to create unique lighting situations where portions of the model's body merge seamlessly with the background. This adds an air of mystery to the image. It is as if the model is sculpted in shadows.

Pose

This pose is unique because the model's head is tilted back, almost entirely obscuring her face. The light hits the neck and right breast, illuminating only portions of the body. This brings an artistic, almost abstract quality to the image. The arm behind the head adds another interesting angle, as do her bent legs.

Camera: Nikon D100

Lens: Nikon 28/75

Shutter Speed: 60th Second

F-Stop: 2.8

Mode: Digital color conversion

Model: Carlotta

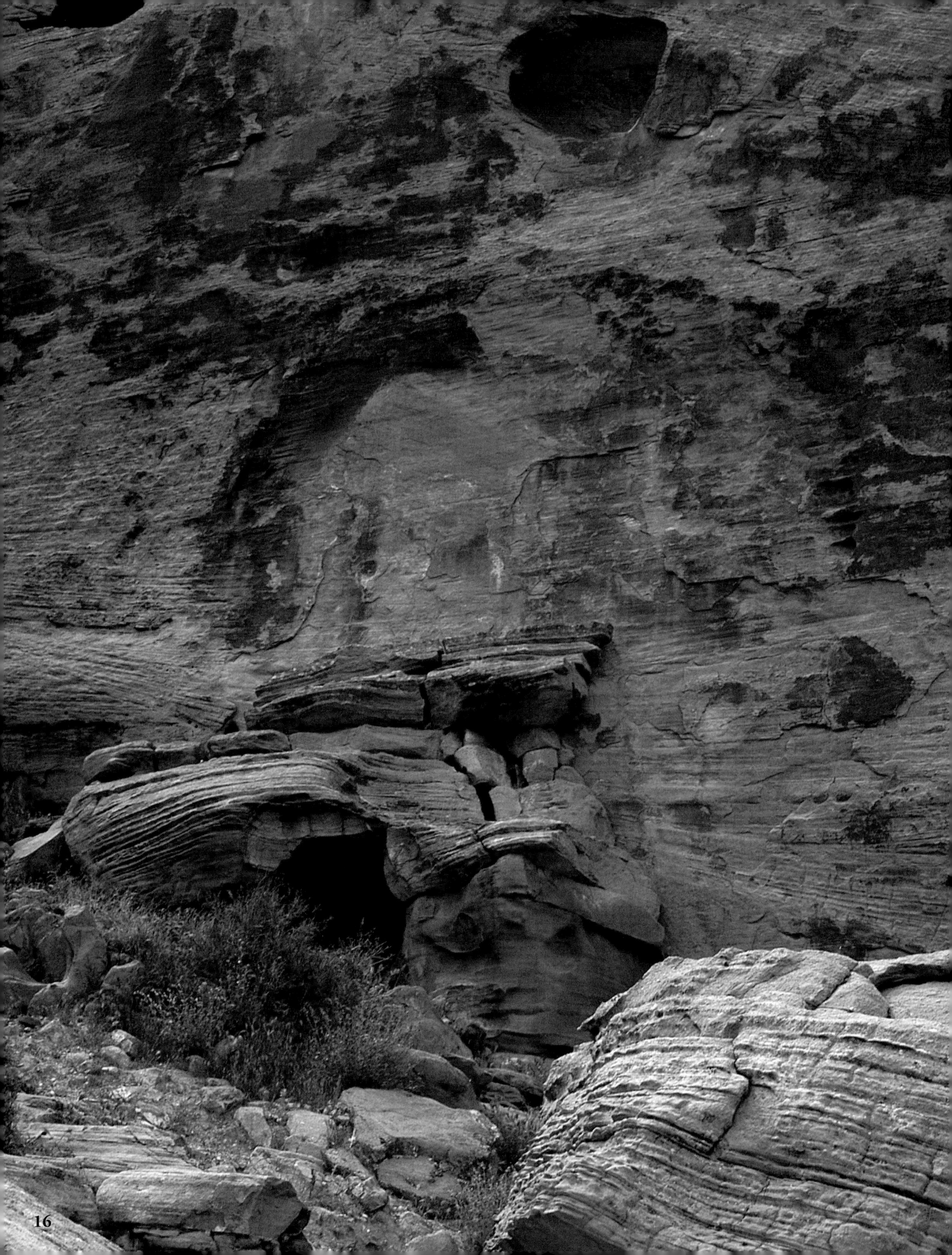

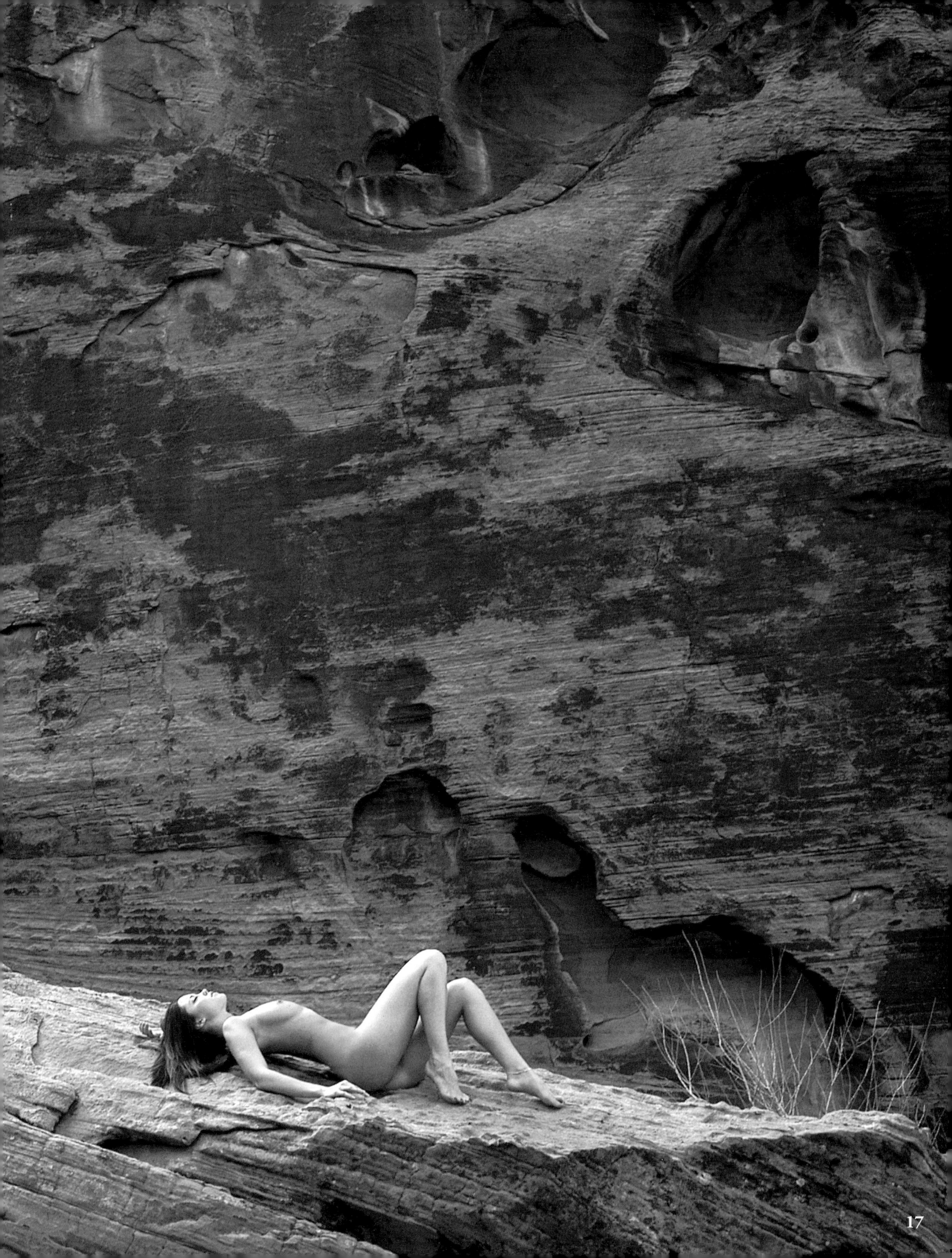

Landscape

The double-spread image on pages 16 and 17 was shot in the Valley of Fire in Nevada. My goal was to capture the immenseness and beauty of the area. When on location, it is a good ides to take in the whole area and look for opportunities to capture scenic backgrounds. Outdoor glamour photography does not always have to focus solely on the model. Shooting from a distance with the model smaller in the foreground creates a fresh, vibrant type of image.

Composition

By not placing the model in the center of the image, I have created a flowing left-to-right image. Notice the prevalence of horizontal lines in the striations of the rocks and the angle of the model's body. This was done intentionally to present an image of beauty in harmony with nature.

Pose

The elongated pose is very artistic and dramatic. The arched back and bent legs help create additional shadows to add definition. The model's dark hair provides exceptional contrast with the rock she is laying on; it also provides a focal point and helps anchor the image.

Camera: Nikon D100

Lens: Tamron 28/75

Shutter Speed: 125th Second

F-Stop: 8.0

Mode: Digital color conversion

Model: Brooke

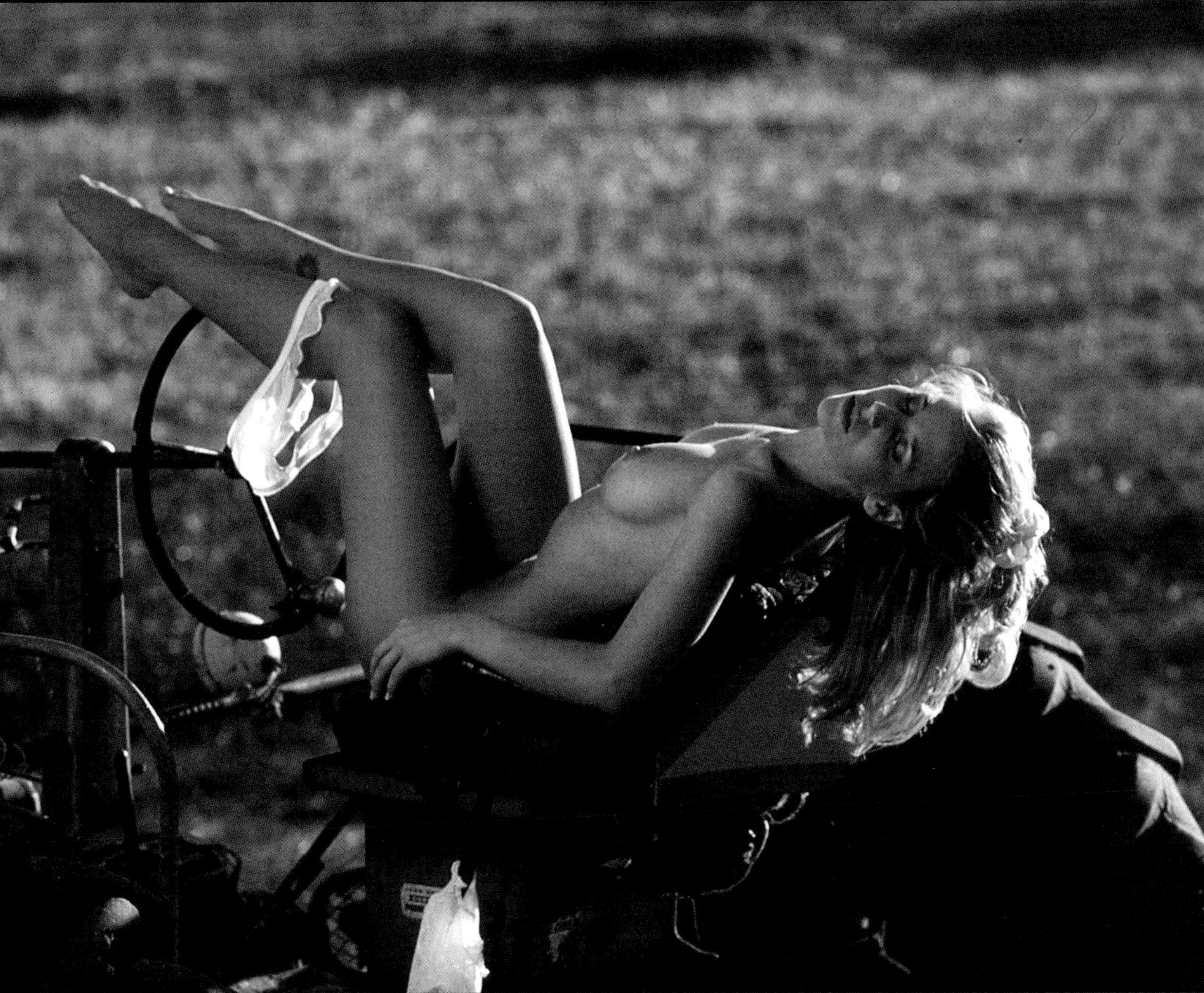

Lighting

This image was taken as part of series for *Playboy*®. It was shot in the late afternoon so the model would be back lit. A reflector was used to light the front portion of the scene. The gentle play of sunlight on the model's hair and her pose lends to a feeling of relaxation and basking in the warmth of the day.

Clothing

The model started fully clothed and slowly disrobed. This image is particularly alluring with just the white panties on her leg, adding a bit of mystery to the image.

Shades of Gray

Black and white photography is composed of a multitude of gray tones. A successful image has true black blacks and white whites as well as a wide range of grays. Although this image was shot with color Kodak Ektachrome film, it converts well to black and white. The tire provides rich darkness while the highlights from the sun and stark whiteness of the discarded lingerie provide white. The field in the background creates an abstract textured background to contrast with the model's smooth skin.

Camera: Nikon FM

Lens: Nikon 80/200 mm

Mode: Ektachrome film

Model: Kirstin

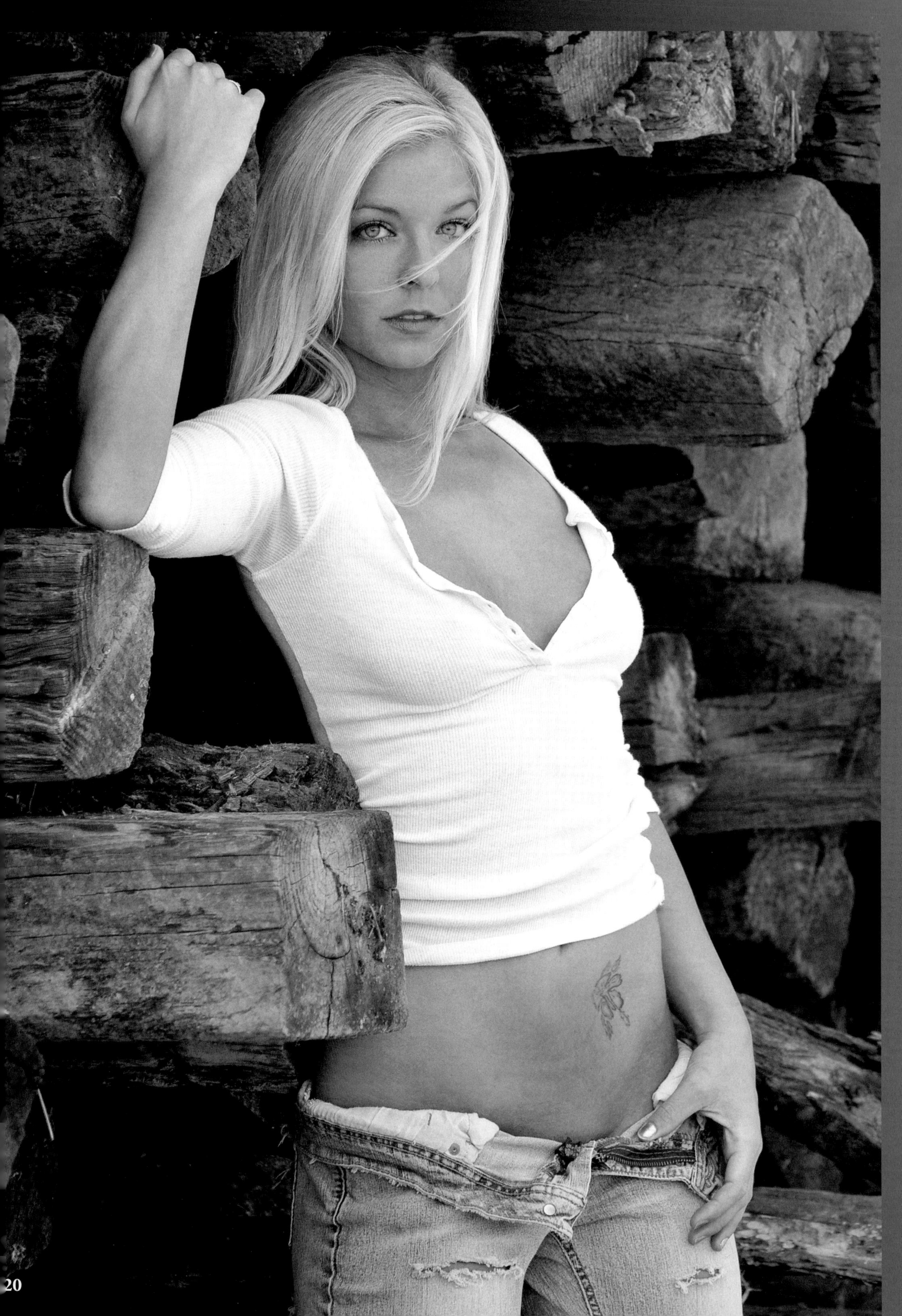

Setting

This image, shot in Sonoma County, shows the model in front of a stack of old railroad ties. I chose the background specifically because it provides outstanding contrast for this model. With her light hair, light skin, and white clothing, the shadows behind her create separation from the background. In addition, the rough wood grain adds another dimension of texture to the image. Keep in mind that a simple setting can yield outstanding results.

Clothing

When shooting glamour photography, don't discredit the allure of everyday clothing. Here the model is wearing a plain white henley, and unbuttoning it added sensuality. The seductive feeling is enhanced by her unbuttoned, slightly lowered, ripped jeans.

Camera: Nikon D300

Lens: Nikon 70-300VR

Shutter Speed: 125th Second

F-Stop: 6.3

Mode: Digital color conversion

Model: Tina

tip

There are many ways to convert color digital photography to black and white (see the color inset section of this book for a detailed description). Adobe Photoshop® has a "convert to grayscale" function. However, for this image I used the plugin Nik Silver Efex Pro®, which allows added control, more precision, and has excellent time-saving pre-sets.

Communicating with Models

The images on pages 22 and 23 were taken during the same photo session, shot in Sonoma. The location is a field of yellow California poppies, which provide a soft, feminine, beautiful backdrop. It is an area of natural, wild beauty. In both images, I used flash fill to properly light the model.

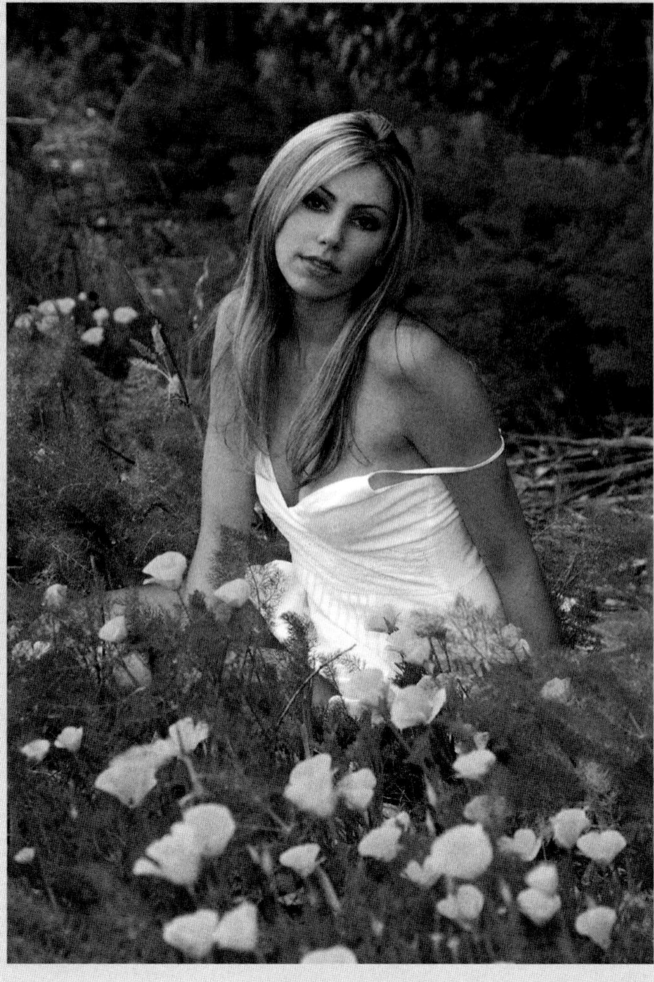

While obviously very similar, small nuances change the entire feel of the image. To achieve results like these, it is very important to establish clear communication with the model and be able to express exactly the type of image you want.

In the smaller image on this page, the feel is sweet, virginal, and softly seductive. It is more straightforward: a beautiful girl in a lovely location. I instructed the model to let her strap fall, but keep her breast covered to preserve the modest feel.

In the larger image at right, the feeling has changed completely. The image is still feminine, but now much more seductive. Some of the changes are obvious, some more subtle. Below is a list of directions I gave the model to change the effect of the image.

1. *Lean back and bring your right arm up to your neck.* This exposes more of the thighs and torso and shows that her dress has been pushed up slightly. Having the model lean back is more inviting and opens her body language. A woman touching her own skin, even her neck, makes the image much more sensual.

2. *Leave your strap on your arm and pull the front of the dress down on one side.* This makes the image overtly more suggestive. Be sure to discuss nudity with your model in advance so you know what she is comfortable with.

3. *Look into the camera, muss your hair, and give me a 'come hither' expression.* In the first image, the model tilted her head, which makes her look more girlish. Next she straightened her head and looked directly into the camera, which is much bolder. Her slightly rumpled hair gives her a more sexual air. The model obviously mastered the facial expression.

Camera: Nikon D300

Lens: Nikon 24/120VR

Shutter Speed: 250th Second

F-Stop: 6.3

Mode: Digital color conversion

Model: Sarah Rae

In a photo session, communication with the model is usually quick and fluid. You won't break it down into steps, but keep giving suggestions and tips until you achieve the look you want. Keep shooting as the model poses and moves. If a particular look is very striking, ask her to hold it. Give the model feedback and encouragement throughout the photo session and be open to her ideas and suggestions.

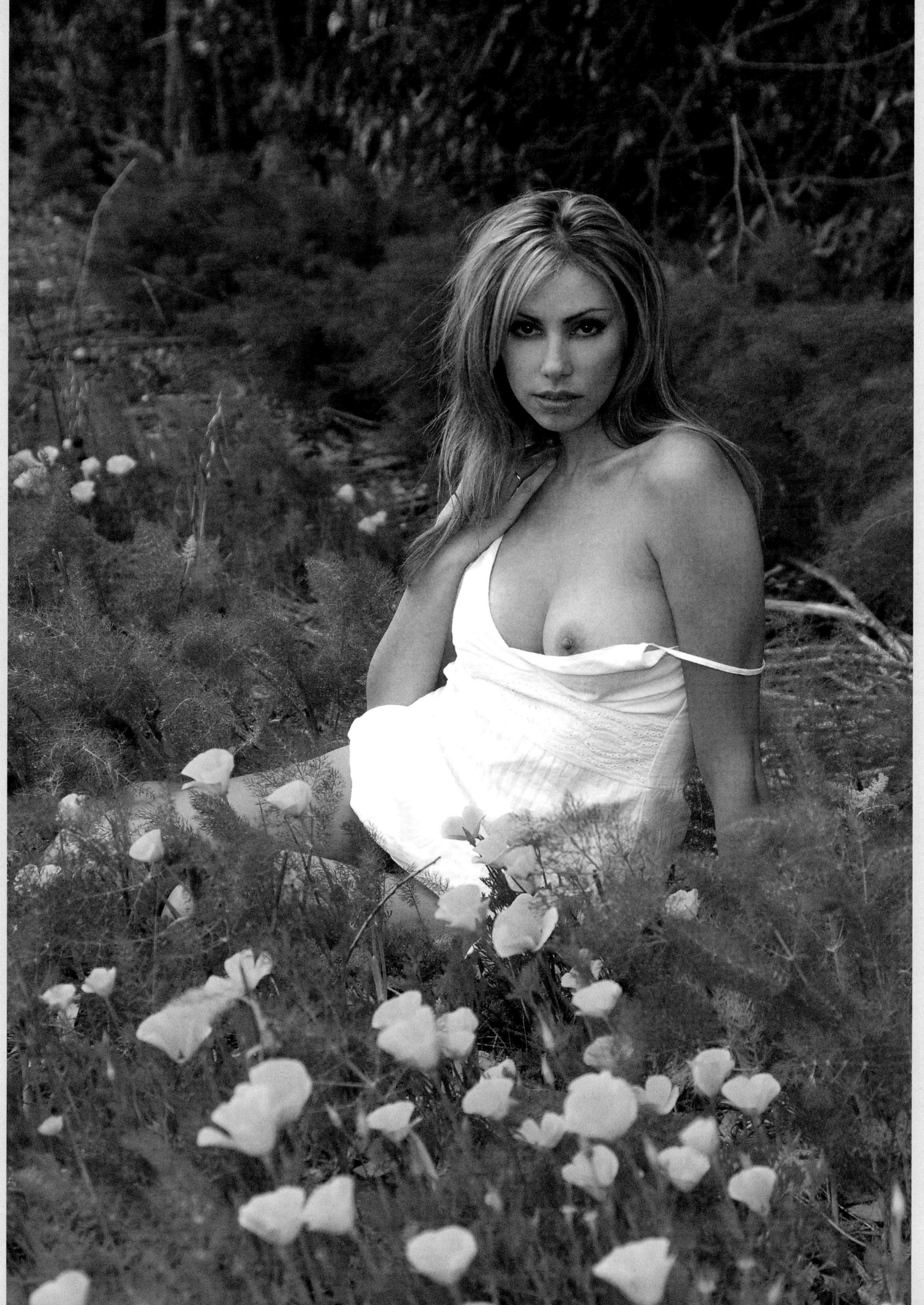

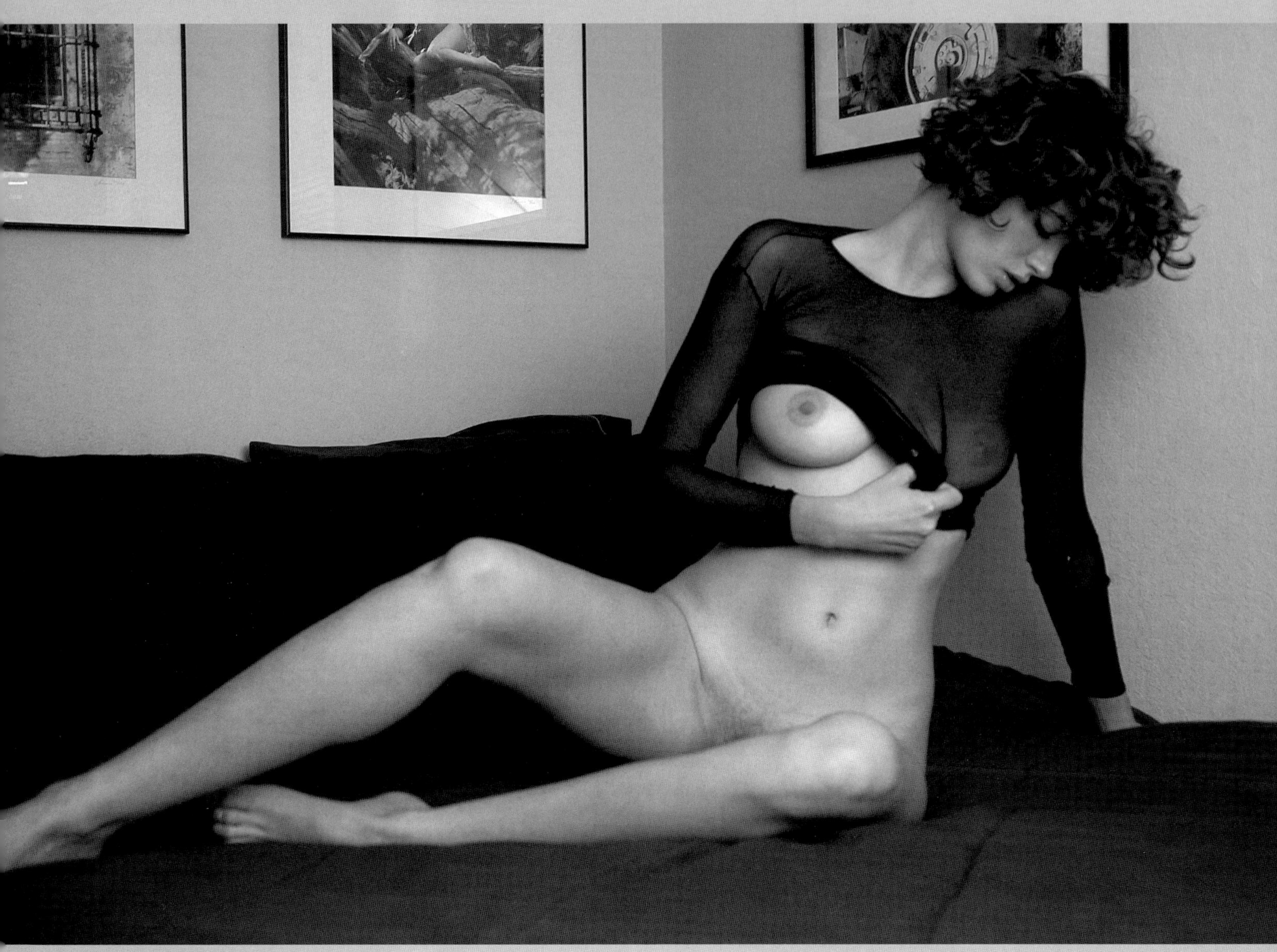

Composition

This studio shot was lit with a flash for even, constant lighting. It is a top-to-bottom study of contrasts. The viewer's eye flows from the model's dark hair, to the black shirt, to the black bedding, which enhances and sets off the model's fair skin and long legs. The black picture frames on the wall add continuity.

Cropping

Be aware of cropping. In this image, the model's right foot is cut off at the toes, something I typically try to avoid.

Expression

This is a unique image because it is slightly suggestive and intimate, while not being sexual or erotic. The model's short, curly hair has a tousled feeling and her half-dressed gesture lends to this. It is as if we have captured an introspective moment at the start of a beautiful woman's day. Effective glamour photography can have a voyeuristic, unposed feel to it, as this image demonstrates.

Camera: Nikon D100

Lens: Tamron 28/75

Shutter Speed: 125th Second

F-Stop: 3.2

Mode: Digital color conversion

Model: Helena

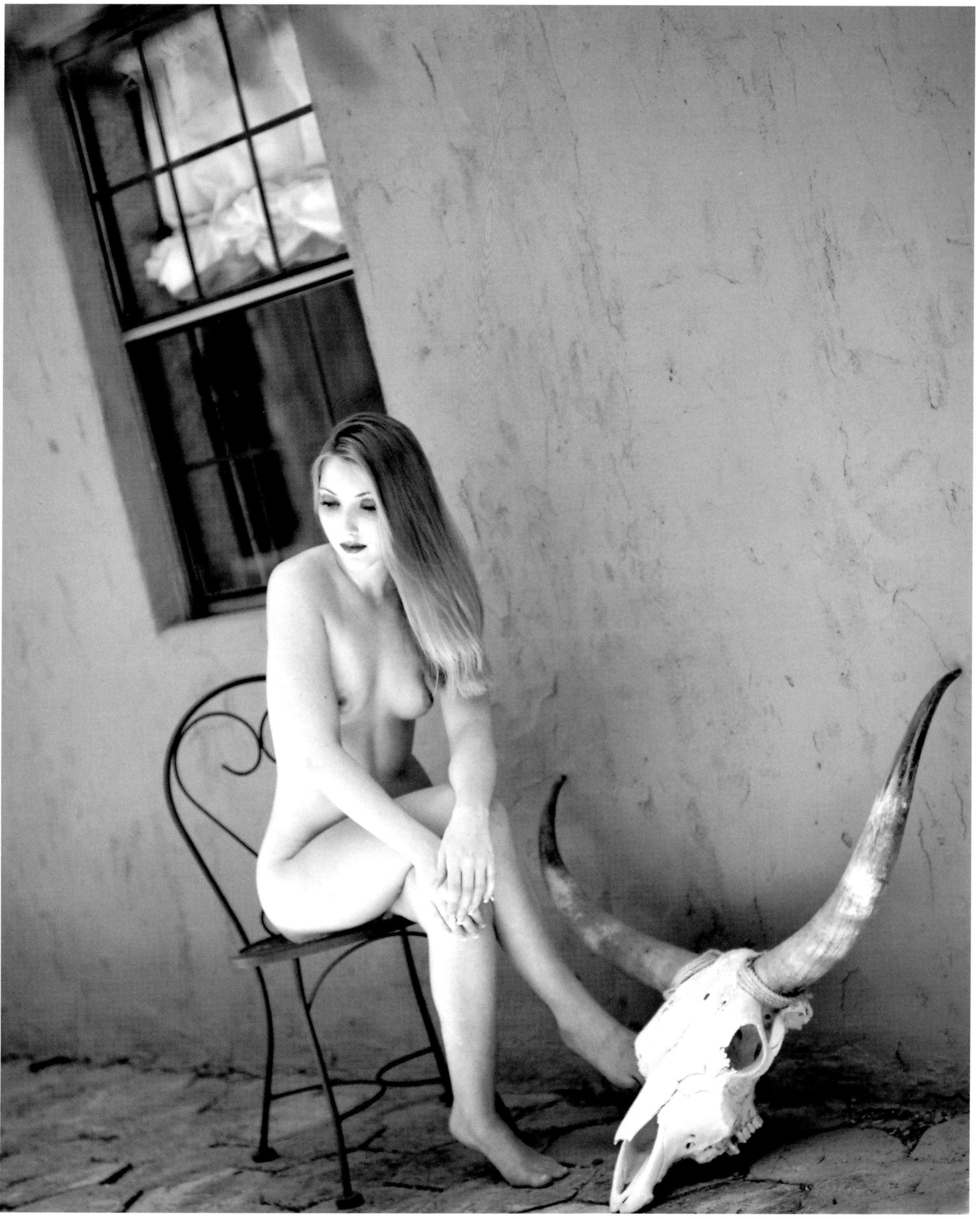

Location

Shot in Cave Creek, Arizona, the image on page 25 has a distinct Southwestern feel. The location was chosen for the available props and background textures. The rough stucco wall provides a subtle textured backdrop to contrast with the model's smooth, fair skin. Positioning the chair directly beneath the window leads the eye directly to the model.

Pose

The seated pose creates a sense of calm relaxation. Since the model is looking away from the camera it is also very introspective. Note how the model has her heel raised, which helps create definition in the leg. Her crossed legs also add to the wonderful, sensual curve of the waist and hip.

Camera: Pentax 67

Lens: 135 mm

Mode: Black and White Film

Model: Kara

hint

Props are a great way to create a sense of location or a certain feeling in a photo. When you are on location, look for props you can move to create the image you are seeking. For example, in this shot the skull was brought in to accent the Southwestern feel.

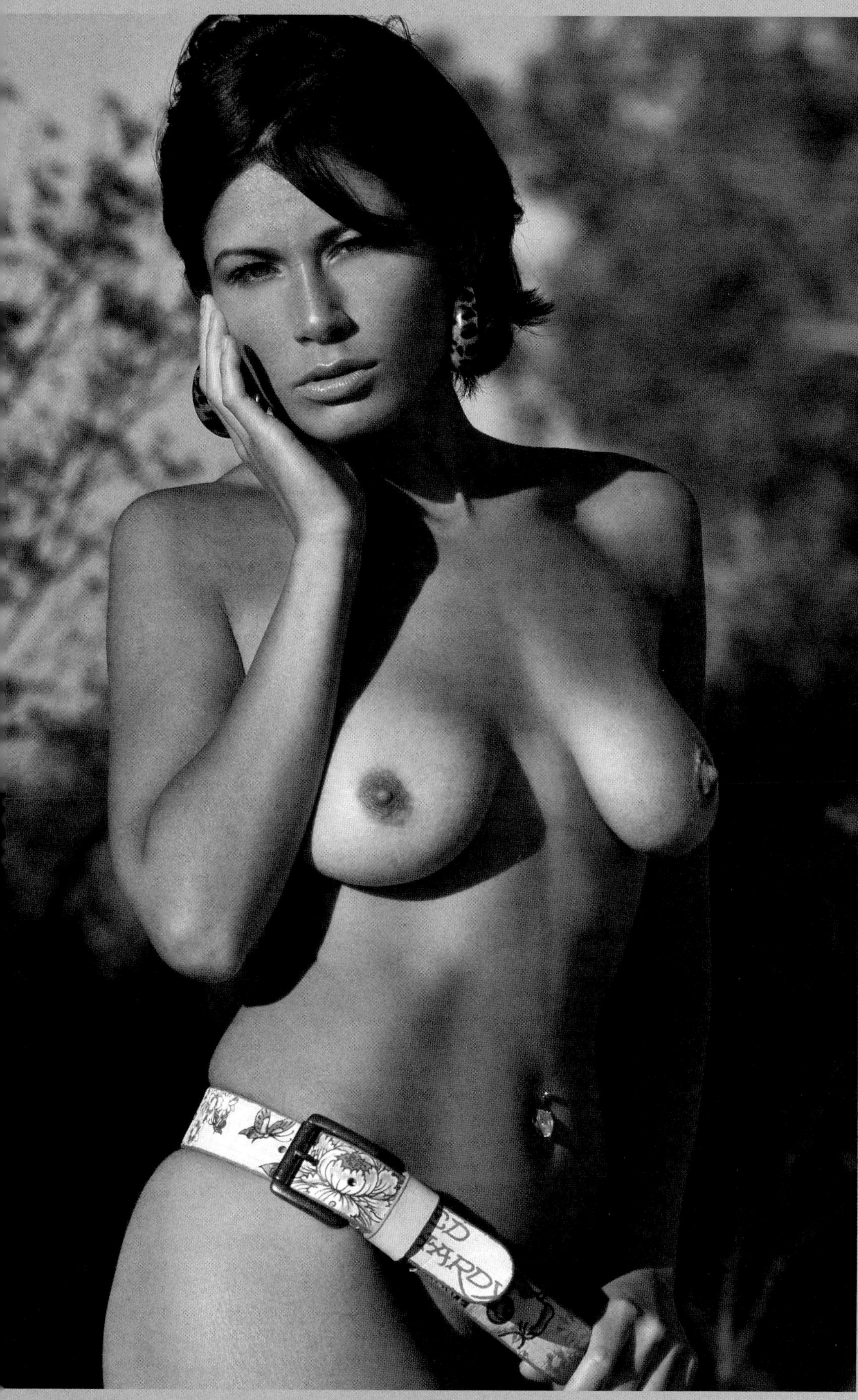

Gradient

This location was chosen for the strong light-to-dark gradient background. It provides exceptional top-to-bottom contrast and balance against the model's dark hair.

The background also affected other facets of the shot. The focus is tight on the model, so the depth of field is short, which causes the background to blur almost to the point of abstraction. This also affected the cropping. Normally I would not cut off the model's hand, but opening the frame would have lost the gradient background. Remember, there are no strict rules in glamour photography. Trying something slightly different can yield amazing results.

Accessories

Try unusual accessories, such as a belt, necklace or scarf. The Ed Hardy belt added a nice accent and gave the model a place to rest her hand. It also helped separate the upper and lower torso, defining the model's hip.

Camera: Nikon D300

Lens: Nikon 70/300 VR

Shutter Speed: 500th Second

F-Stop: 11.0

Mode: Digital color conversion

Model: Aurie

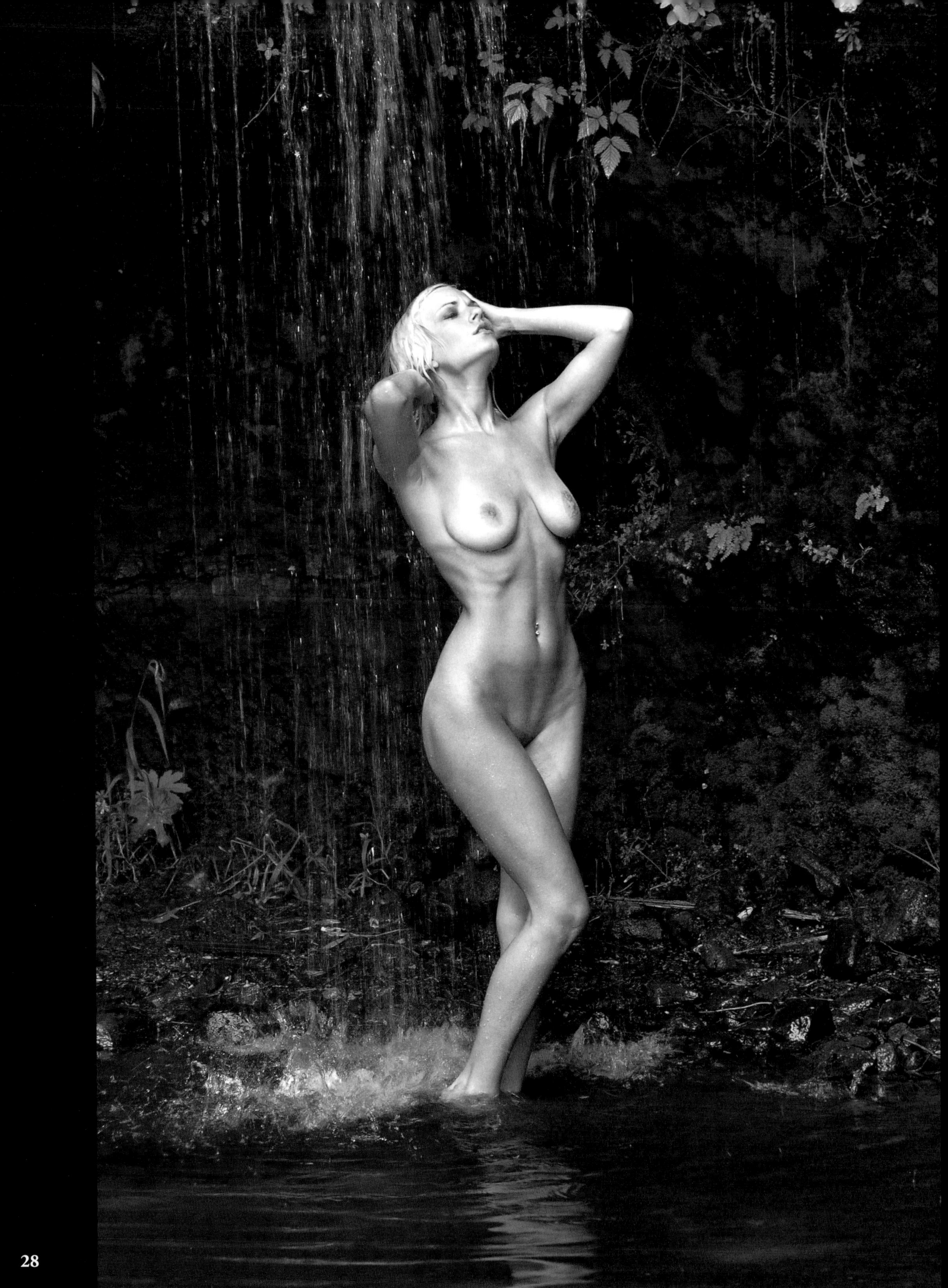

Location

This image was shot during a workshop in Mount Hood, Oregon. The model is standing under a natural waterfall. The affect of the water on her skin is very sensual. The various textures of the foliage provide a marvelous background, creating a sense of isolation and serenity with nature. The model's solitary reflection in the water enhances this feeling.

Lighting

Since this was shot in the late afternoon, there was not enough natural light to capture the location and illuminate the model. I used a portable strobe above the model. This produced a number of desired results. First, there is no shadow under the model's neck. Second, the falling water and uppermost leaves are illuminated, drawing the viewer's eye down the image. Finally, it amplified the model's fair skin, making her almost seem to glow.

Retouching

Many photos need minor retouching, so I tend not to go into detail about it unless I do something out of the ordinary. Here it was necessary to remove the shadow caused by the strobe light to maintain the natural setting and feeling. I also darkened the background slightly to accent to the model.

Camera: Nikon D300

Lens: Nikon 70/300 VR

Shutter Speed: 30th Second

F-Stop: 7.1

Mode: Digital color conversion

Model: Danielle

Contrast

I was looking to shoot a studio portrait that deviated from the norm. With a willing model and a bucket of mud, we created a number of striking, appealing images. The key was the simplicity of the images highlighted the texture. The custom painted background was slightly textured but subtle. The mud on the model's skin created texture all over her body and contrasted with her smooth skin. By framing her face with her hands and tilting her head, there is a very sensual, erotic quality to this image.

Lighting

This image was shot in my Novato studio using a large soft box for lighting. It was positioned about 45 degrees from the model at the left of the camera. This allowed for her hair to blend into the background and created shadows on the right side of her body with a defined edge on the right.

Camera: Pentax 67

Lens: 35mm

Mode: Black and White Film

Model: Jewel

hint

Introduce an unexpected element (like the mud) into a glamour photograph for new, unique results. Many models are willing to do something different to make their finished work stand out. Be creative and adventurous!

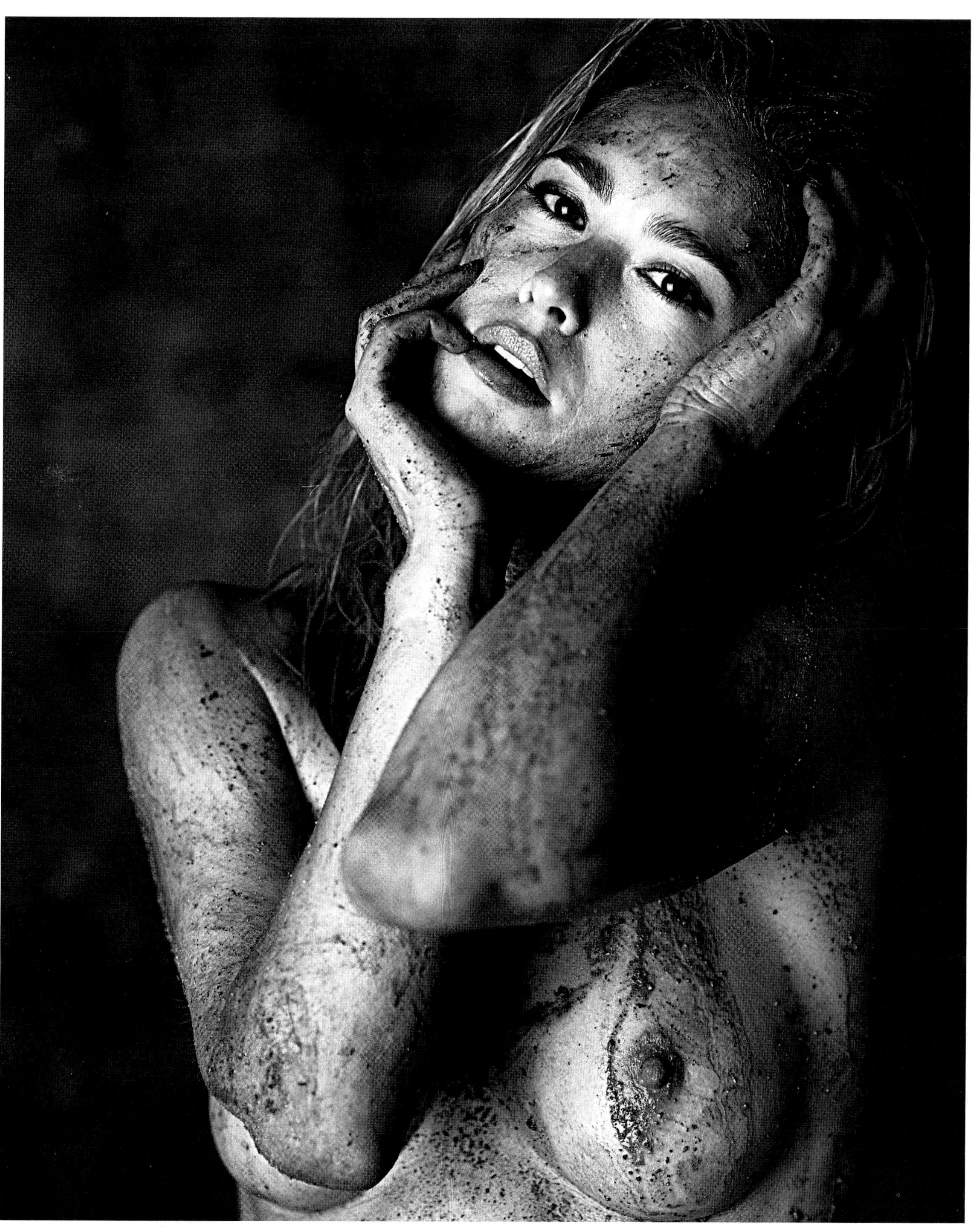

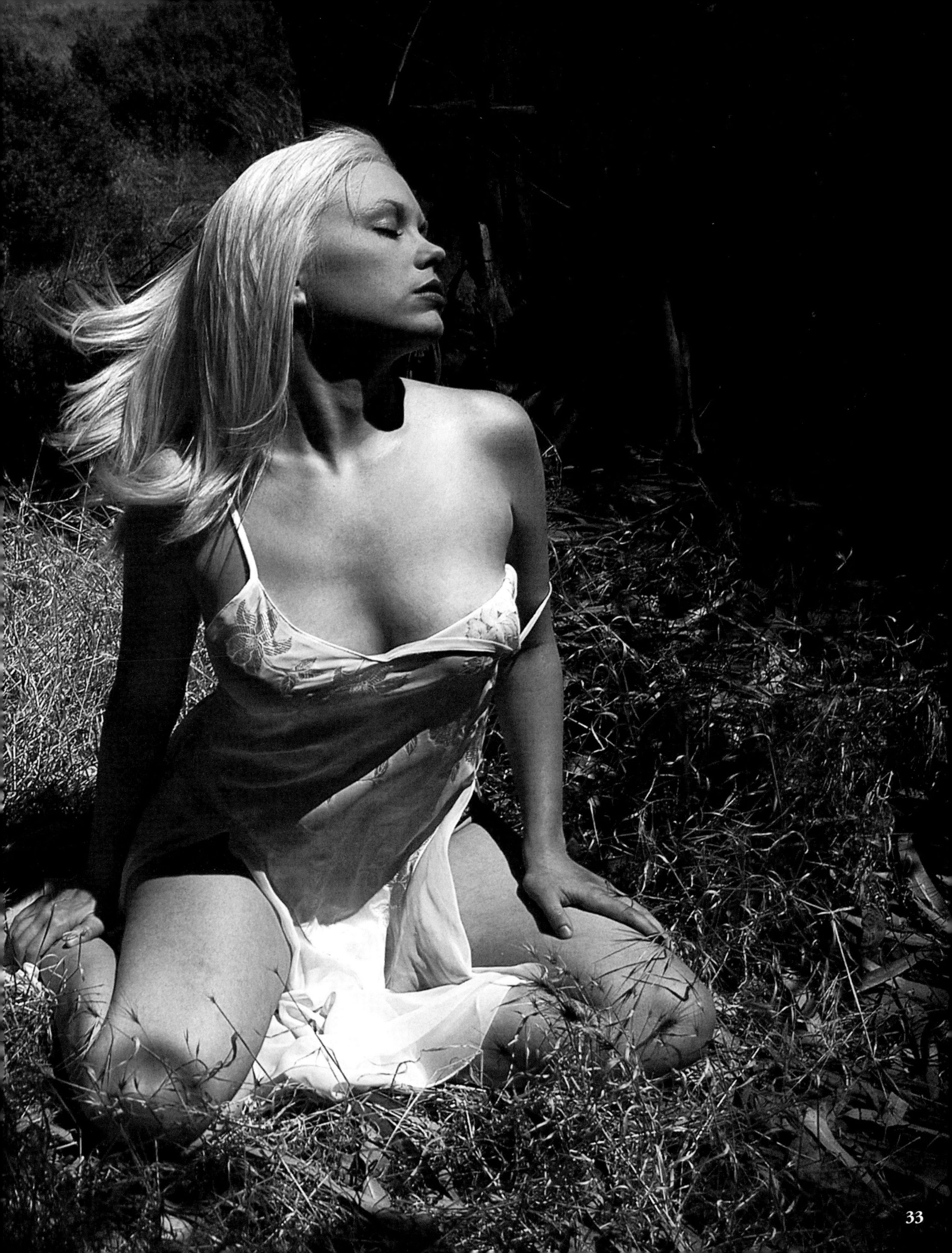

Setting

The double-spread image on the preceding pages was shot during the mid-afternoon in Sonoma County. This setting was chosen for the remarkable light pattern. The sun was creating a warm highlight in a patch of grass, while the background faded into deep shadows. This image is actually much more effective in black and white than color because of the intense light on the subject and the grass in the foreground. Black and white reduce the image to only gray tones and darkens the shadows, making it more dramatic.

Feeling

Even though the lighting is dramatic, this image has a soft, sensual feel. The clothing accentuates the feeling since it is soft, flowing, and delicate. The model has her head turned and eyes closed, which leads to the feeling of romance, but also helps fully light her face and avoid squinting.

Camera: Nikon D100

Lens: Tamron 28/75

Shutter Speed: 1,000th Second

F-Stop: 5.6

Mode: Digital color conversion

Model: Sarah K.

hint

When shooting outdoor glamour photography, look for unique lighting situations such as strong patches of sun or distinct shadow patterns. Place your model accordingly. You cannot plan light like this; take advantage when you find it.

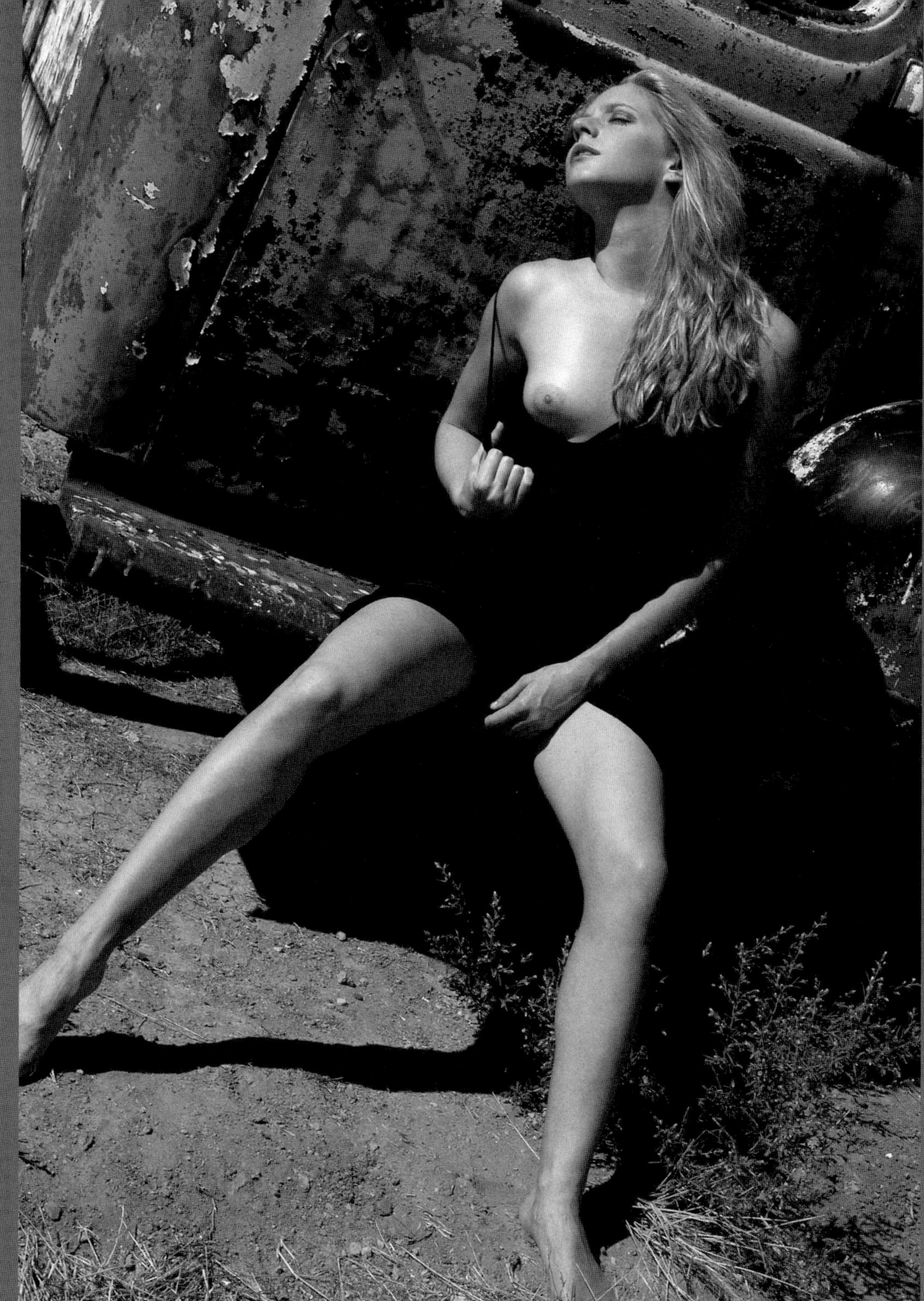

Camera: Nikon D100

Lens: Nikon 28/75

Shutter Speed: 1,200th Second

F-Stop: 9.0

Mode: Digital color conversion

Model: Kaya

Contrast

Shot using only natural, mid-afternoon southern light, this image takes advantage of a plethora of contrasts. The direct sunlight creates rich, dark directional shadows under and behind the model. The dark lingerie adds another dimension, splitting the model's body and allowing her midsection to blend into the background. Finally, her soft, smooth skin against the peeling paint of the metal truck in the background creates another layer of contrasting textures.

Cropping

Try to avoid cropping off hands and feet. Notice how the model's right foot is cropped. I normally try to avoid doing that. However, this is such a strong image in so many others ways it makes the cropping acceptable. Also, widening this shot to include her foot changed the background significantly in the upper left corner and was distracting. It is important to find the right balance.

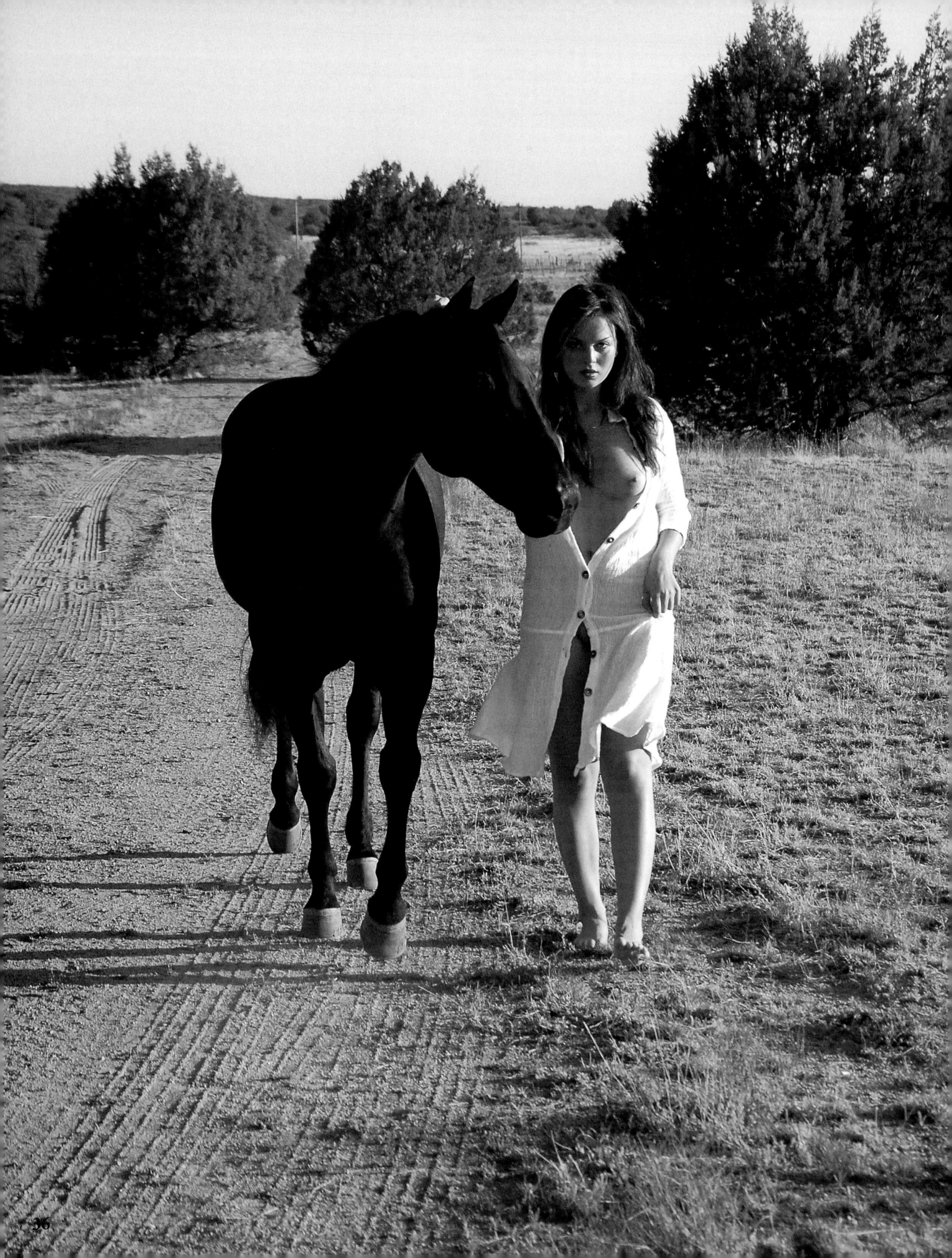

Movement

This image was shot in Skull Valley, Arizona, as part of a one-on-one teaching session. Both the model and the horse are walking toward the camera (notice that the horse's front left hoof is off the ground). The shot captures movement without distortion, which can be difficult.

Contrast and Harmony

This image is a study in contrast and harmony. The dark horse matches the model's dark hair and the bushes in the background. I added the white clothing so the model would have an area of true white, which helps balance the light colored sky.

Horizontal Lines

This location has no straight true horizontal lines. The horizon line in the background is obscured by the foliage. The only horizontal lines are created by the shadows on the ground from the early evening light. This is an excellent example of how natural light can add direction and angles to an image, making the time of day a critical factor.

Camera: Nikon D200

Lens: Nikon 24/120 VR

Shutter Speed: 250th Second

F-Stop: 6.3

Mode: Digital color conversion

Model: Betcee May

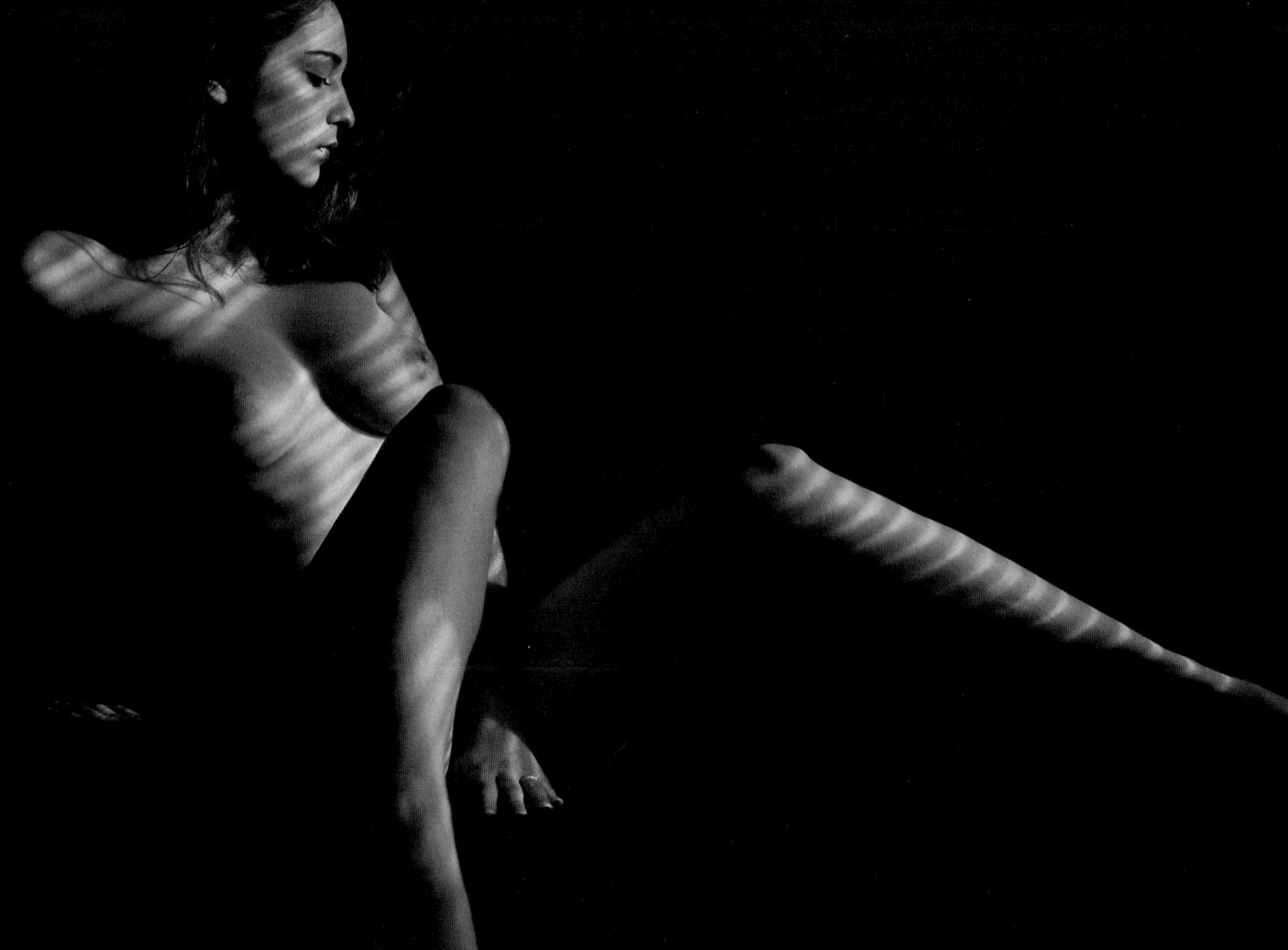

Light Patterns

This image was shot in my Novato studio. Captured in the early morning, it uses all natural window lighting with shadow patterns from the venetian blinds. The model created this pose, which is more of an artistic nude and accentuates the long line of her leg.

Model

This simple yet feminine setting works well for this model. She has a very strong, classic profile. Her dark, sleek hair blends into the background and helps frame her face. It is important to be aware of your model's strengths and weaknesses and adjust your shots accordingly.

Camera: Nikon D100

Lens: Tamron 28/75

Shutter Speed: 60th Second

F-Stop: 3.5

Mode: Digital color conversion

Model: Carlotta

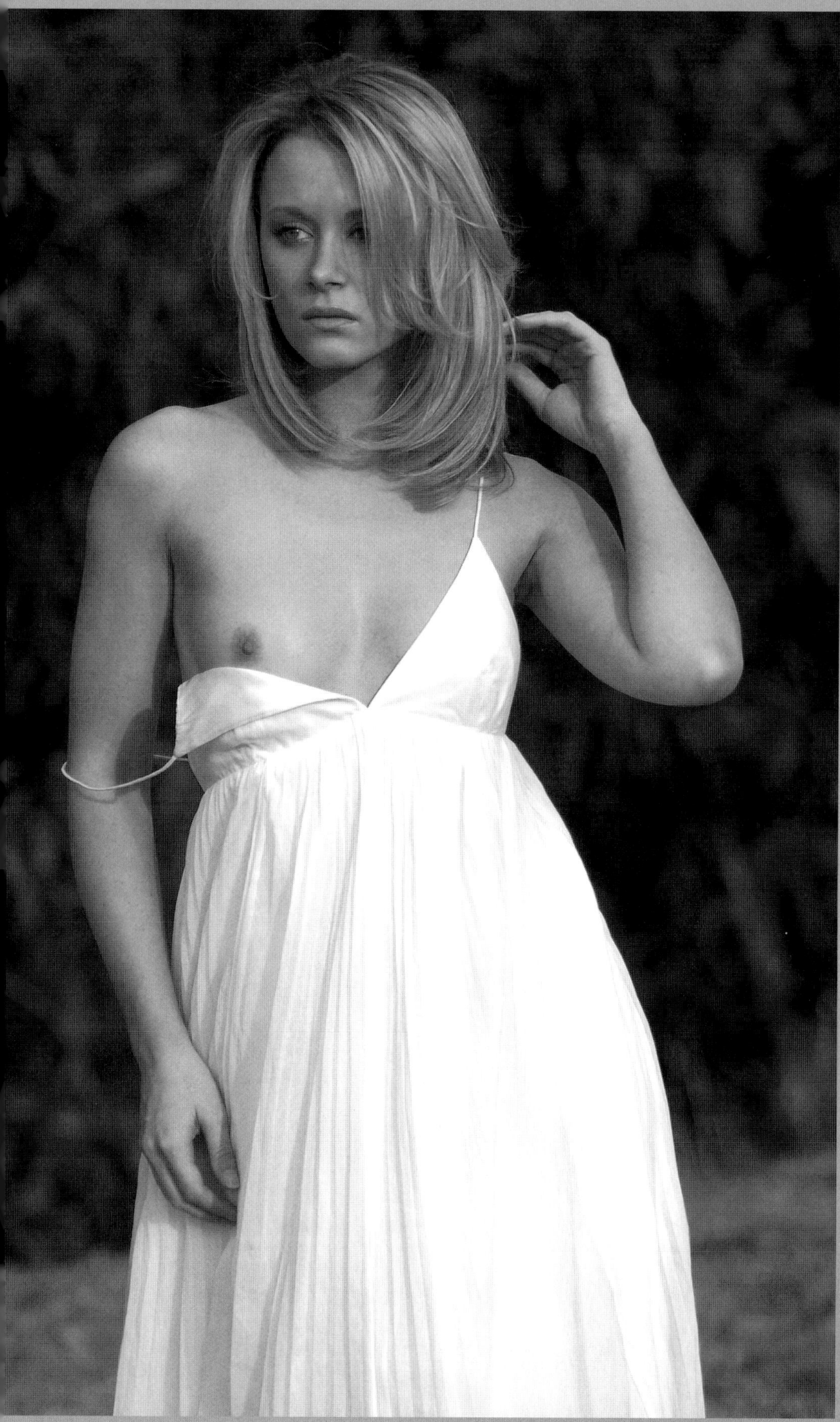

Expression

This model has a very evocative face and her expression sets the mood for the entire image. By looking away from the camera she conveys a feeling of melancholy and introspection. Her hair and clothing add to this feeling of disheveled, ethereal beauty. The fallen strap and exposed breast convey vulnerability. All of the elements work together to unify the image.

When working to develop a specific theme or feeling, be sure to strive for unity in all the elements. For example, if the model was wearing black, sexy, provocative lingerie, this image would have had an entirely different, less innocent feel.

Background

Because the emotion in this image is so strong, the background is purposely subtle and understated. The model is standing in front of a grove of eucalyptus trees which, when shot in soft focus, provides interesting, contrasting texture without being overbearing or distracting.

Camera: Nikon D200

Lens: Nikon 70/300 VR

Shutter Speed: 125th Second

F-Stop: 5.6

Mode: Digital color conversion

Model: Jamie

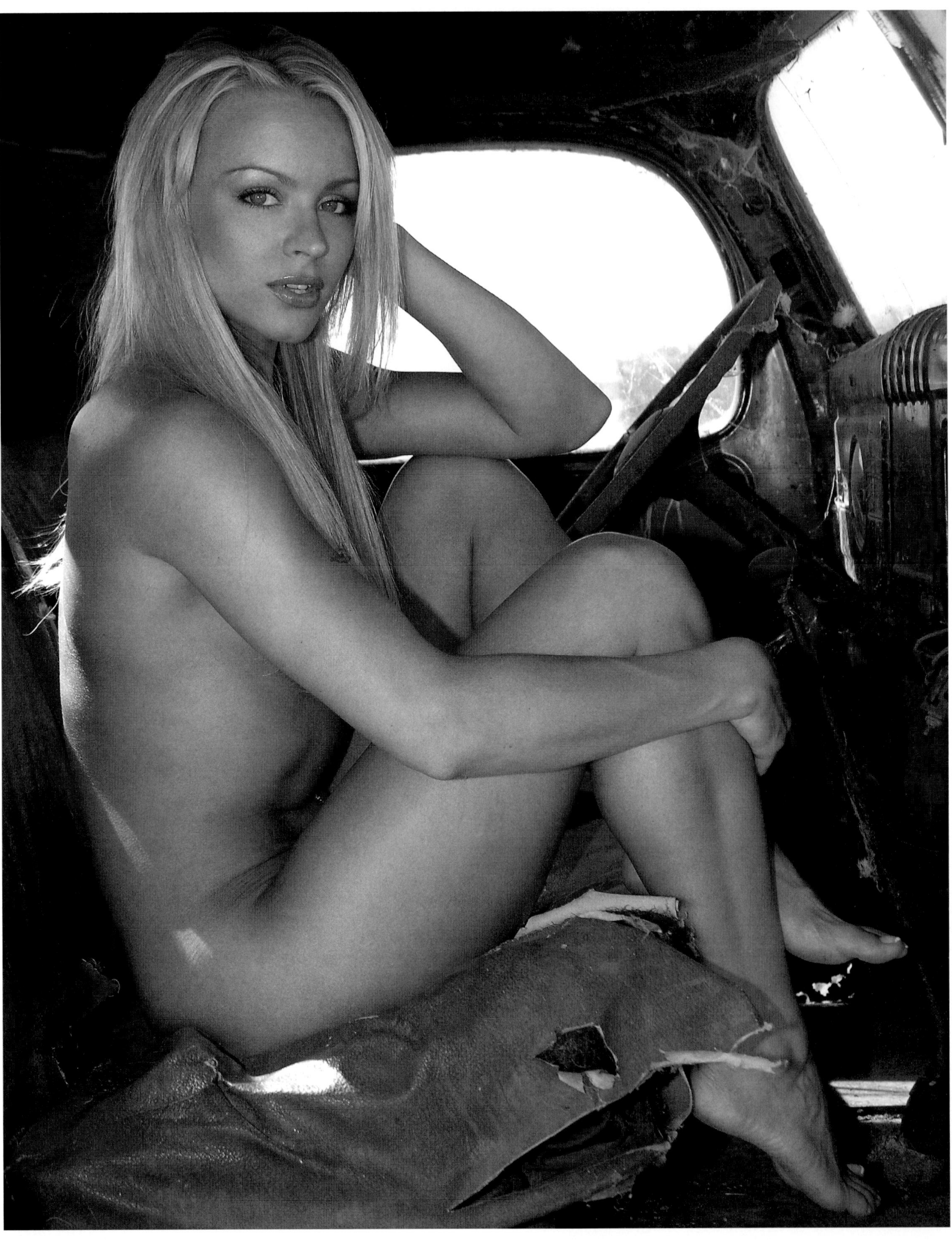

Setting

This image was shot in Sonoma in the late afternoon. This old abandoned truck was full of rust, rips, and imperfections, and created a great contrasting background for the lovely model.

Pose

The position of the model's body emphasizes the smallness of the space. Her left arm raised adds a sense of balance and also breaks up the starkness of the window in the background. By arching her foot, the muscles of the leg are accented.

Lighting

Shot in the late afternoon, this image utilized flash fill lighting. Flash fill was necessary to accentuate details of the cab and minimize the effect of the natural light coming through the back window of the truck.

Camera: Nikon D200

Lens: Nikon 24/120

Shutter Speed: 125th Second

F-Stop: 5.6

Mode: Digital color conversion

Model: Ali

tip

I have shot some very beautiful outdoor glamour photography in very small and unusual spaces. Be sure to talk to your model first before asking her to crawl into a pipe, culvert, or fallen log to avoid any claustrophobic situations.

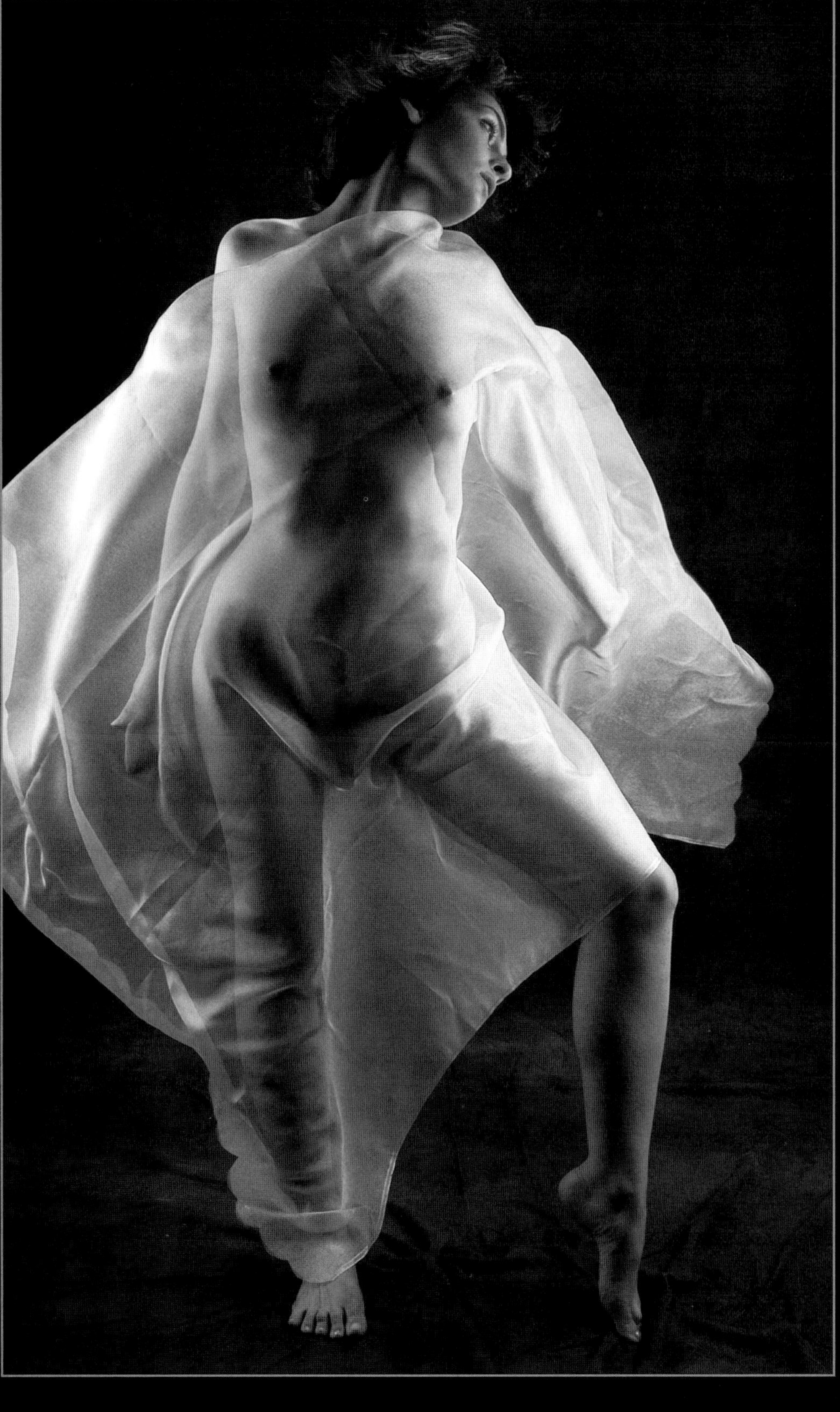

Creation

Shot in a studio in Dallas, Texas, this image was carefully crafted to create a unique visual effect. It is a study of contrasts: the black backdrop and the model interacting with sheer white fabric. I used a fan to adhere the fabric to the skin and create a sensual feeling combining movement and mystery. The model chose the pose and was able to move very gracefully and work with the fabric.

Lighting

The lighting played a critical role in this shot. Lights were positioned crosswise, about 90 degrees to both camera right and left. There was a small additional hair light, just enough to add separation from the background at the crown of the model's head. Note how the model's face is turned back and into the light. This helped illuminate her face while still maintaining the shadows on her body.

Camera: Nikon D100

Lens: 28/75 Tamron

Shutter Speed: 125th Second

F-Stop: 8.0

Mode: Digital color conversion

Model: Miriana

Location

This image was shot inside an old concrete bunker that overlooks the entrance to San Francisco Bay. The room was very small, only about 8' x 8' and the light source was a window. This was taken in the afternoon with the light coming from the west. The sun created a diagonal swatch of light and the model crafted a series of different poses working within the light.

Space

Because the area was so small, there was very little area to maneuver. To make the shot more dramatic, I shot through another window looking down at the model. The angle added interest and gave the model more freedom to try different poses.

Black & Gray

This image has a large concentration of solid blacks shadows, which lend drama to the image. In addition to the shadows, there are a number of other dark areas on the model's face, which were enhanced by her makeup. Dark mascara always frames a model's eyes, but lipstick color plays an important role as well, even in black and white photography. A light, glossy lipstick is going to reflect the light and create a highlight on the lips. A darker red lipstick, as this model is wearing, is going to convert as a deeper gray tone, bringing additional contrast to the face.

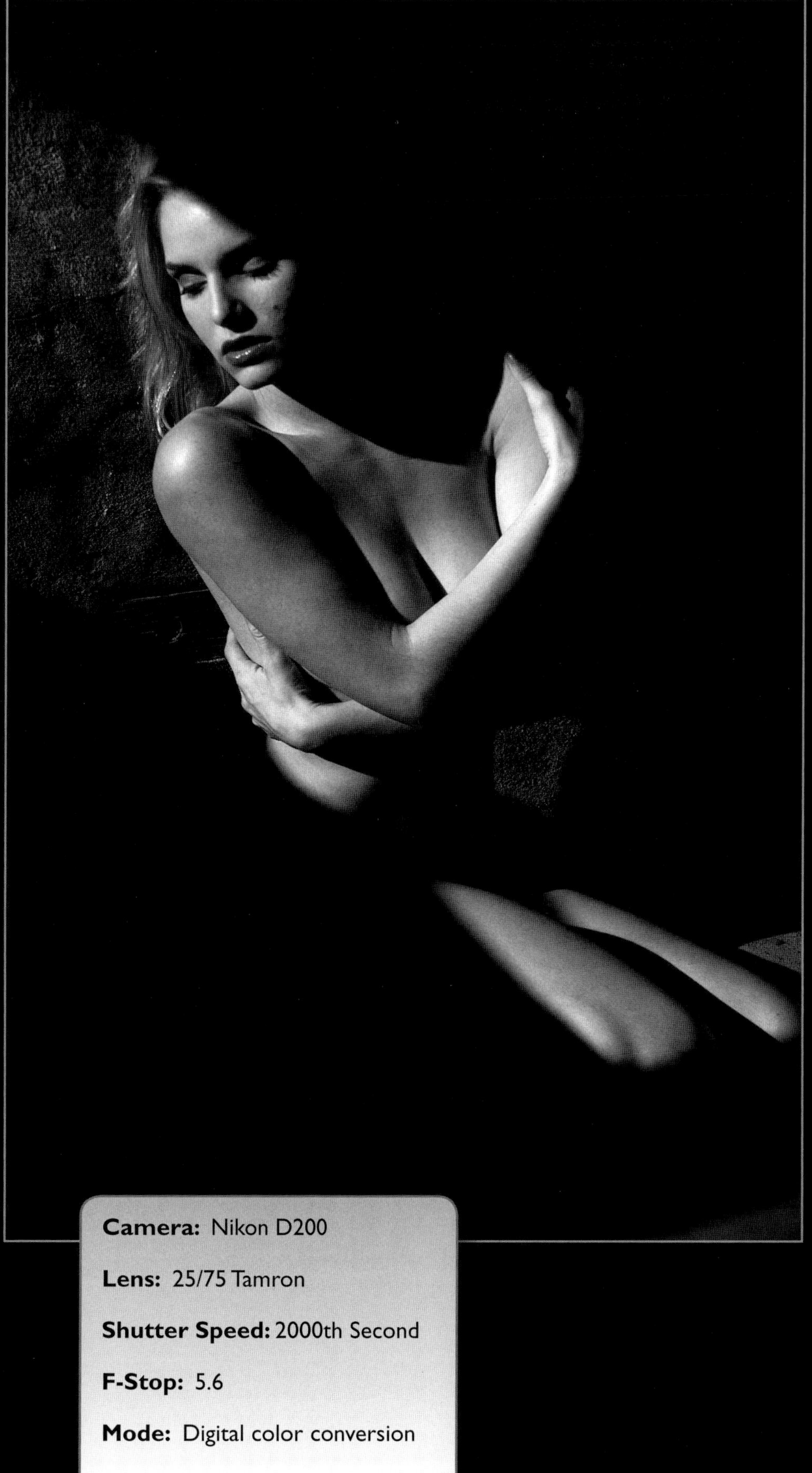

Camera: Nikon D200

Lens: 25/75 Tamron

Shutter Speed: 2000th Second

F-Stop: 5.6

Mode: Digital color conversion

Model: Liz

Negative Shapes

I choose this background because of the of interesting angular, negative shapes created by the machinery. They provide strong black areas and exceptional contrast for the model. The rusted metal surface has additional texture and contrast.

Positioning

It was critical to position the model for the maximum contrast against the background. Her light blond hair was highlighted best against the darkest area, so I had her tilt her head back and up.

Angles

This image is juxtaposition of angles, both natural and man-made. The kneeling pose creates good opposing angles with the legs, as do the bent arms. Her lifted neck also creates another angle (and shadow area) by her head.

Camera: Nikon D100

Lens: 28/75 Tamron

Shutter Speed: 180th Second

F-Stop: 8.0

Mode: Digital color conversion

Model: Anika

hint *Watch your model's hands. They can be graceful or look claw-like. In this image, the hands are slightly awkward. It might have been more effective to have the model's left hand on her knee rather than having her arms crossed.*

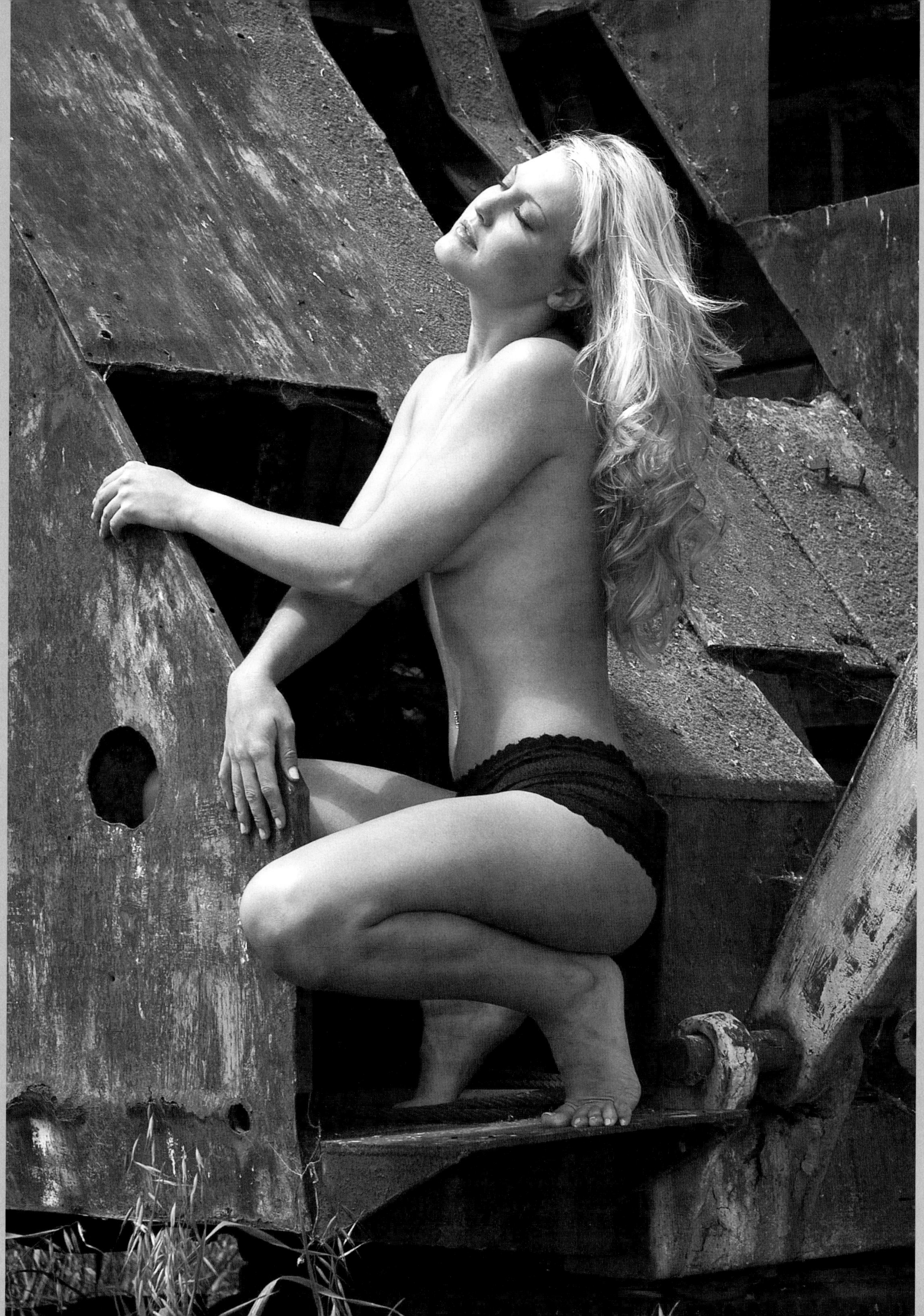

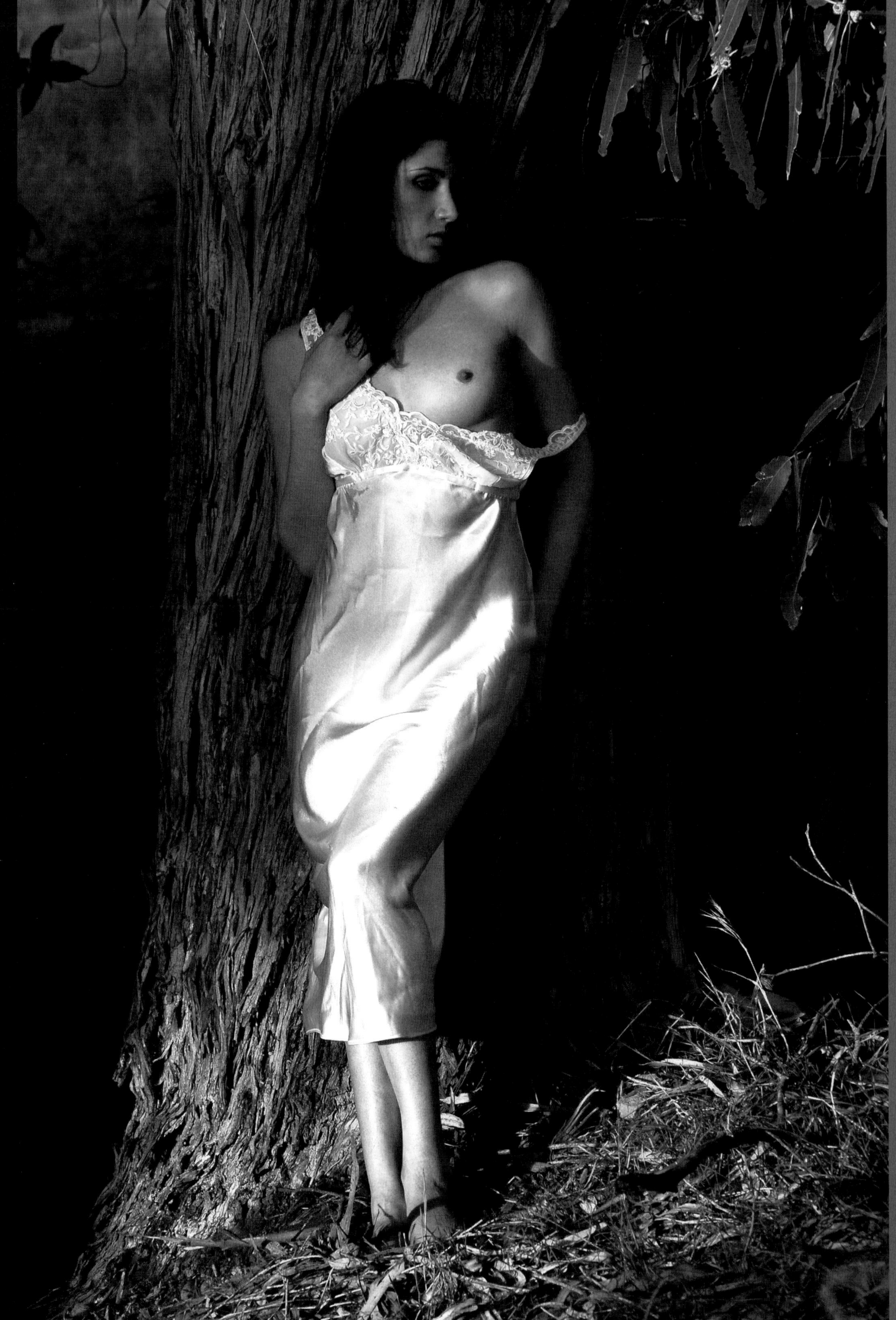

Texture

This image was shot in the early afternoon light in Sonoma. The location was chosen for the multiple layers of texture in this natural setting. The tree bark is extremely rough, which contrasts well with the deep, almost solid, shadow areas on either side of the model. The grasses in the foreground are another layer of texture — different from the bark and creating a contrasting pattern in the foreground.

Fabric

Part of the reason this image is so effective and engaging is the fabric of the model's clothing. The white satin has a bright sheen that shows up well and has wonderful reflective qualities. It also has very sensual gathers, following the model's body and the line of the tree. The model's bent leg accentuates the fabric and adds more wrinkles and shadow areas.

Camera: Nikon D300

Lens: Nikon 70/300 VR

Shutter Speed: 250th Second

F-Stop: 8.0

Mode: Digital color conversion

Model: Elle

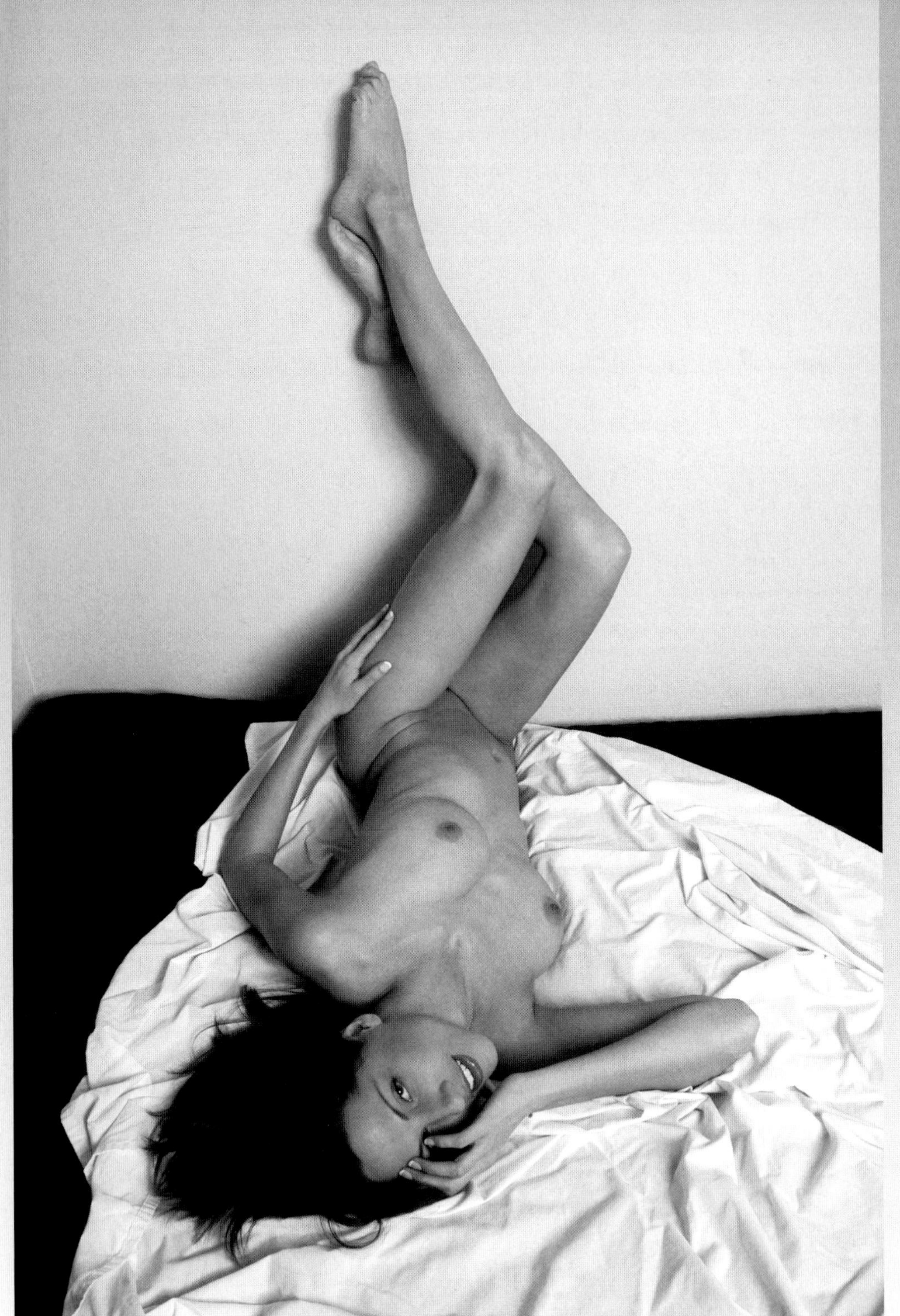

Camera: Nikon D100

Lens: 19/35 mm

Shutter Speed: 125th Second

F-Stop: 9.0

Mode: Digital color conversion

Model: Jennifer

Creating Different Feelings in Studio

The images on pages 48 and 49 are examples of similar studio poses that convey completely different feelings. Both models have their arms up, bent, and touching the face. The image on this page has a more playful feeling as if the pose is candid and the model has been caught unaware. The key to creating this feeling is the facial expression and how the model approaches the camera. Here the model's mouth is open and she is smiling slightly, looking directly at the camera. On page 49, the feeling is much more voyeuristic and introspective because the model's eyes are closed and her head is angled away from the camera. It is as if I have captured a private moment and the model is unaware of the camera. Also, compare the body language in both images. The image at left is much more open, while the right image is more of an implied nude. The model's right hand and leg cover her breasts and add to the mystique of the image.

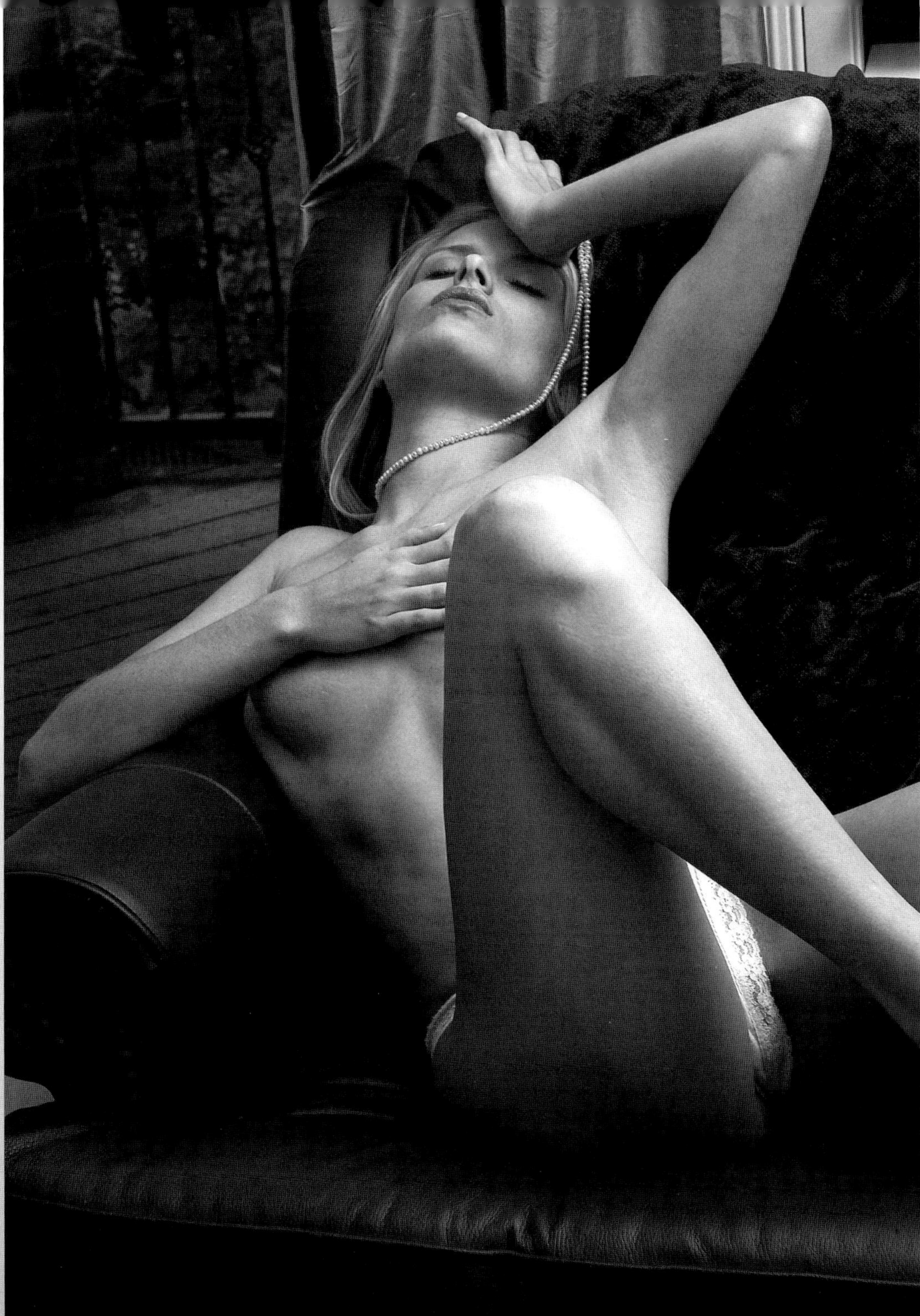

Camera: Nikon D100

Lens: Nikon 28/75

Shutter Speed: 100th Second

F-Stop: 11.0

Mode: Digital color conversion

Model: Reanna

Creating Contrast

Both of these images are effective because there are good areas of contrast. The image at left is more starkly black and white. The majority of gray tones are in the model's skin. I added another layer of contrast by spreading a simple white cloth over the black background while still leaving the back visible on the sides. The primary purpose was set off the model's dark hair, but it also added some nice wrinkles and shadow areas to accentuate the casual, unposed feel of the image.

The image on this page is composed of more gray tones and the model is the lightest area. This makes it more sensual, which works well with the dramatic pose. Note in both these images the model is reclining. Using a chair or bed as a prop has the potential for numerous positions — sometimes the more unconventional, the more striking the end result.

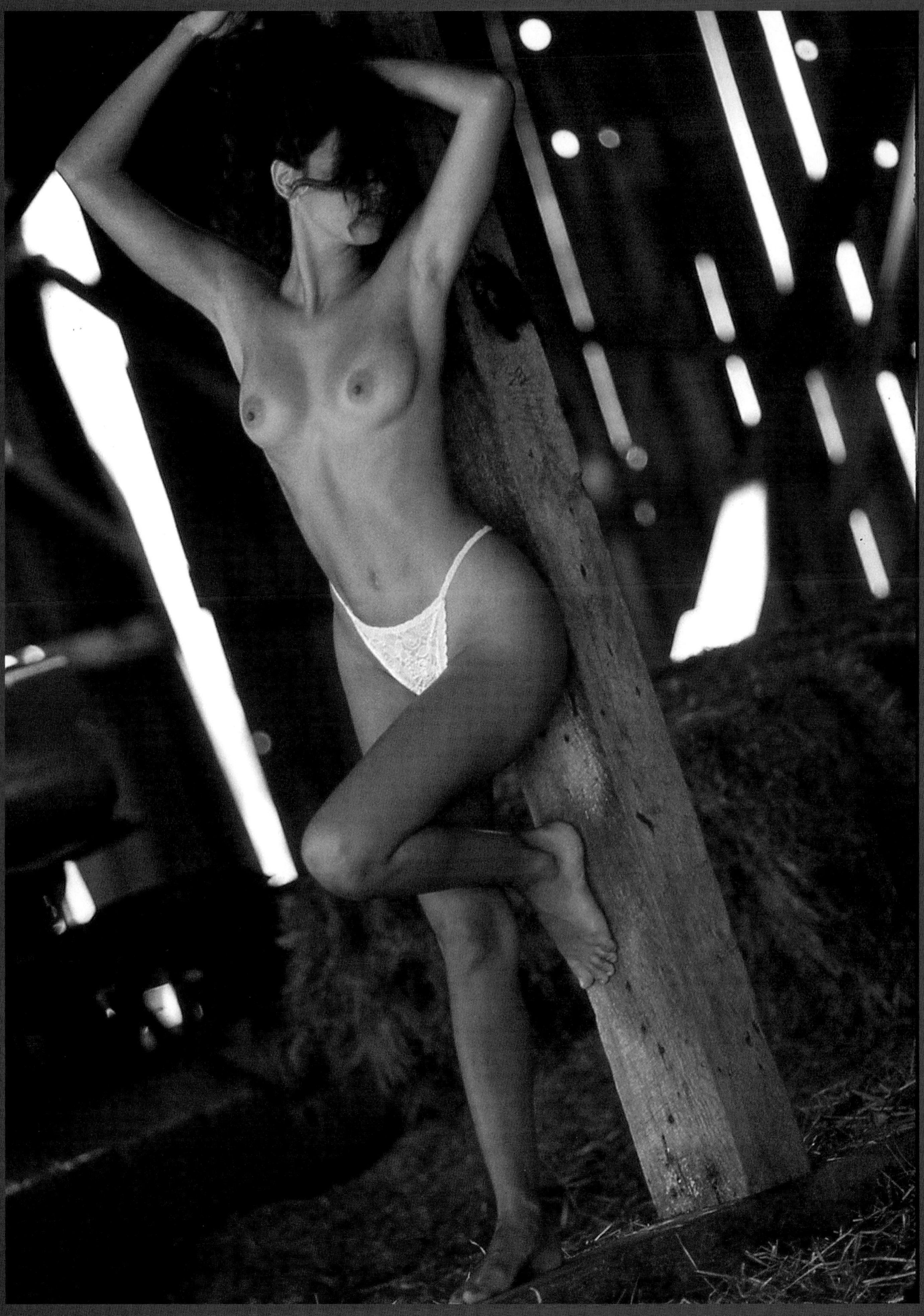

Location

This image was shot in an old, rather decrepit barn in Sonoma. I chose it for two reasons: light and texture. There was a lot of light coming in between the wooden slats, causing patterns of very bright areas. In addition, the hay, tractor, and wooden beam all have interesting contrasting textures.

Pose

The wooden beam gave the model something to lean against and a place to rest the foot of her bent leg. I asked her to bend her leg and arms to help offset the predominance of vertical lines in the image. Her raised arms also framed her head, which helped elongate the line of the body.

White

This image has a number of strong white areas, mainly from the background light. To help balance this and draw the eye to the model, I wanted to have some white clothing on the model as well. The white panties added a touch of feminine sensuality, while preserving the long, clean line of her body.

Camera: Pentax 67

Lens: 135 mm

Mode: Black and White Film

Model: Lalanya

hint

I tilted the camera a bit when taking this shot. Try angling your camera slightly when you are shooting in an area with strong vertical or horizontal lines. It softens the angles and gives unexpected results.

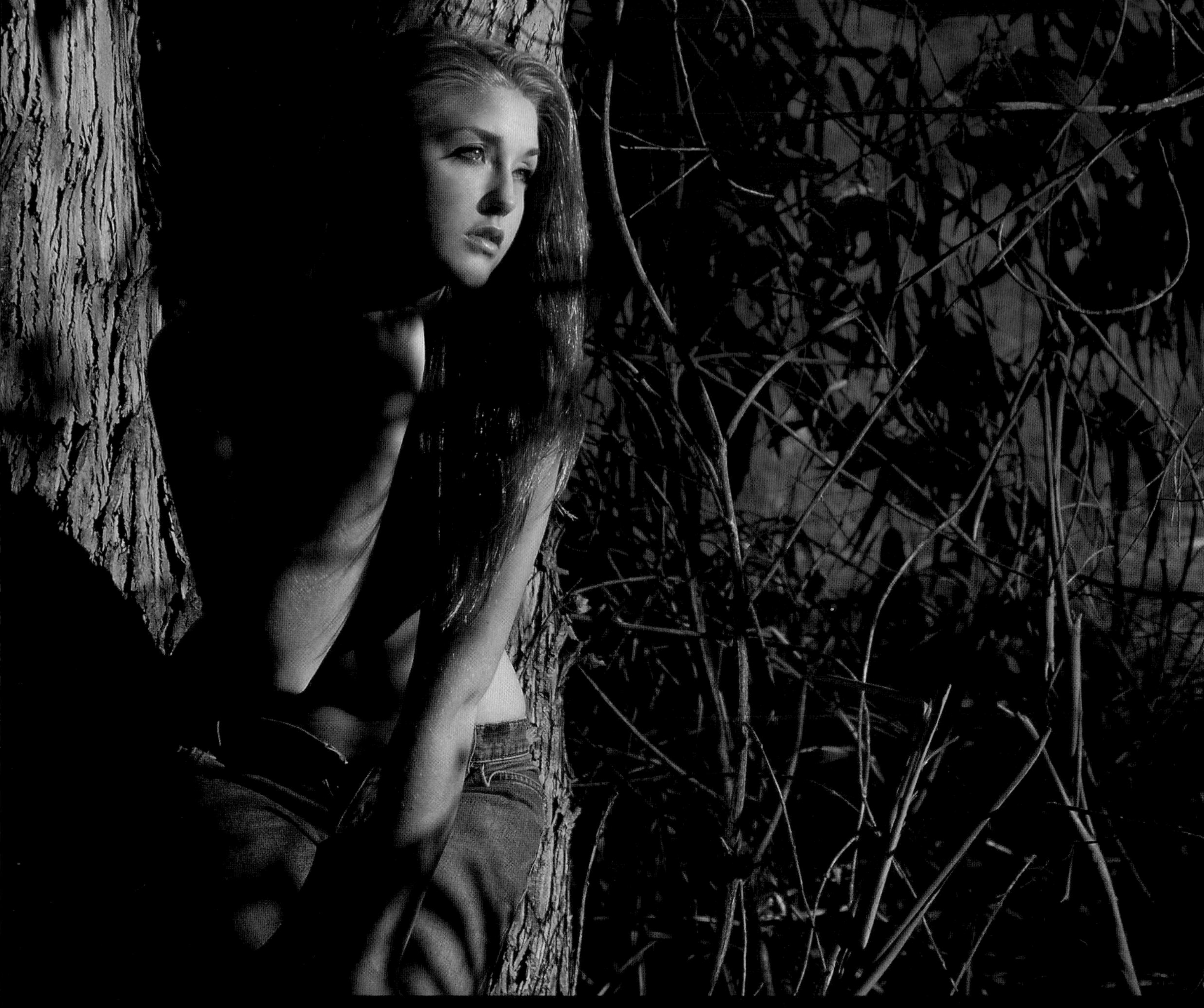

Trees

You will find a number of my images with the model in, against, or near trees. It is because most bark has such rugged texture that it contrasts amazingly well with the model's smooth skin. This image is no exception. However, this tree served an additional purpose: camouflage. This model was not comfortable doing nude shots, so we looked for a setting where she could create an implied nude. This tree gave her a place to sit and lean forward, concealing her breasts in shadow. It is always important to work with your model and find a pose she is comfortable with.

This setting was also critical for the quality of the light. Shot in the late afternoon, the soft, gentle light illuminated only portions of the model, accentuating her beautiful, pensive face. It also created interesting shadow patterns on her legs and torso.

Camera: Nikon D200

Lens: Tamron 24/120VR

Shutter Speed: 500th Second

F-Stop: 5.6

Mode: Digital color conversion

Model: Courtenay

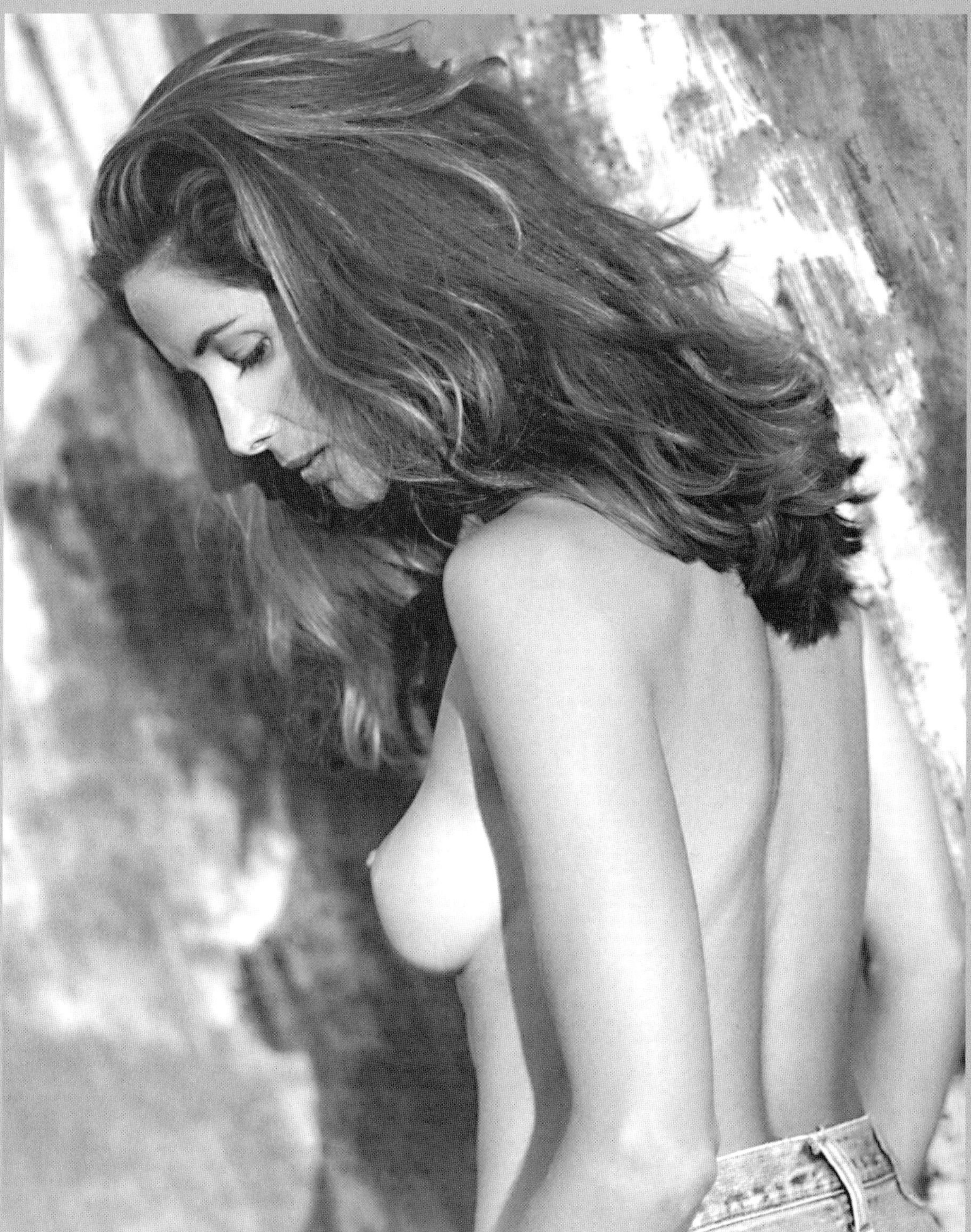

Camera:
Hasselblad 503

Lens: 150 mm

Shutter Speed:
500th Second

F-Stop: 5.6

Mode: Agfa Pan 100 Film

Model: Jane

Sunlight

This image was shot in the early afternoon in bright sunlight. The sun was at the model's side, which created the very clear shadow on the back drop. When shooting in bright sunlight, it is best if the model does not look at the camera. It is much easier and effective if the model is looking down or away. You will avoid squinting and still have the benefits of bright sunlight.

Shadows

I often utilize the " in my work to add drama and intense areas of black to the image. In this image, the shadow is created by the model; it is a twin of her pose. The shadow also helps clearly define the model's profile and body, creating separation from the background.

SETTING

This image was shot in my Novato studio. The goal was to capture the essence of female beauty and the sensuality of the model without any noticeable props or background. I cropped it as tightly as possible to capture the model's expression and a good portion of the body.

LIGHTING

I shot this using a beauty dish. It was 22" in diameter and painted flat white for soft, white light. This created the catch light in the eyes, which really helps draw the viewer into the image.

EXPRESSION

The model's expression helps make this image so effective. Her mouth is slightly open, creating a sensual warmer feeling. It creates a very natural, relaxed look.

Camera: Nikon D300

Lens: Nikon 24/120

Shutter Speed: 250th Second

F-Stop: 8.0

Mode: Digital color conversion

Model: Harley

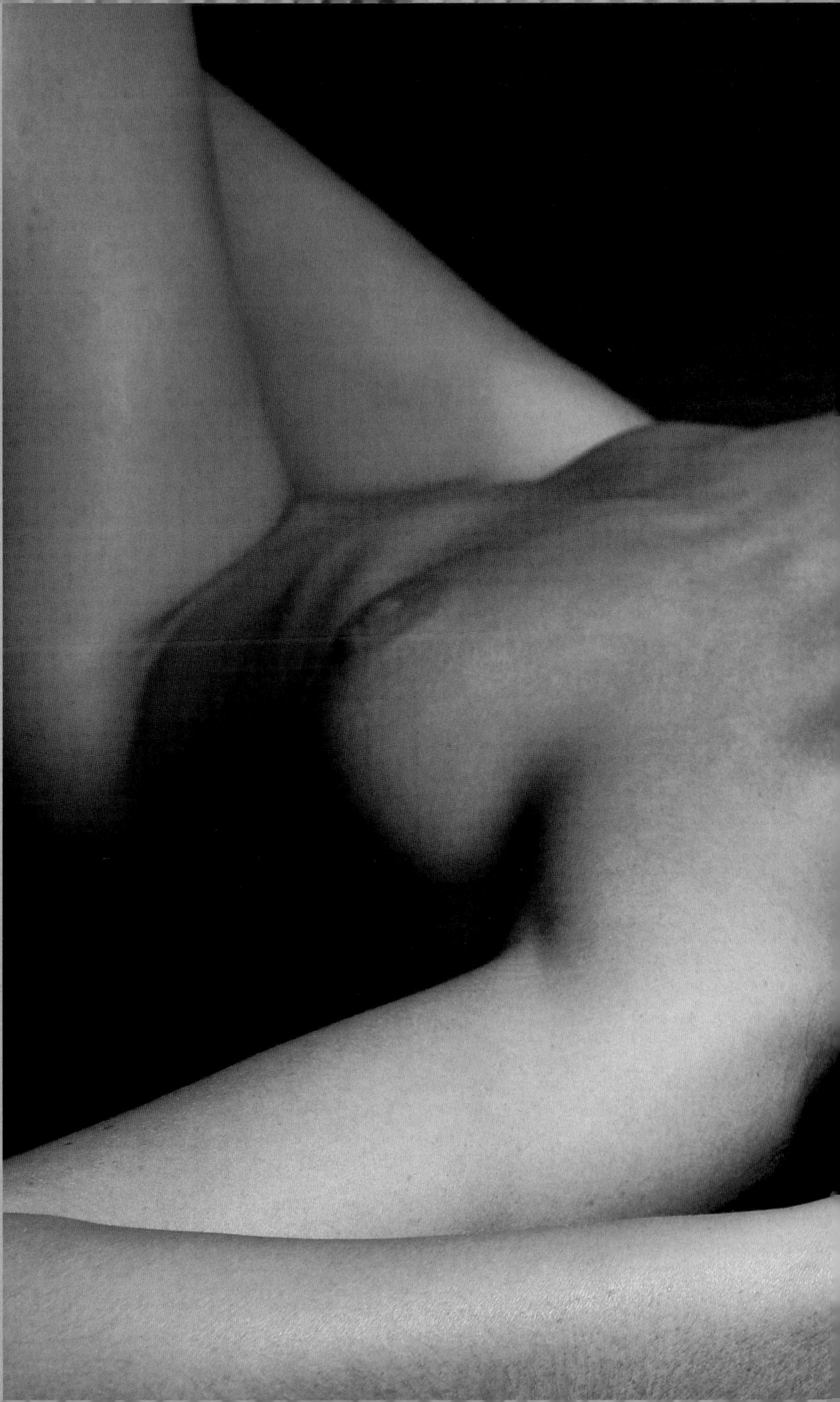

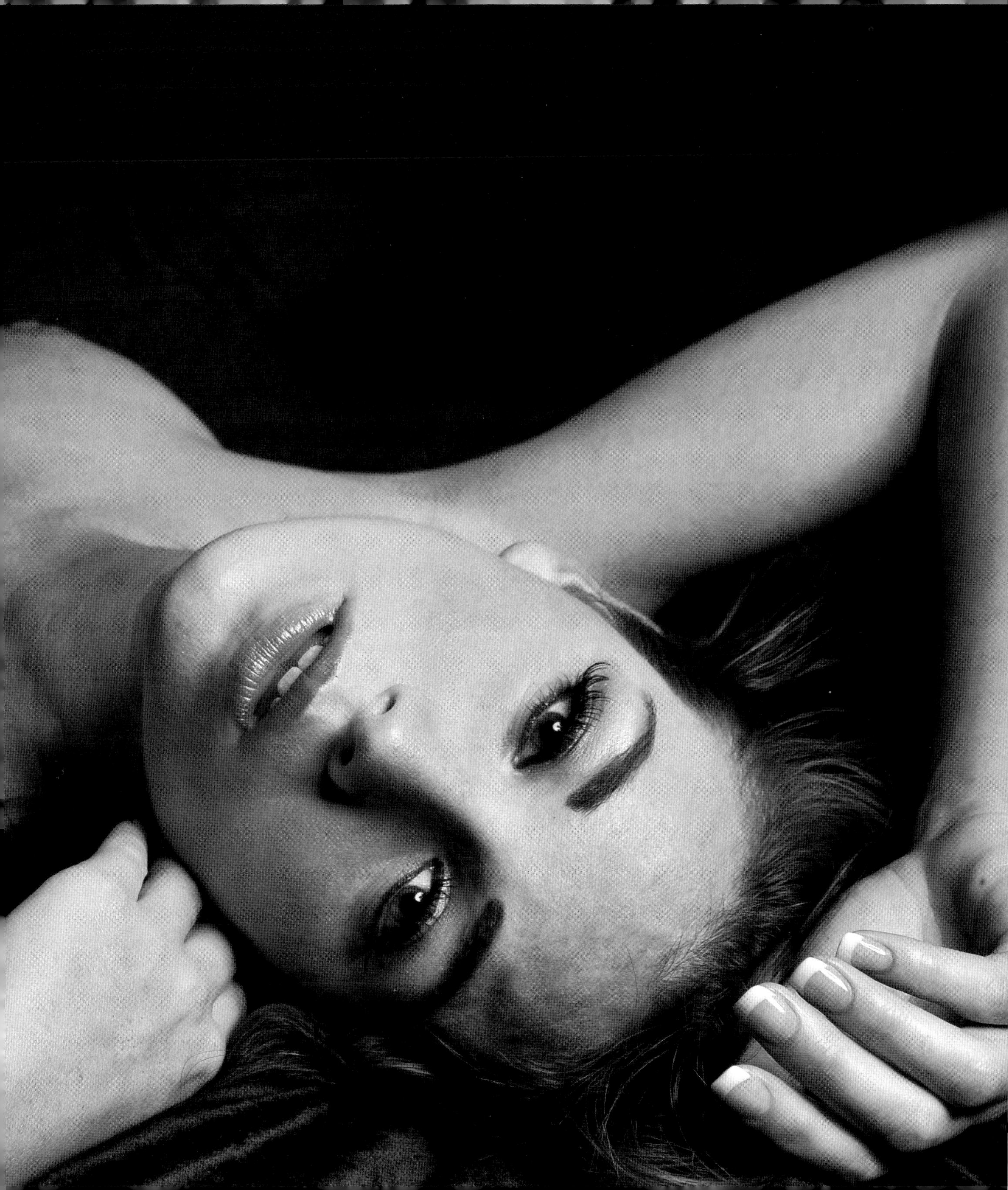

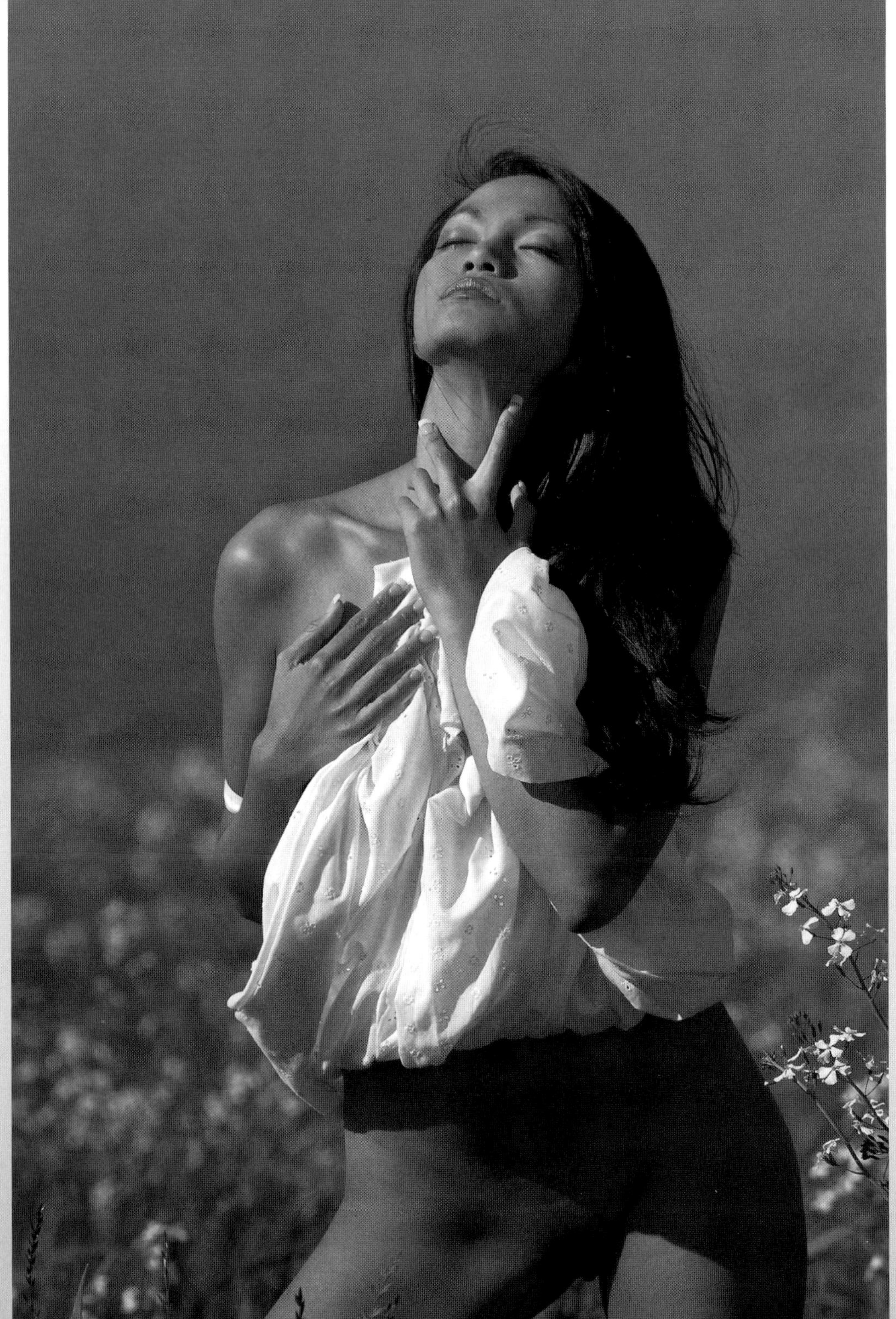

Camera: Nikon D200

Lens: Nikon 70/300 VR

Shutter Speed: 500th Second

F-Stop: 7.1

Mode: Digital color conversion

Model: Iris

Skin Tone

I have shot models of all shapes, sizes, and colors. Skin tone is always a key factor in determining the type of shot, lighting, and background. In outdoor glamour photography, getting the right background for a model's skin tone can be tricky, especially when working in a wide open location. The photos on pages 56 and 57 show models of opposite skin tones in outdoor locations. Generally, you want to shoot a brunette model against a lighter sky or background to get optimal separation as in the example above. This can be tricky when looking at a color subject, because you must imagine how the scene will convert to black and white. Remember, colors define edges. A warm blue sky and a rich, taupe skin tone may have the same gray density when converted to black and white. It can be hard to determine where one color ends and the other begins. This is why a brilliant color photograph can look flat and lifeless when converted. However, black and white photography does have advantages in regard to skin tone. It flattens undertones and tends to smooth imperfections.

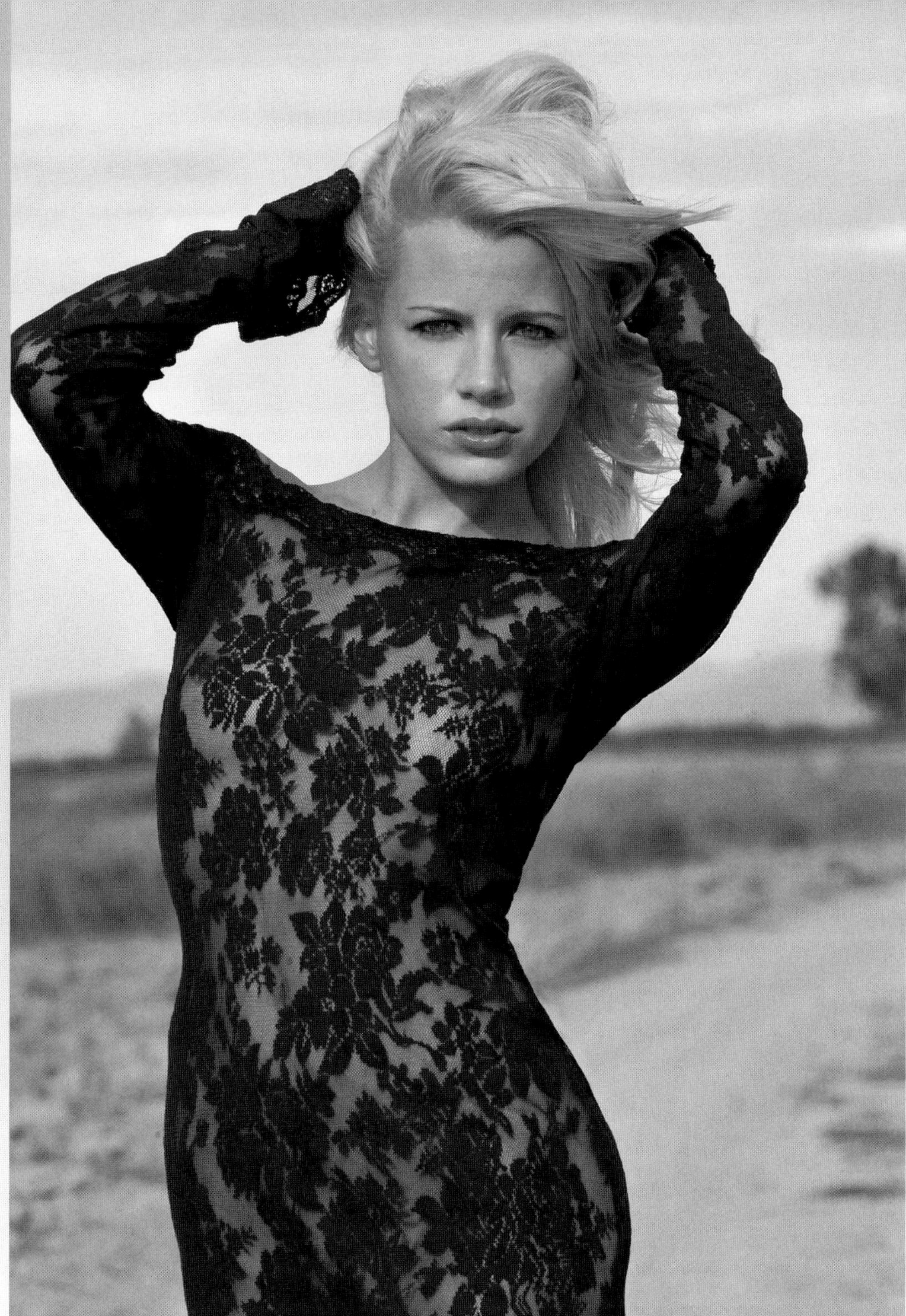

Camera: Nikon D300

Lens: Nikon 70/300 VR

Shutter Speed: 500th Second

F-Stop: 9.0

Mode: Digital color conversion

Model: Jaimie

Clothing

Clothing, even minimal items such as simple white panties, are an excellent way to balance skin tone and created needed areas of separation in black and white photography. The photo on page 56 is a good example of adding clothing to create differentiation and contrast. This location was lush with green grasses, yellow flowers, and a warm blue sky. However, I knew when converted to black and white the tones would be very similar. That works for the bottom of the image. The shadows and similar tones make the model's lower body blend in with the background. The white dress adds contrast to the image and enhances the pose, making it very feminine and dramatic. In the image above, I took the opposite approach. The model has fair, light skin and hair. The background is also very light. The sheer lace black dress creates contrast and offsets the medium grays of the rather barren location. The tight cropping allows the pattern in the dress to really pop and helps reveal the sensual lines and curves of the body.

Mystery

This image was shot in the late afternoon inside an old barn in Sonoma County. I chose the location because sunlight was leaking in from distressed areas of the barn, which created broken sections of light. This type of lighting is very effective for creating an image that is more mysterious, as with this image. Only certain areas of the body are well lit, while others are in shadow. This creates an almost abstract feel to the entire composition. The background is indistinct; the viewer only gets a hint of it from the post that the model is leaning against.

Face

The dramatic shadows on the model's face add to the mystique of the image. The model tilted her head up and partially into the patch of sun, which lights only her brow and a portion of her face. Her expression is also enigmatic; she is not only looking into the camera, but seemingly beyond it. This model is excellent at posing and matching her facial expression to the type of mood the entire image is trying to convey, which really helps make this image work.

Camera: Nikon D200

Lens: 24/120 VR

Shutter Speed: 500th Second

F-Stop: 9.0

Mode: Digital color conversion

Model: Liz

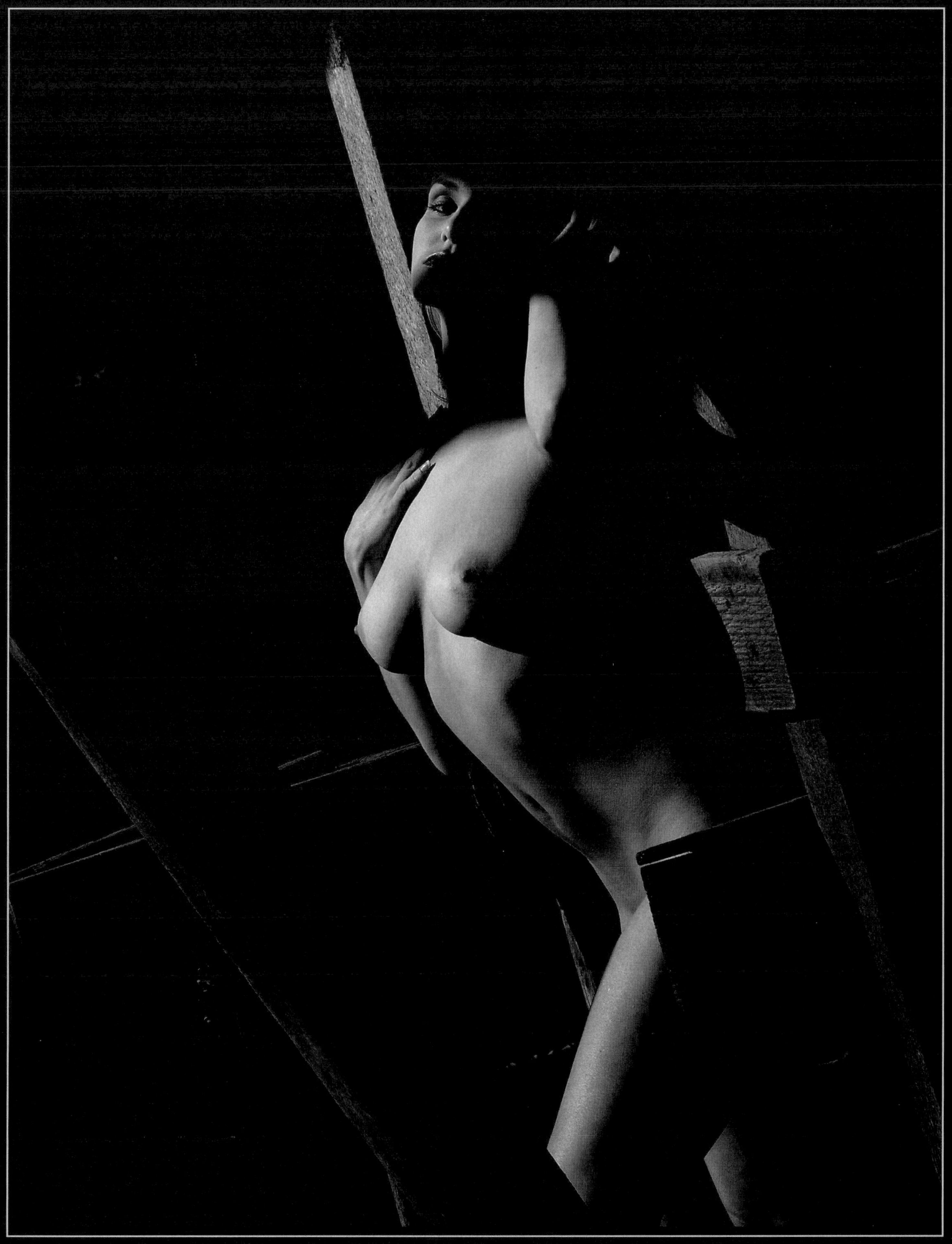

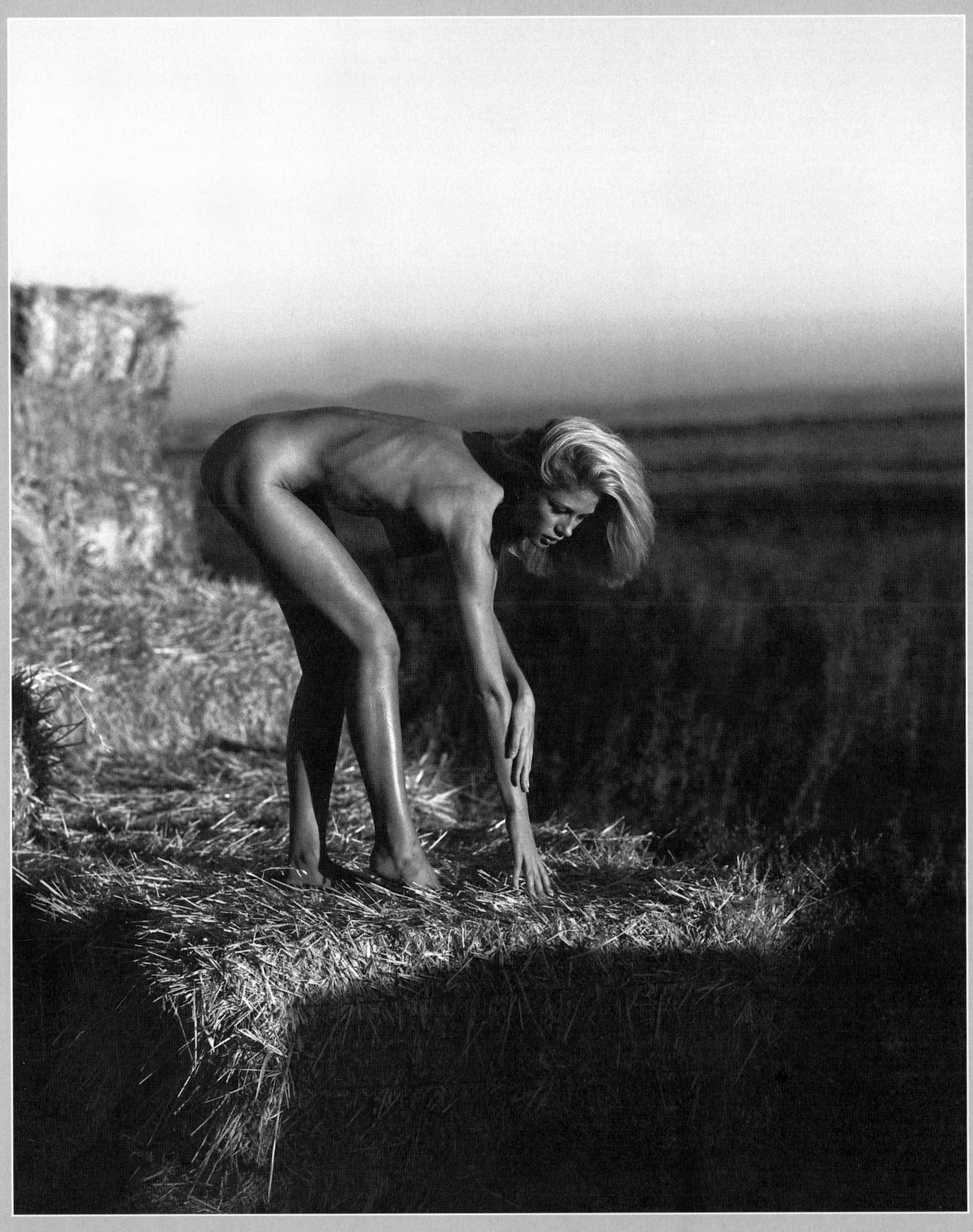

Setting

This image was shot in the early evening in Sonoma. The sun was setting and the fog was rolling in. The fading sun lit up the hay, casting a warm soft glow across the hay bales, accentuating the texture. The fog helped soften the harshness of the horizon line, creating almost a gradient effect to the background.

Hair

Hair color, length, and texture impacts glamour photography in a number of ways. In this image, the model's hair adds another dimension of light, catching the sun. It also frames the face, and the shadow helps define the model's profile.

Camera: Pentax

Lens: 135 mm

Mode: Film

Model: Rowan

hint *Long lines of the female body are beautiful. Try non-traditional poses (such as bending or stretching) to accentuate the lines of the body.*

Skin Tone

Working with a model with either an extremely dark skin tone or an extremely light skin tones makes converting a color image to black and white fairly simple because it is easy to contrast the skin tone with the background. This image, shot at a workshop in Cody, Wyoming, demonstrates that principle. The model is very fair and she is posed against a rusty old vehicle in a junk yard. The background provides interest and texture. The model's skin tone provides the excellent contrast that makes an outstanding black and white image.

Shape

Models come in all shapes and sizes. This lovely model is naturally curvaceous and the pose is meant to draw attention to her shape and the beauty of the female form. With her legs bent and slightly crossed, and the feet on top of each other, the legs elongate the whole line of the body, accentuating the supple curves of the waist and hip. Her arms cradle her breasts, which adds balance and additional angles to the upper body. Always encourage a model to pose in ways that flatter her natural shape.

Camera: Nikon D200

Lens: 24/120VR

Shutter Speed: 250th Second

F-Stop: 10.0

Mode: Digital color conversion

Model: Tiana

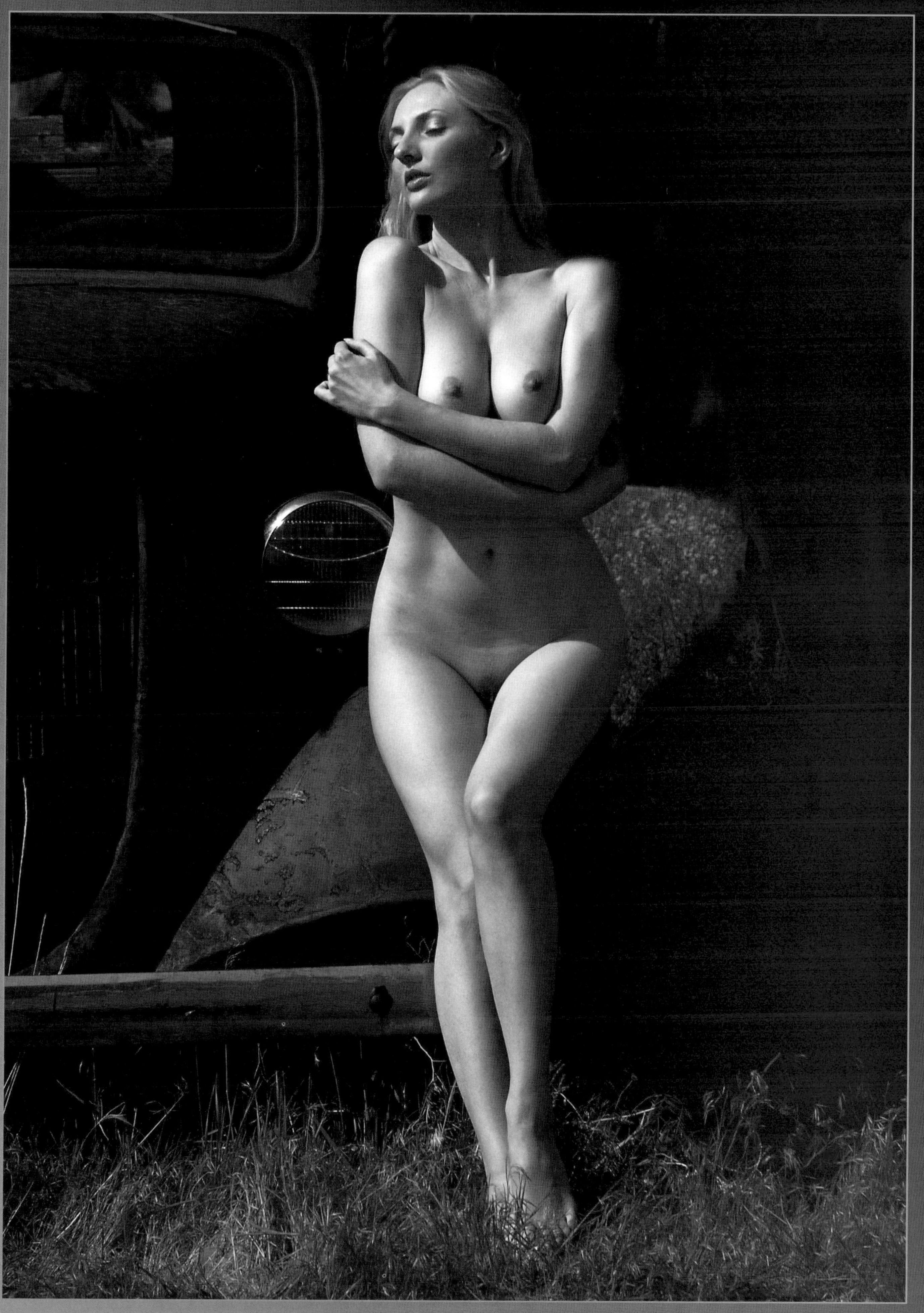

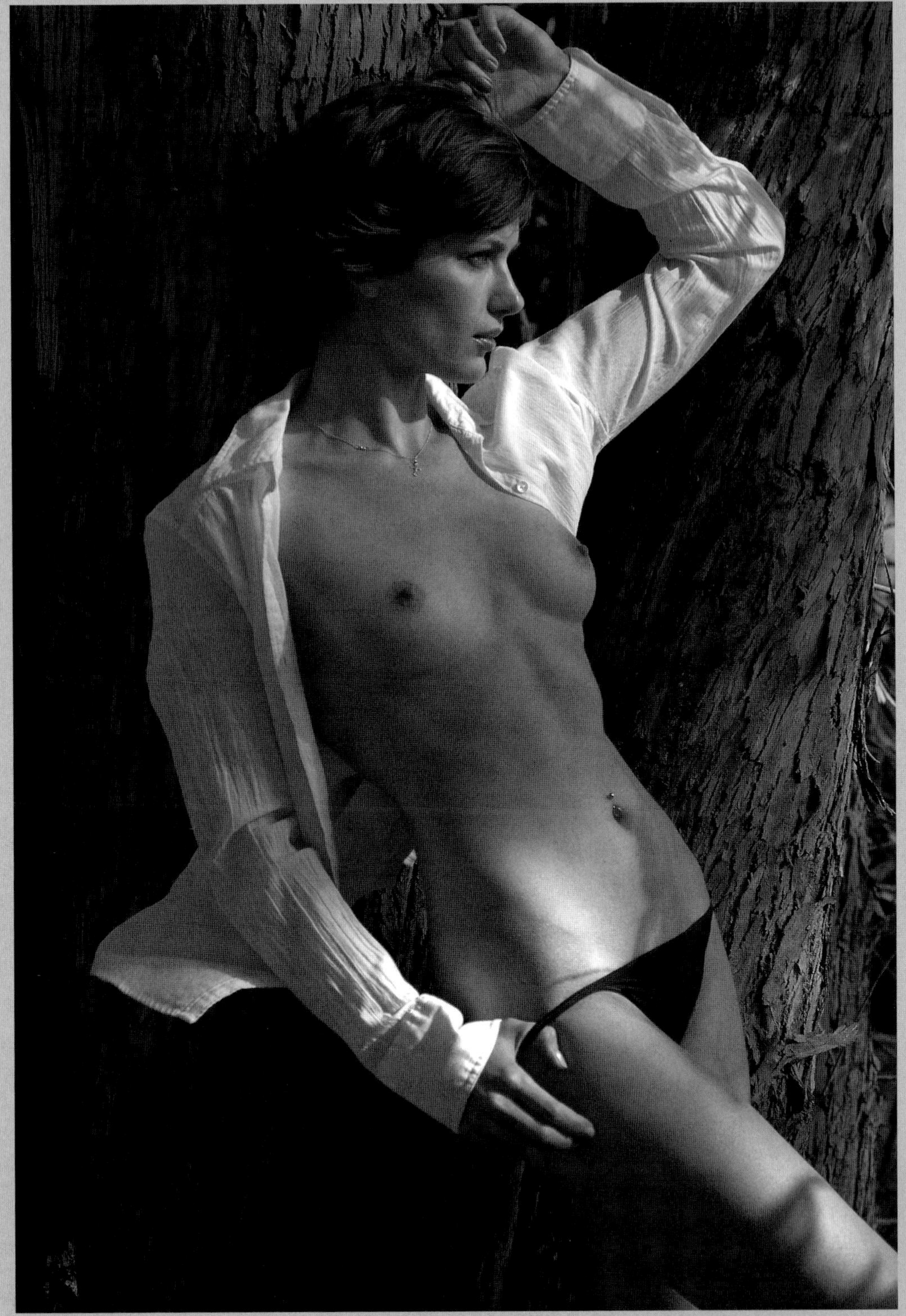

Camera: Nikon D200

Lens: Nikon 70-300VR

Shutter Speed: 250th Second

F-Stop: 5.3

Mode: Digital color conversion

Model: Katya

Lighting

This image, shot in Sonoma County, makes use of the natural light spreading out between the trees. In this particular case, I placed the model in a naturally occurring pattern of lighting. The light, entering from the west, creates increasingly darker shadows down her lower body There is a hot spot located on her right hip, in the core of her pose. The result is an image in which the model appears to be looking toward a light source, touched by only parts of it.

Texture

The texture in this image, provided by the bark of the trees against which she is leaning, is increased by the lighting and the varying shadows, putting the lighter parts of her skin into even sharper contrast with the tree bark. Originally, the image was shot in color. I changed it to black and white in Adobe Photoshop®. This boosted the contrast, which made the shirt whiter and the shadows deeper.

Pose

The sensuality of this shot is enhanced by the pose and the slender frame of the model. She's looking away from the camera, toward that light source and thinking about something the viewer can only guess at — providing an enhanced artistic value to the image.

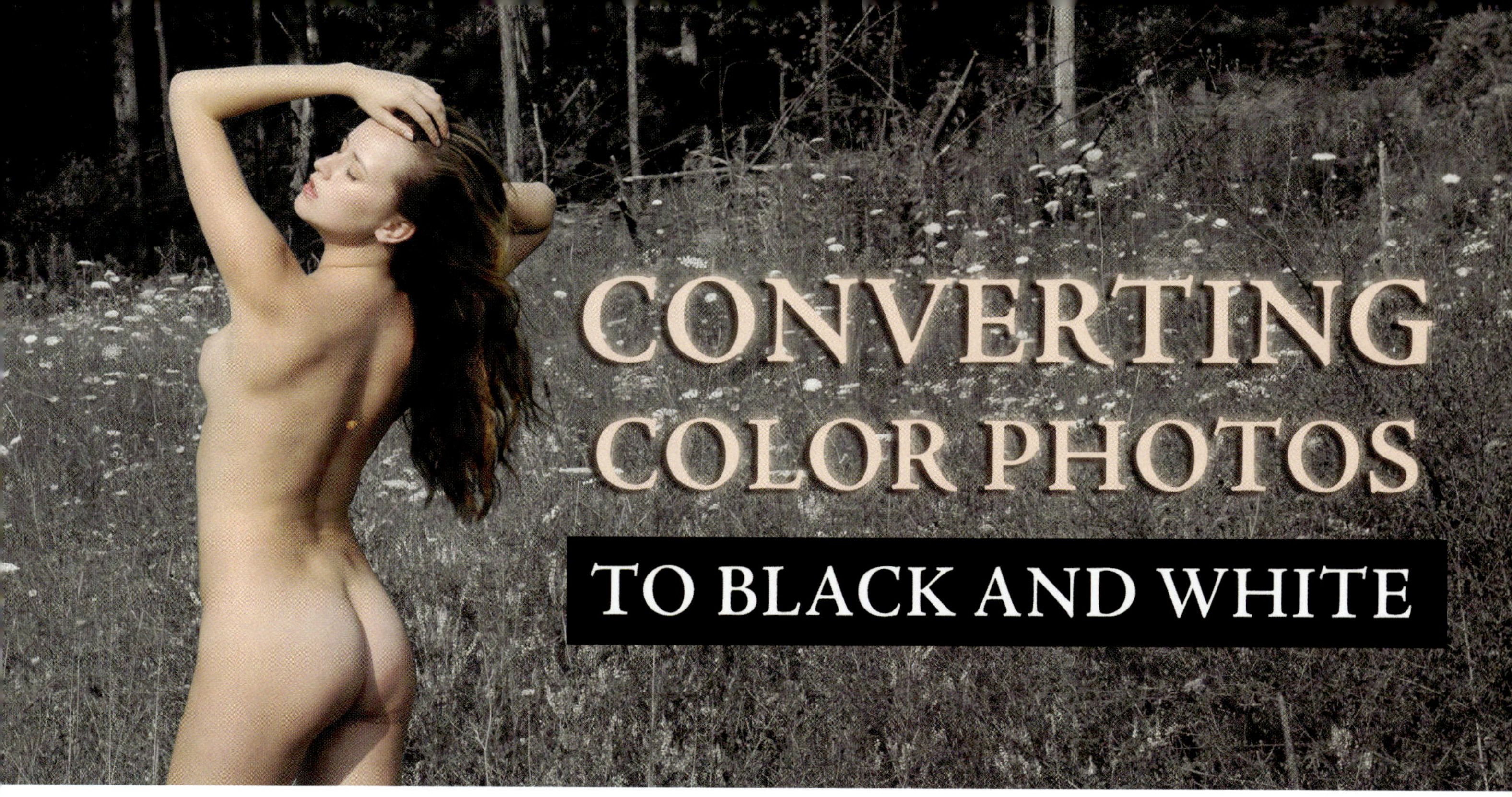

Many of the images in this book were taken digitally. If you want to convert your digital photos to black and white images, there are a number of ways to do it. In this section, I have outlined my two favorite ways.

I use Photoshop® CS4 to edit, correct, and tone my images. There are many other software programs available, but I like the Photoshop® features, especially some of the third-party plug-ins.

Gorman/Holbert Method

One of the best ways I have found for converting images in Photoshop® is the Gorman/Holbert method. You can turn this method into an automated action in Photoshop® and have every photo convert automatically by simply applying the action.

However, be aware that every image has different amounts of tones and contrasts. It is a good idea to keep a layered version of your file so you can individually adjust the curves and levels to fine tune the final photograph.

Here is the step-by-step Greg Gorman method from **www.gormanphotography.com/bw_conversion.pdf**:

- Open the image you want to convert in Photoshop®. Under the image menu, select mode>lab color
- Click (highlight) the lightness channel
- Under the image menu, select mode>gray scale (discard color information)
- Command/control click on the gray channel (to load the selection)
- Under the select menu, choose image>inverse to select the shadows
- Under image menu, choose mode>RGB color
- In the adjustment layers palette, choose solid color
- Select a color from the color picker or from the swatches palette (which I prefer because you can save a custom color)
- Your choice of color should be based on the tonal range you wish to see in your final toned black and white
- Go to your layers palette and change your blending mode to multiply
- Because your color fill is on a layer, you may adjust the opacity to dial back the color that you desire
- In addition, you may add a curves or levels adjustment to achieve the desired contrast
- Should you wish to change the color of your black and white "duotone," simply double click the color
- Fill and reselect the color
- Create a new layer

- While holding the option button, go to the pop-out menu and select merge visible
- Change the blending mode to overlay
- Reduce the opacity to 20 percent
- Choose filter-other. Then select-high pass. Set radius at 50 pixels
- Double click the new layer to bring up properties
- Bring the black point arrow in to 70. Next option/click the black point arrow to split them
- Pull one half of the arrow back to 50
- Bring the white point arrow in to 185. Next option/click the white point arrow to split them
- Pull one half of the arrow back to 205. Click OK
- If necessary, the opacity may be varied to reach your desired adjustment
- Under the file, menu select save as and choose your file and location (for example, desktop>new folder> black and white conversions)
- If you choose not to flatten your file at this time, you can change the tonal and contrast adjustments to different settings in the future if desired

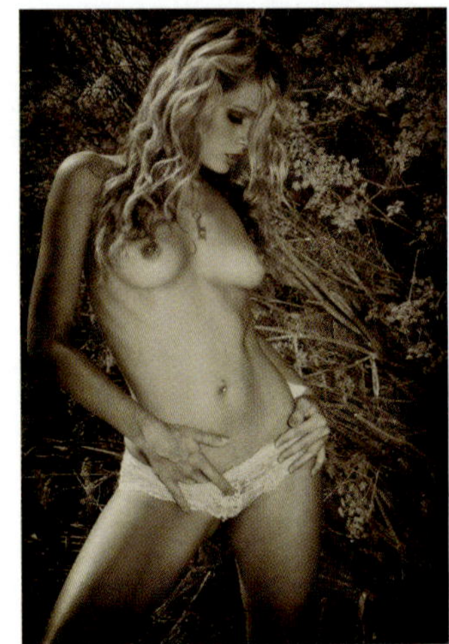

Antique Plate I

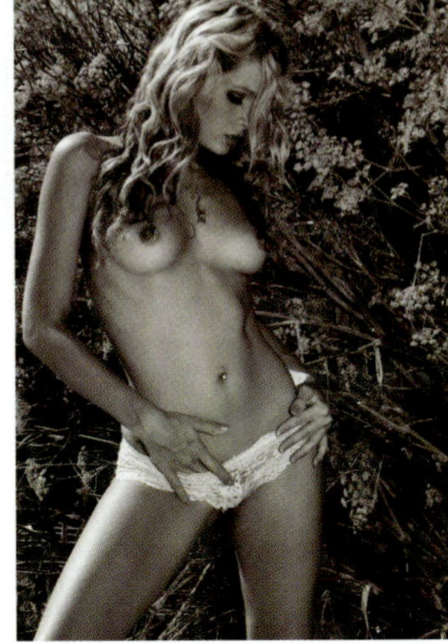

High Contrast Red Filter

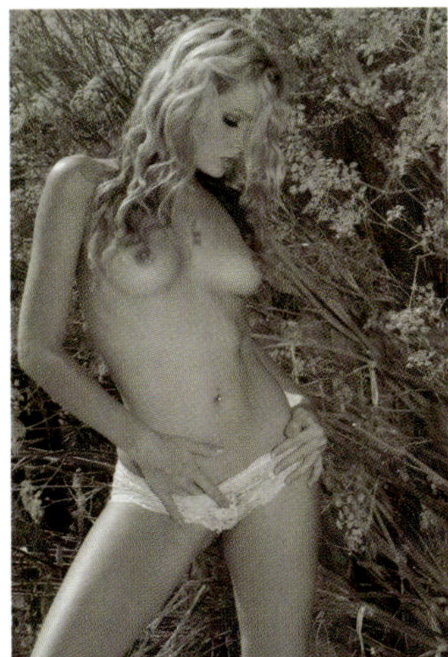

Soft Skin

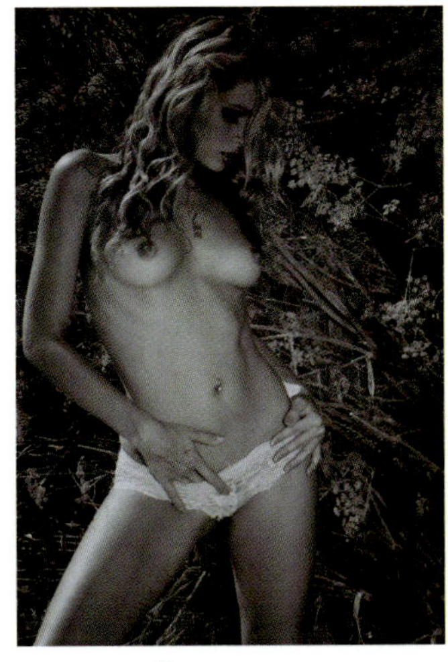

Cyanotype

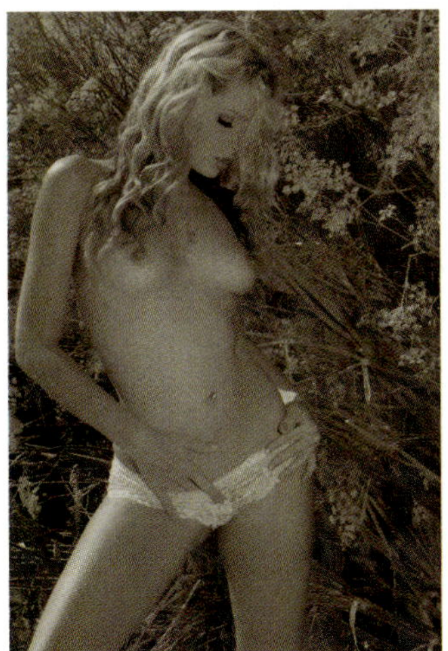

Soft Sepia

Photoshop® Plug-ins

I recently started using Nik Software Silver Efex Pro™ specifically for black and white image conversion. This Photoshop® plug-in streamlines the conversion process, while still allowing me to control a variety of aspects, such as brightness, contrast, structure, shadows, and highlights. The software also simulates film and paper types as well as warming and cooling filters. In addition, you can create your own presets or choose from the 20 different default presets. The small images at right show some of the standard presets, with the pre-set name listed below the image. You can see the wide of results that can be achieved with the same image.

The Web site **www.niksoftware.com** is also very helpful. You can download a free 15-day trial of the software, watch video demonstrations on how to use it, or download the comprehensive user guide. If you are interested in purchasing any of the Nik plug-ins, use the promo code BLEMON and receive a 15 percent discount.

The following pages contain a brief overview of how I typically use Silver Efex Pro™ to convert an image. I have included screenshots of each step of the process.

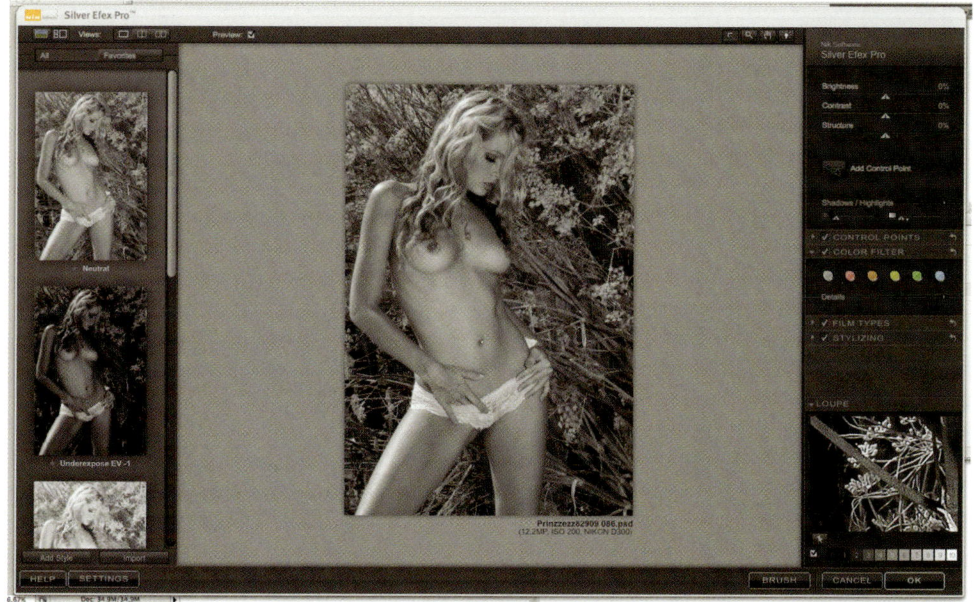

STEP 1

Working in RGB color mode, click to open Silver Efex Pro™. The large center screen will show your basic conversion. The standard pre-sets are on the left. The function controls are on the right.

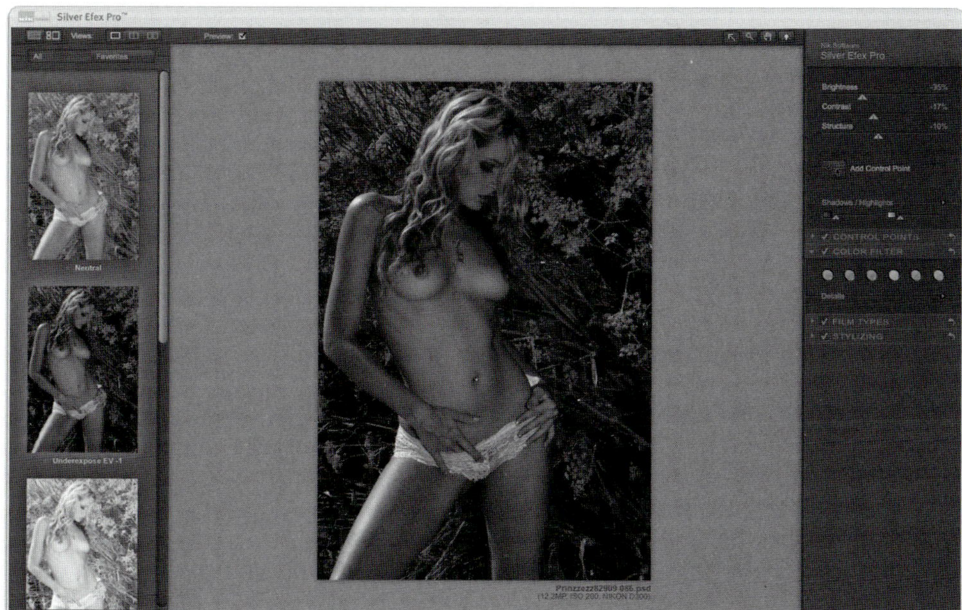

STEP 2

With my images, I start by using the pre-set UnderExpose EV-1. This will darken the image and give me areas of rich black.

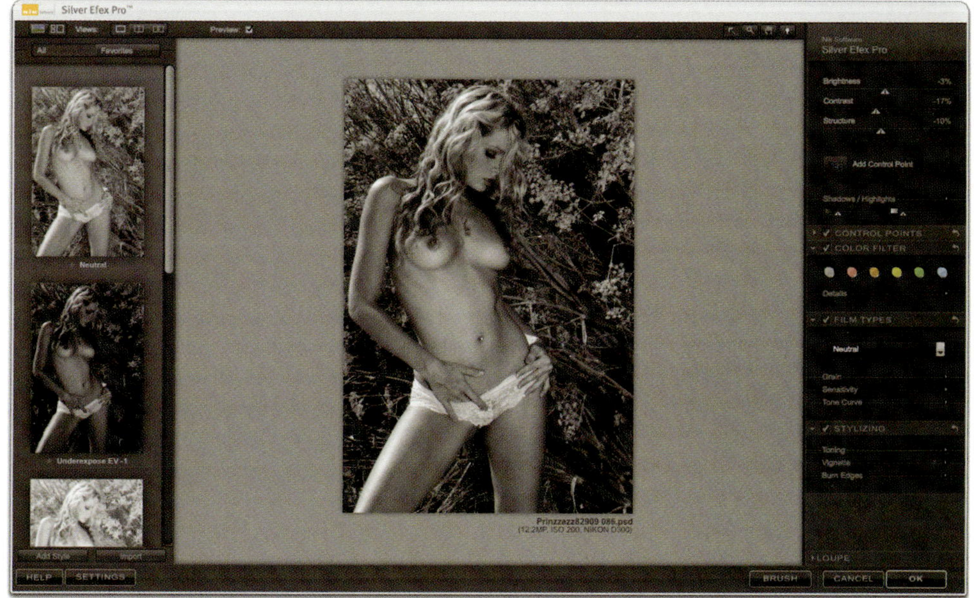

STEP 3

Finally, I adjust the brightness, contrast, and structure with the slider bars on the right. For this image, the brightness is -3, the contrast is -17, and the structure is -10. It is a very simple, yet effective way to convert the image.

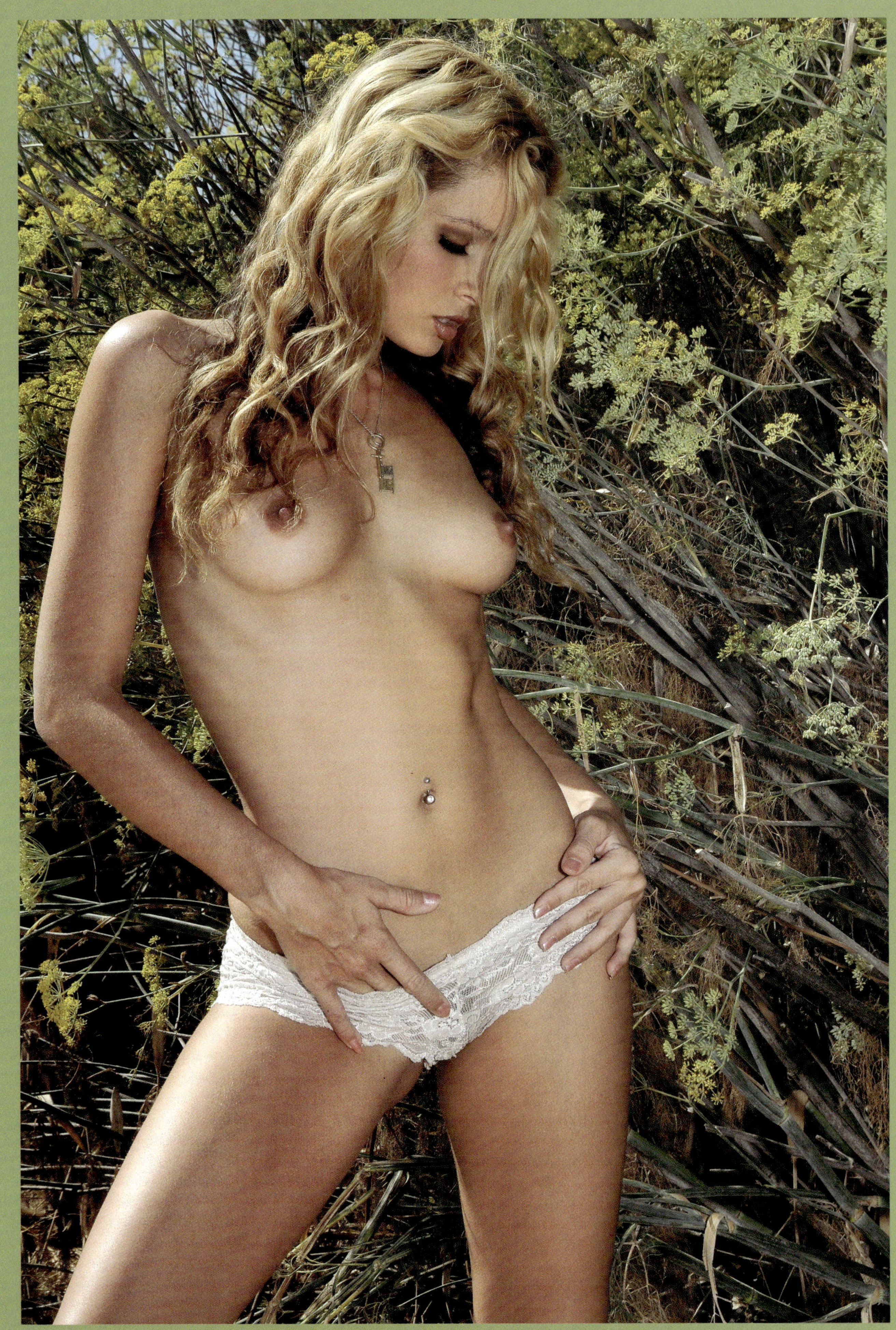

Original Color Image

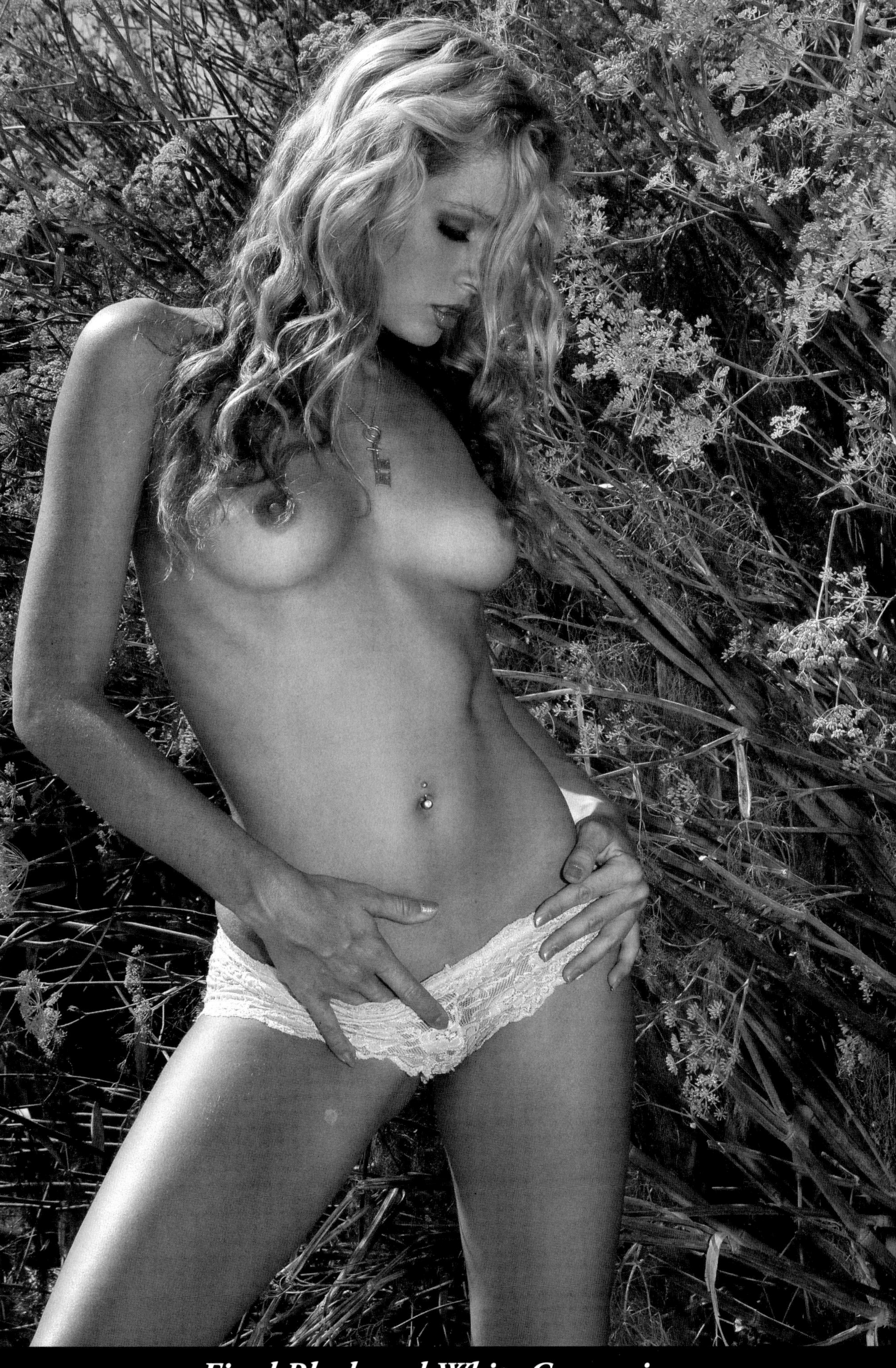

Final Black and White Conversion

Not All Images Convert Well to Black and White

You can convert any image to black and white, but not every image will look good. In fact, some very beautiful color images do not look good in black and white. Here are some basic qualities your image must have to look good when converted:

- **Contrast.** Your image should have strong areas of white and black or it will look flat and washed out. In glamour photography, you can add contrast with either black or white clothing. See pages 56 and 57 for examples.

- **Tonal range.** The tonal range refers to the shades of gray in an image. The more varied tones in an image, the more interest and depth in the image. Lighting can be a key factor in creating a range of tones on skin by creating shadows. If colors are different but the tones are the same, the image will not have separation and won't convert well.

- **Texture.** An image with a lot of texture will convert well to black and white. Also, contrasting textures within an image are very effective. This is why outdoor glamour photography can be so effective in black and white. Nature offers many beautiful textures such as tree bark, grass, and foliage, which contrast with a model's smooth skin.

- **Areas of separation.** If an image has many shades of gray but they all run together, the image may not work well in black and white. An effective image needs to have multiple areas of separation (such as clearly defined edges) to give it dimension and depth.

The following pages have examples of color photos that do not convert well to black and white. It is possible to work with these images in Photoshop® and Silver Efex Pro™ to improve the final result, but they require significantly more editing than most of my images.

EXAMPLE 1

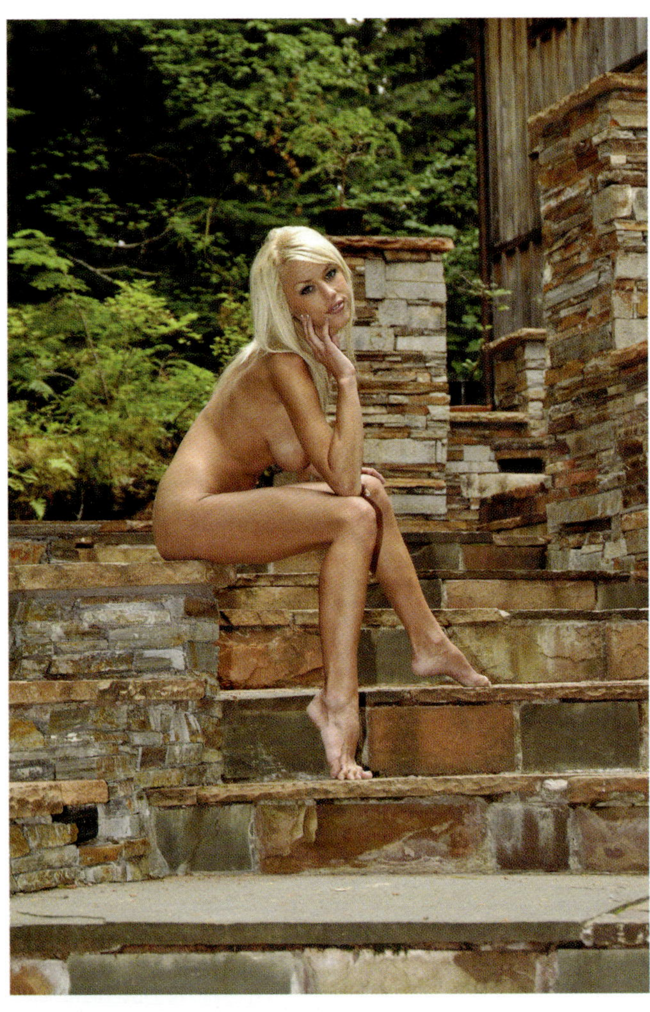

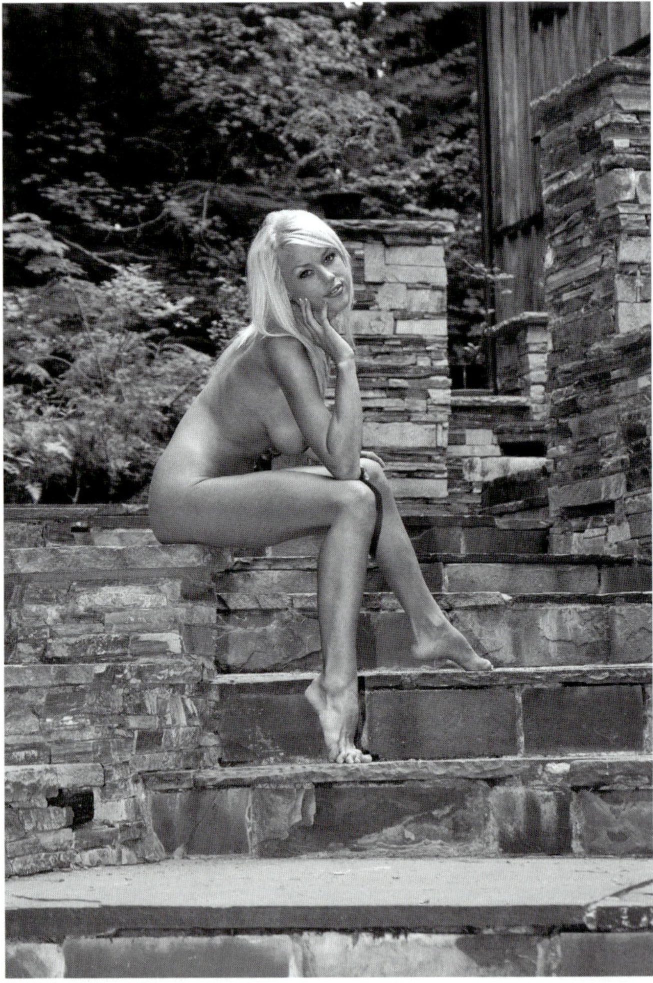

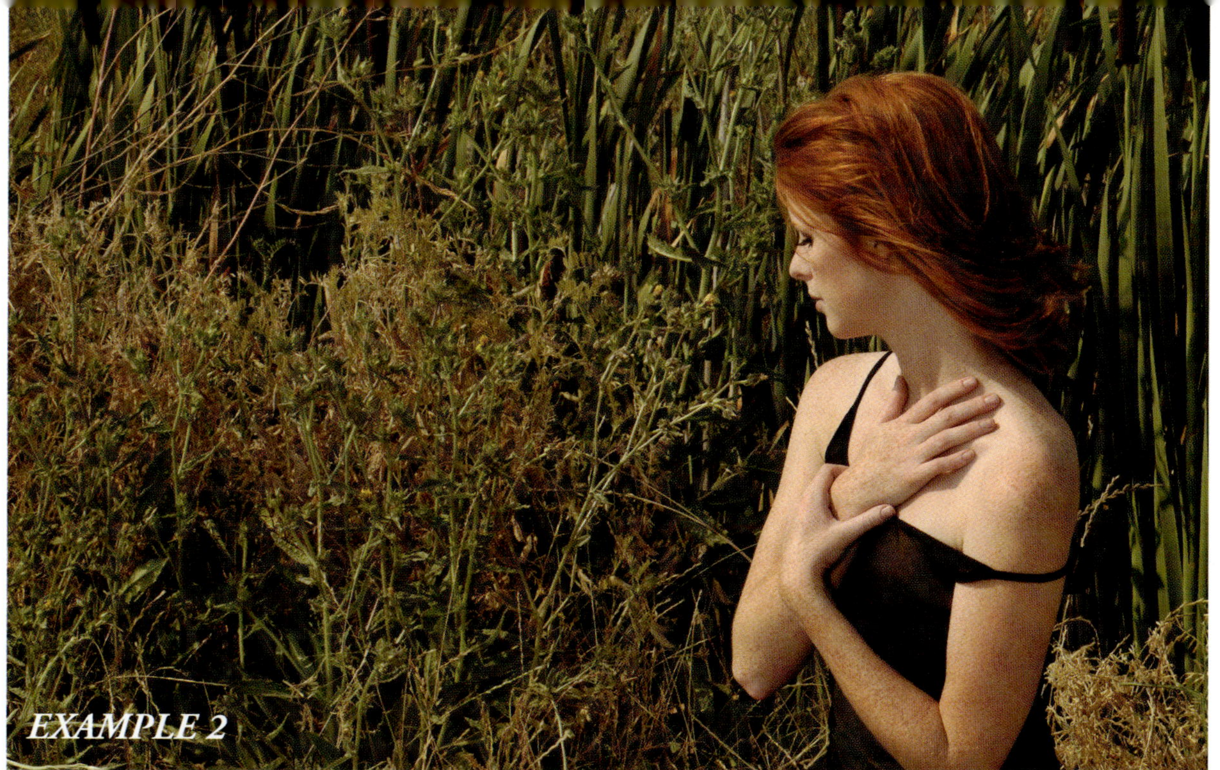

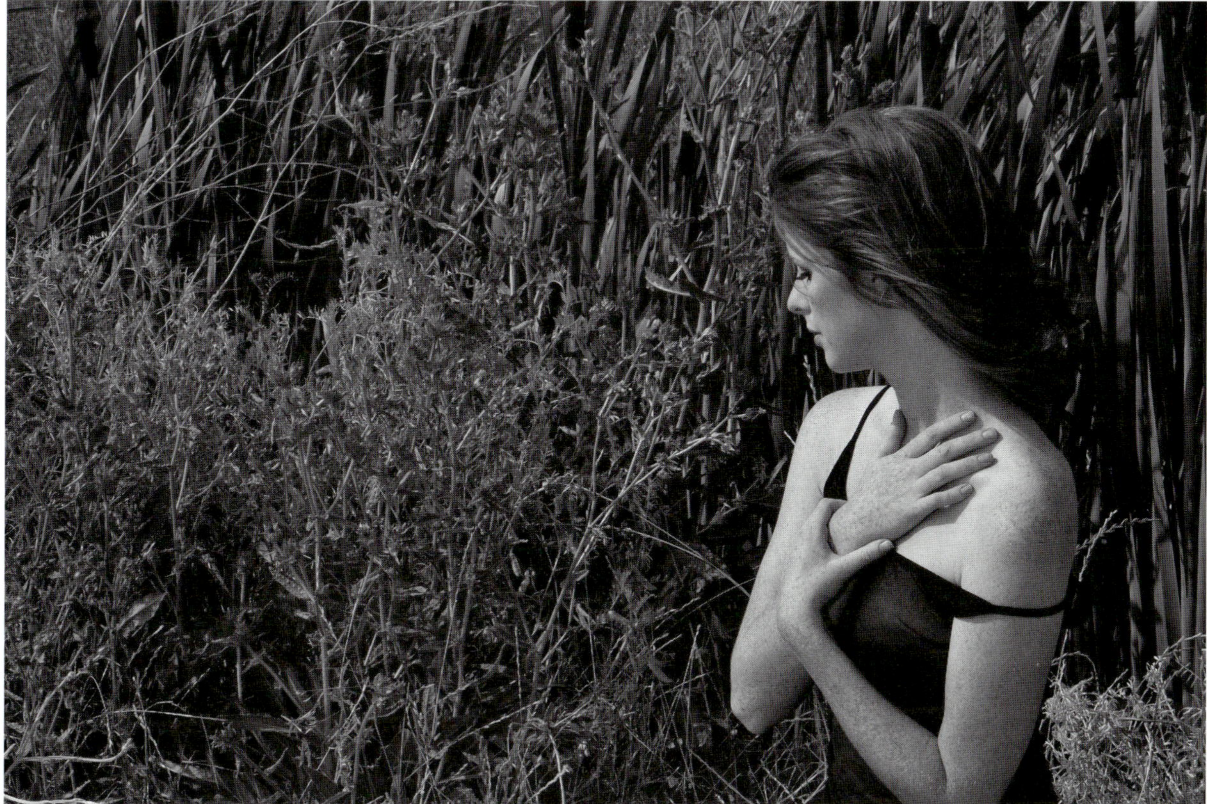

Why It Doesn't Work

In ***Example 1***, the model is very tan and her skin has almost the same tone as the stone steps she is sitting on. The image has great textures, with nice dark areas in the trees and good white areas in the hair. However, the foreground has marginal contrast, so the model's body doesn't separate from the background as much as I would like. This could be fixed in Silver Efex Pro™ by lightening only the skin using the paint feature.

In ***Example 2,*** color plays a key role in the effectiveness of the image. The model's red hair provides vibrant contrast against the dark green of the grasses and is the focal point of the image, bringing out the other red and brown undertones in the foliage. Red and green have almost the same gray value when converted to black and white. When converted, the model's hair no longer stands out, but blends into the background. The photo still has good texture and contrast but not as much impact in black and white.

More Conversion Examples

I encourage you to experiment with black and white conversion in Photoshop® and Silver Efex Pro™. Critically assess the qualities of your photos and take advantage of the digital editing features that allow you to control and improve brightness, contrast, and texture. Below are some additional example of digital photos I have converted. It is valuable to look at the "before" and "after" to see how the conversion process effects and image.

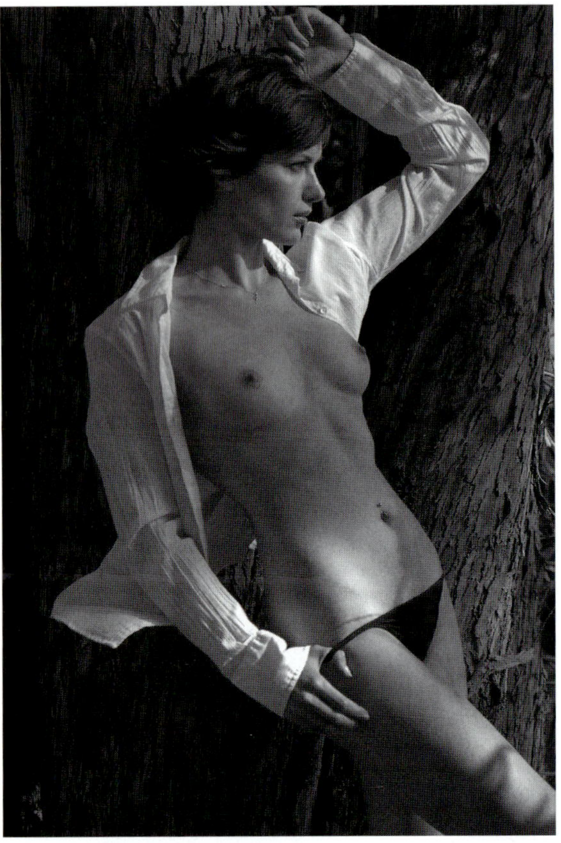

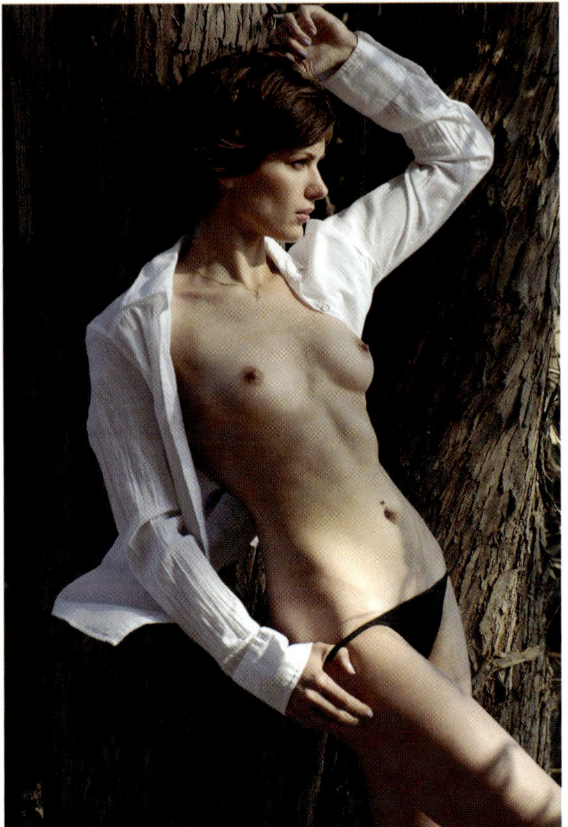

This image works well in black and white because there are very solid dark areas against very light areas. The majority of color is in the skin tone, which converts to many smooth, even shades of gray.

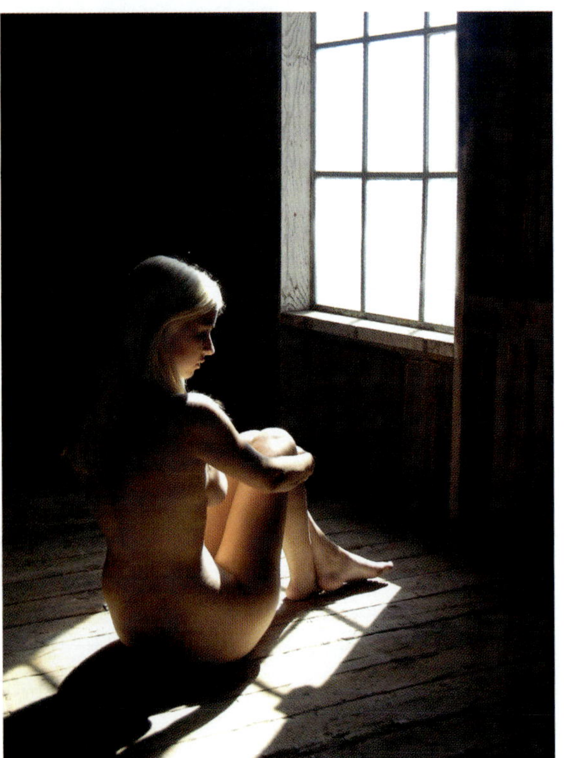

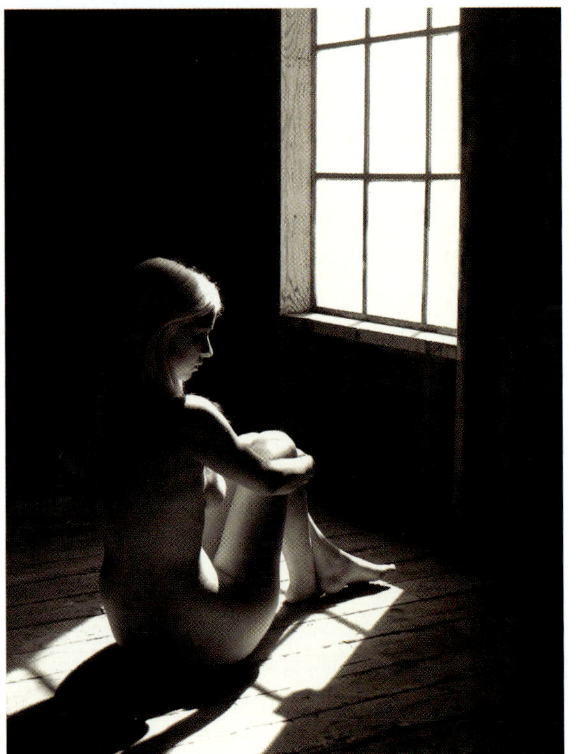

This image works both in black and white and in color. In color, the sunlight emphasizes the warmth of the model's skin. When converted to black and white, the shadow patterns and textures are accentuated because the viewer is no longer distracted by the color.

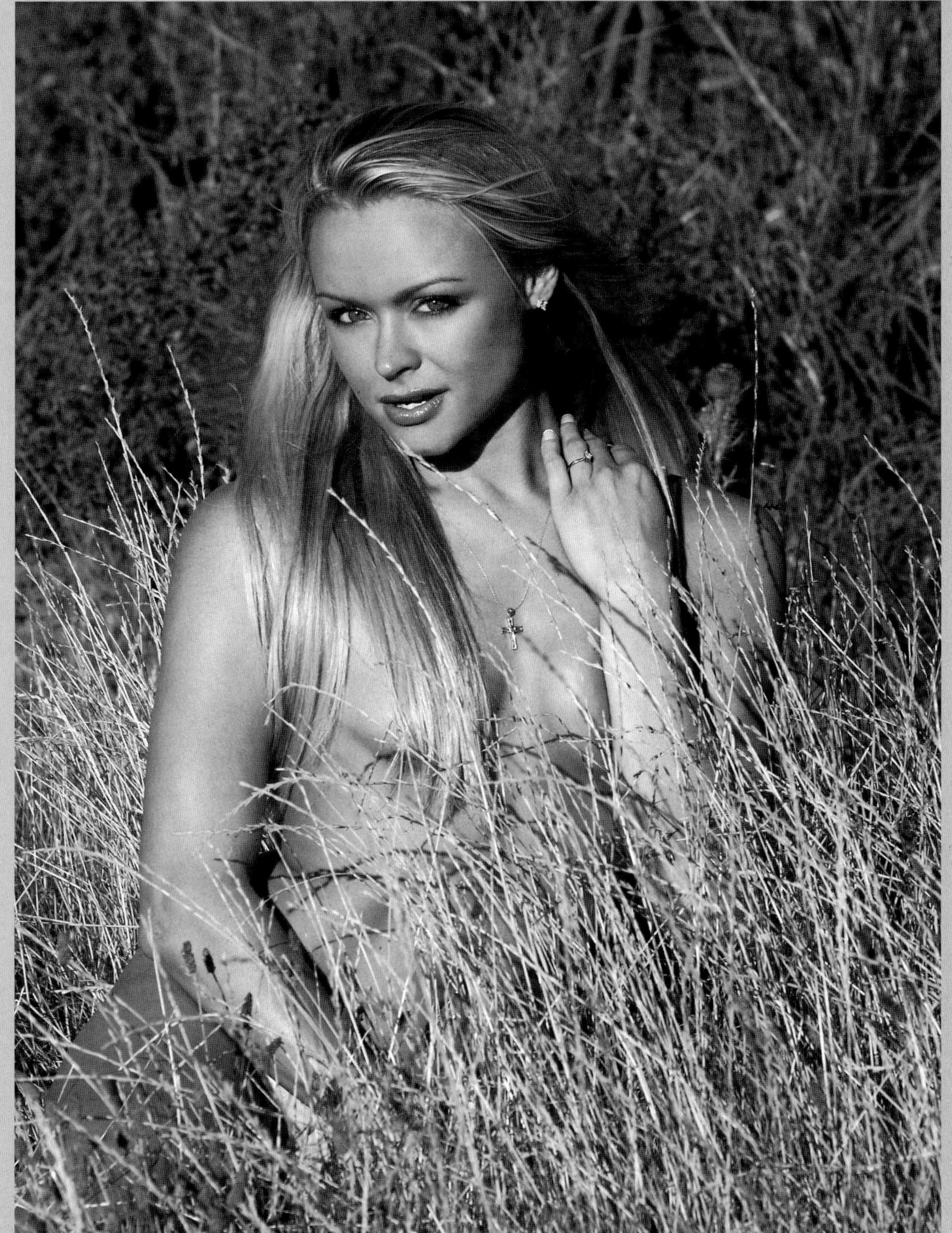

Camera:
Nikon D100

Lens: 70/300VR

Shutter Speed:
250th Second

F-Stop: 10.0

Mode: Digital color conversion

Model: Ali

Texture

This image was shot in the late afternoon in Sonoma County, using flash fill. I chose the location for the tall grass in the foreground. The color matches the model's hair color, creating a very harmonious image. However, it also works well in black and white because there are so many shades of gray and so much texture in the foreground. Much of model's body is hidden in the grass, accentuating her pose and creating an implied nude.

Contrasts

Many of my images have multiple layers of contrast, which is important for creating an effective black and white image. Here, the dark background contrasts with the lighter foreground. The softness of the model's skin contrasts with the foliage. Even the model's expression contrasts with her pose. The arm over her left breast and hair over her right breast add modesty, while her expression is seductive.

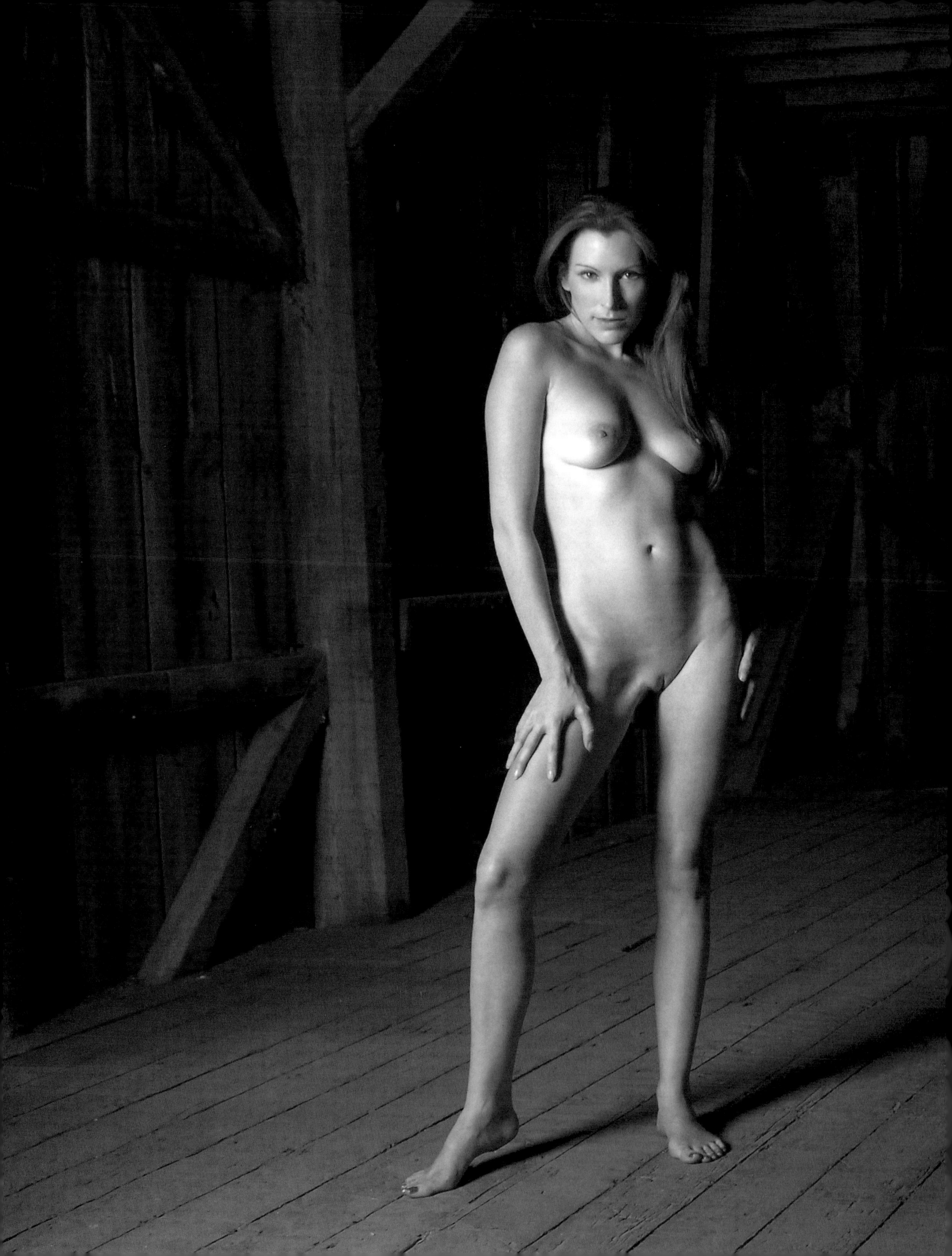

Location

The double-spread image on pages 66 and 67 was shot during a workshop in St. Joseph, Missouri. Taken inside a 125-year-old barn, the setting allowed me to light the model using a portable power pack with a soft box, positioned about 45 degrees from the camera. This created the long shadow across the floor and illuminated the amazing grain of the wood floor and walls. The model also worked with the light, angling her body toward it, creating shadows along her right side.

Depth

This image shows the depth of the interior and clearly creates a sense of space. There are a number of angles that direct the eye. The model's shadow leads to the window. The grooves in the floor give additional perspective.

Exposure

Part of what makes this image exceptional is the exposure. There are two light areas in the image: the model and the window. If you look closely you can see that the exposure of the window is the same as the exposure of the model, so you can clearly see through the window.

Camera: Nikon D200

Lens: 24/120VR

Shutter Speed: 125th Second

F-Stop: 8.0

Mode: Digital color conversion

Model: Serenity

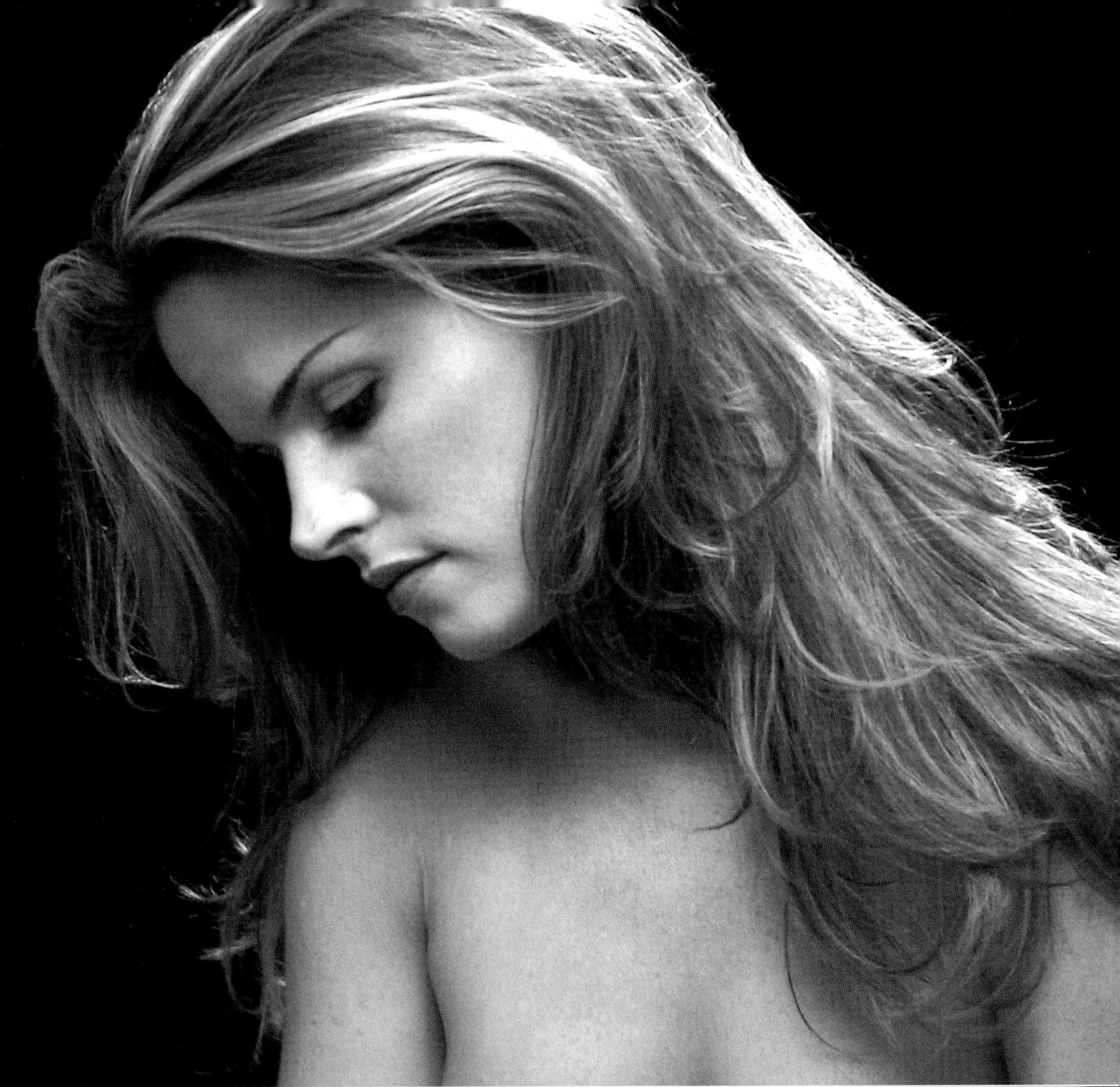

Portrait

This beautiful head shot was taken in my Novato studio. I used a large soft box to camera left and a hair light to create separation from the background. The dramatic lighting contrasted nicely with the simplicity of the background and the reflective expression of the model. Her hair is very soft and feminine and so is her profile. The hint of cleavage makes the image slightly provocative.

Camera: Pentax 6 x 7

Lens: 135 mm

Shutter Speed: 30th Second

F-Stop: 8.0

Mode: Digital color conversion

Model: Julie

Setting

This image was shot in the late morning in Sonoma. The intent was to capture the feeling of warm sunlight on skin in a very natural way. The background is minimal, so it won't distract from the model. The black bushes in the lower part of the background help anchor and stabilize the image. It also provides good balance for the model's dark hair.

Sun

Always be aware of the light and use it to your advantage. Here, the model is positioned so the sun strikes the majority of her body. Her head and arm are up and her shoulders are back, highlighting the chest and torso. Her bent front leg allows the wash of sunlight to flow down her body.

Camera: Nikon D300

Lens: 70/300 VR

Shutter Speed: 500th Second

F-Stop: 8.0

Mode: Digital color conversion

Model: Betcee May

hint *When shooting into the sun, have the model tilt her head up and close her eyes. There will be no shadows under the eyes, just smooth, even lighting.*

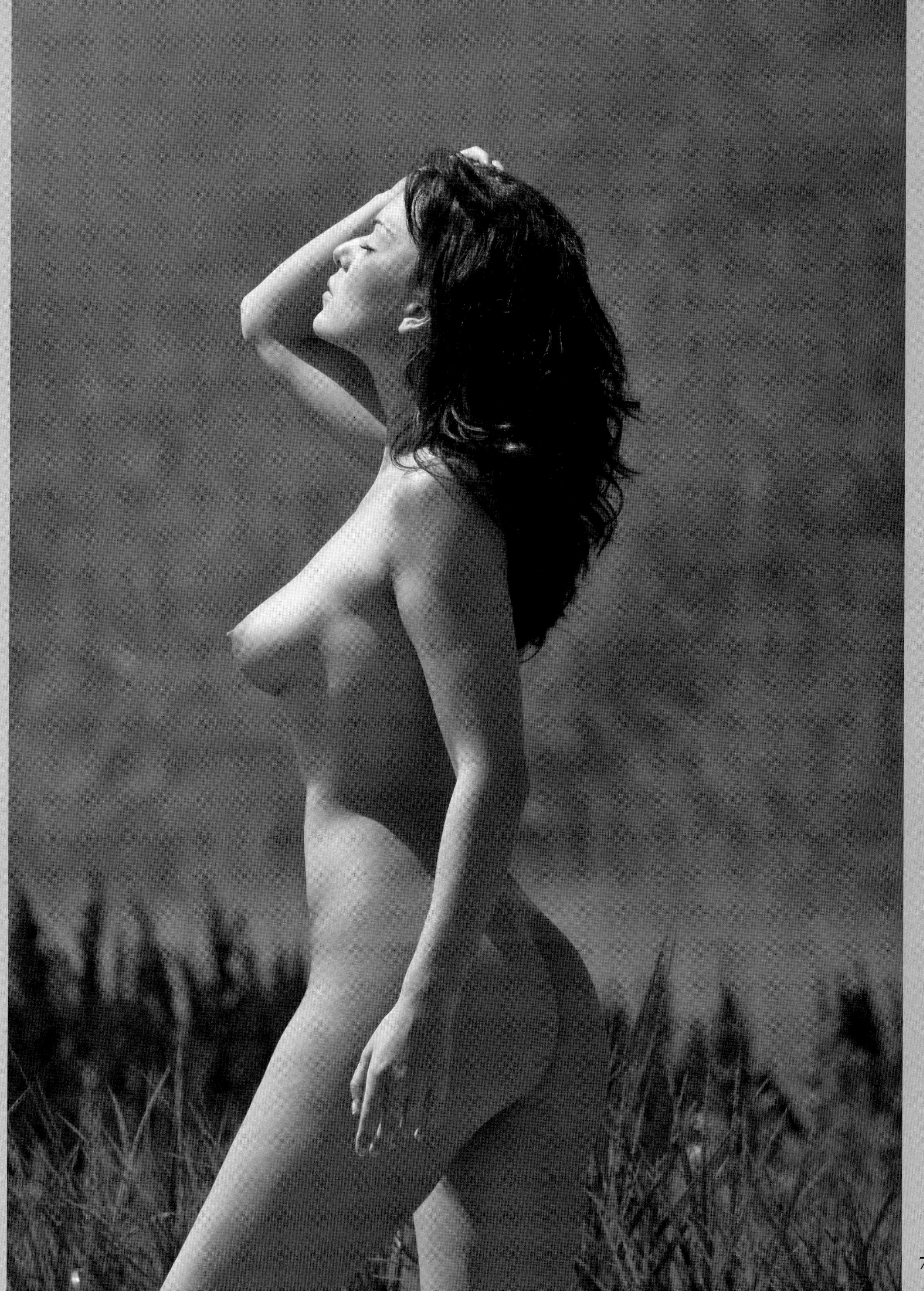

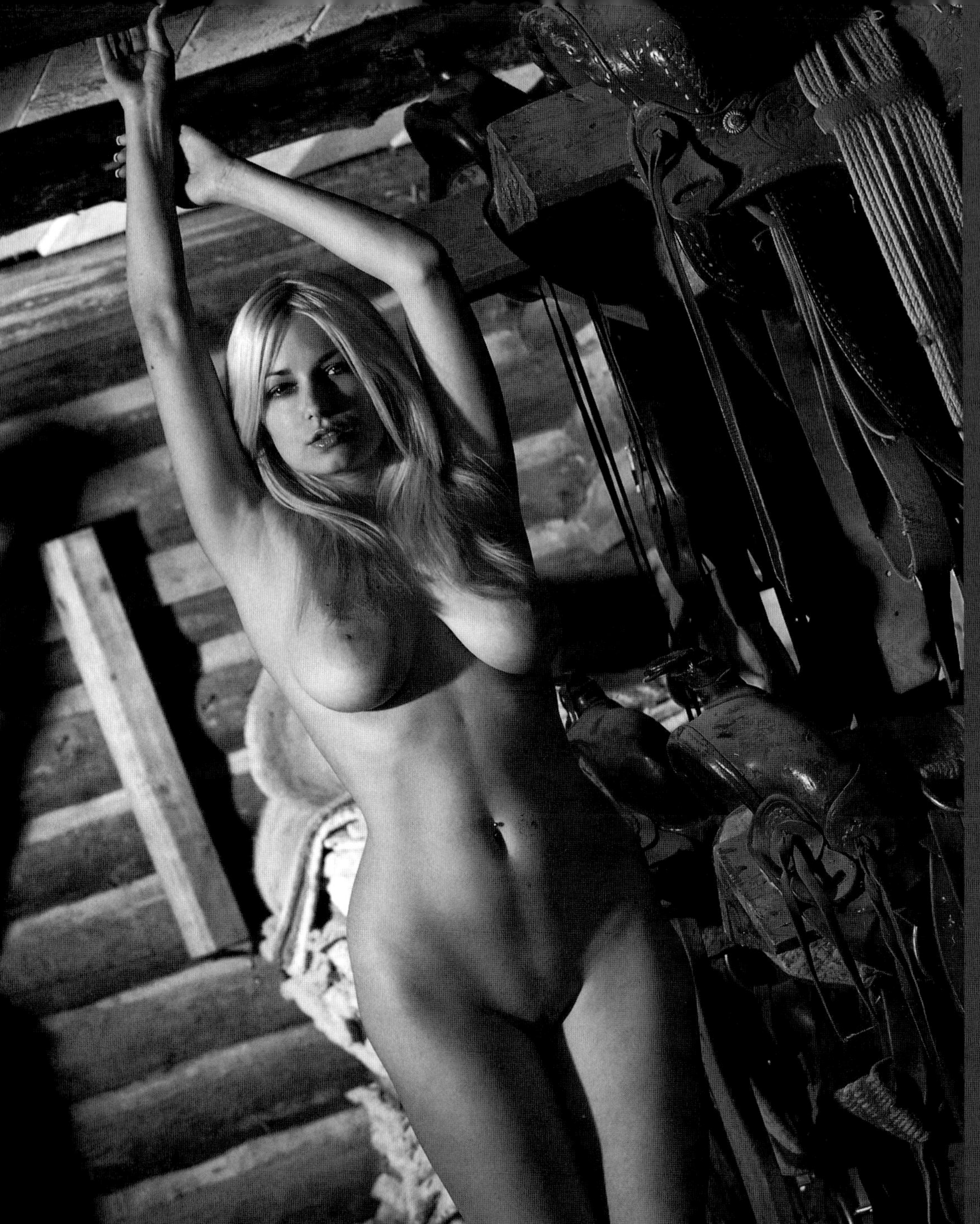

Lighting

This image was shot at a workshop in Cody, Wyoming. Set in an old saddle shop, the chinked logs of the walls and old saddles made a very interesting background. Unfortunately, the natural lighting was not adequate to separate the model from the background. I used supplemental lighting to illuminate the background and add highlights to the model's body. The light was positioned about 90 degrees to the model in order to light her left side. I tilted the camera slightly when shooting so the background angles were not such strong horizontal lines.

Pose

The model created this pose. She is stretching with her arms above her head, which accentuates and lengthens the lines of her body. The pose lifts her breasts and tightens her torso. She is also standing on the balls of her feet, which tightens the muscles of the legs.

tip

If you are not shooting a full body image, always crop above the knee. This will allow you to capture three-fourths of the model's body and will make the image look proportional.

Camera: Nikon D200

Lens: Nikon 24/120 VR

Shutter Speed: 125th Second

F-Stop: 8.0

Mode: Digital color conversion

Model: Danielle

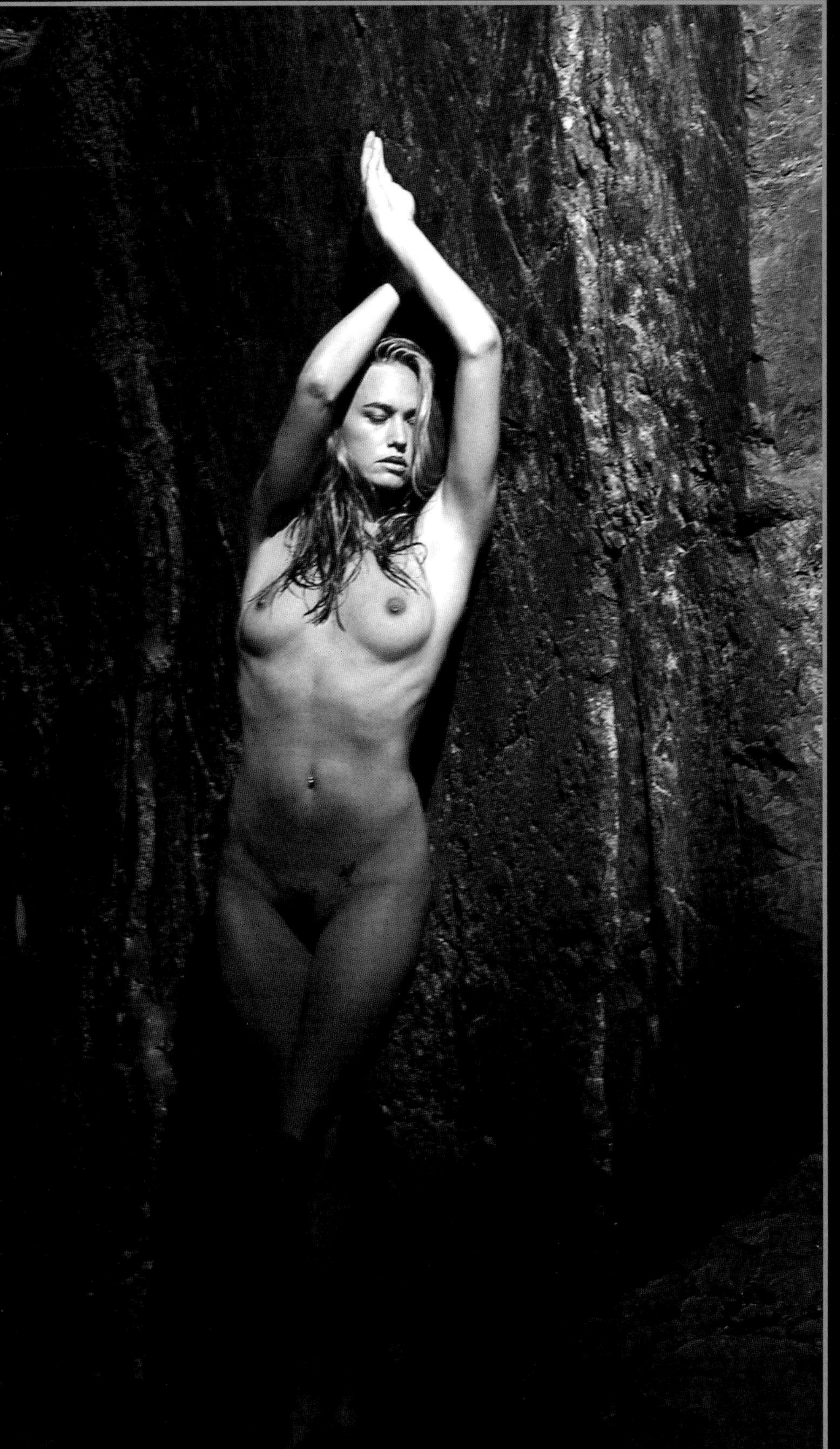

Contrasts

This image was shot in the late afternoon, specifically to take advantage of the beautiful natural light. The setting is all about contrasts: the strength of the granite background against the softness of the female form and the bright sun versus the deep shadows.

Posing

This dramatic pose takes full advantage of the light. The body and face are angled toward the light. The arms bent and crossed over the head create gorgeous, sensual angles, as do the clean line of the hip and leg.

Model

Models are often willing to go to great lengths to get extraordinary shots. In this case, Justine swam across a pond to get to this rocky area near a waterfall.

Camera: Nikon D100

Lens: Nikon 70-300VR

Shutter Speed: 125th Second

F-Stop: 11

Mode: Digital color conversion

Model: Justine

Camera: Nikon D300

Lens: 70/300 VR

Shutter Speed: 250th Second

F-Stop: 16.0

Mode: Digital color conversion

Model: Brooke

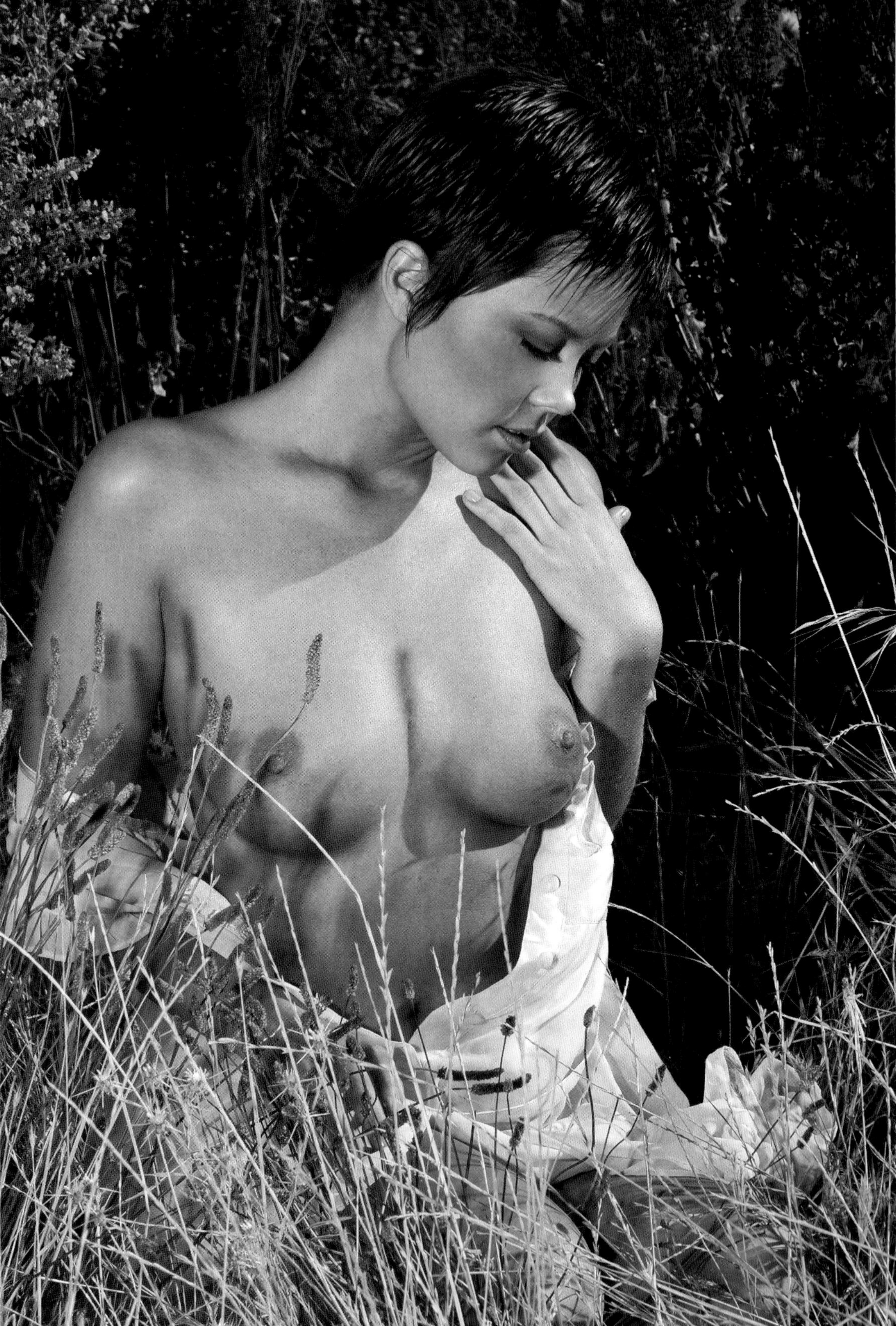

Changing the Look of a Model

The images on pages 74 and 75 are examples of simple ways to change the look of a model. These images were shot on the same day at two separate locations. The first difference is fairly obvious: the hair.

In the image on the left the model has short, dark hair. This worked well with the setting as her hair is very textured and created a contrasting pattern with the dark background. The wisps and shorter strands also caught the light, adding additional highlights. Overall, the short hair gave the model a very gamin-like feel.

In the image at right, the same model is wearing long, lighter-colored wig. A wig can be a good prop. It changed the image completely and added an element of sensuality, in the way the hair nestles between her breasts.

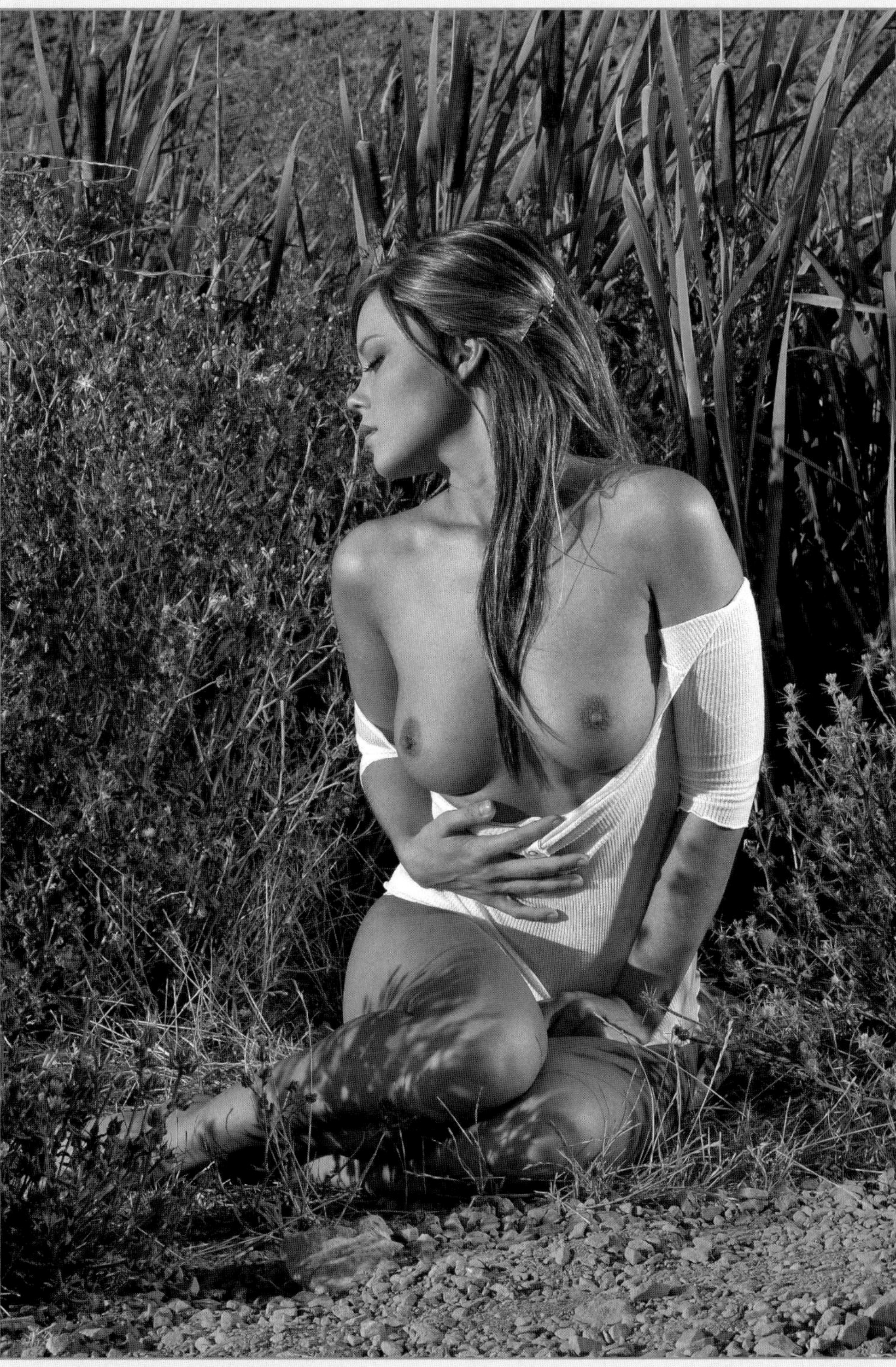

Lighting

The lighting was also a key factor in making the model look different. Both images were lit using a Vagabound II, 110 volt and a portable strobe light. In the image at left, the strobe is closer to the model, making her skin tone look lighter. The strobe made the grasses in front of the model well lit, which helps add texture to the image.

In the image at left, the strobe evened the lighting, creating soft shadows and drawing out the details of the cattails in the background and the rocks in the foreground. There are more shades of gray and less intense areas of black and white. The model's skin tone is a more even gray and contrasts nicely with her white shirt.

Camera: Nikon D300

Lens: 70/300 VR

Shutter Speed: 250th Second

F-Stop: 14.0

Mode: Digital color conversion

Model: Brooke

Sunlight

This is another image meant to convey the feeling of sunlight on skin. It was shot in Sonoma in the late afternoon with southwestern light. The model has raised her face to the sun. Shooting horizontally allowed for the model to stretch her right arm and leg. The shadows on her body are created by the long lines of her limbs. The pose also lengthened the muscles and lines of the model's legs.

Conversion

This image is an excellent example of how colors convert. Note how the dark lingerie around the model's waist almost matches the color of her hair. In color, the lingerie is black and the model has red hair. When converted to black and white, a redhead will usually look like a brunette.

Camera: Nikon D200

Lens: 70/300 VR

Shutter Speed: 500th Second

F-Stop: 6.3

Mode: Digital color conversion

Model: Rebecca

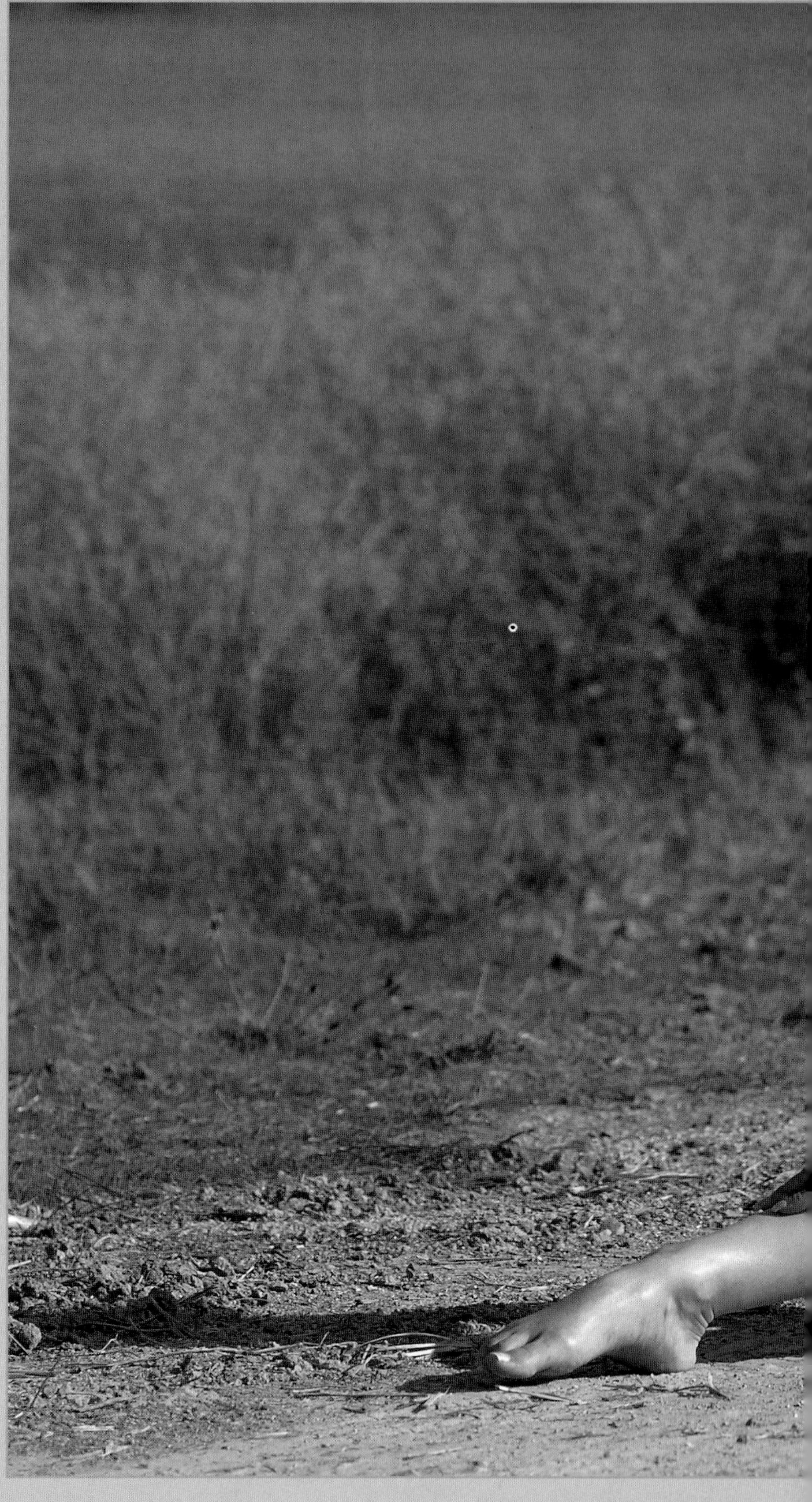

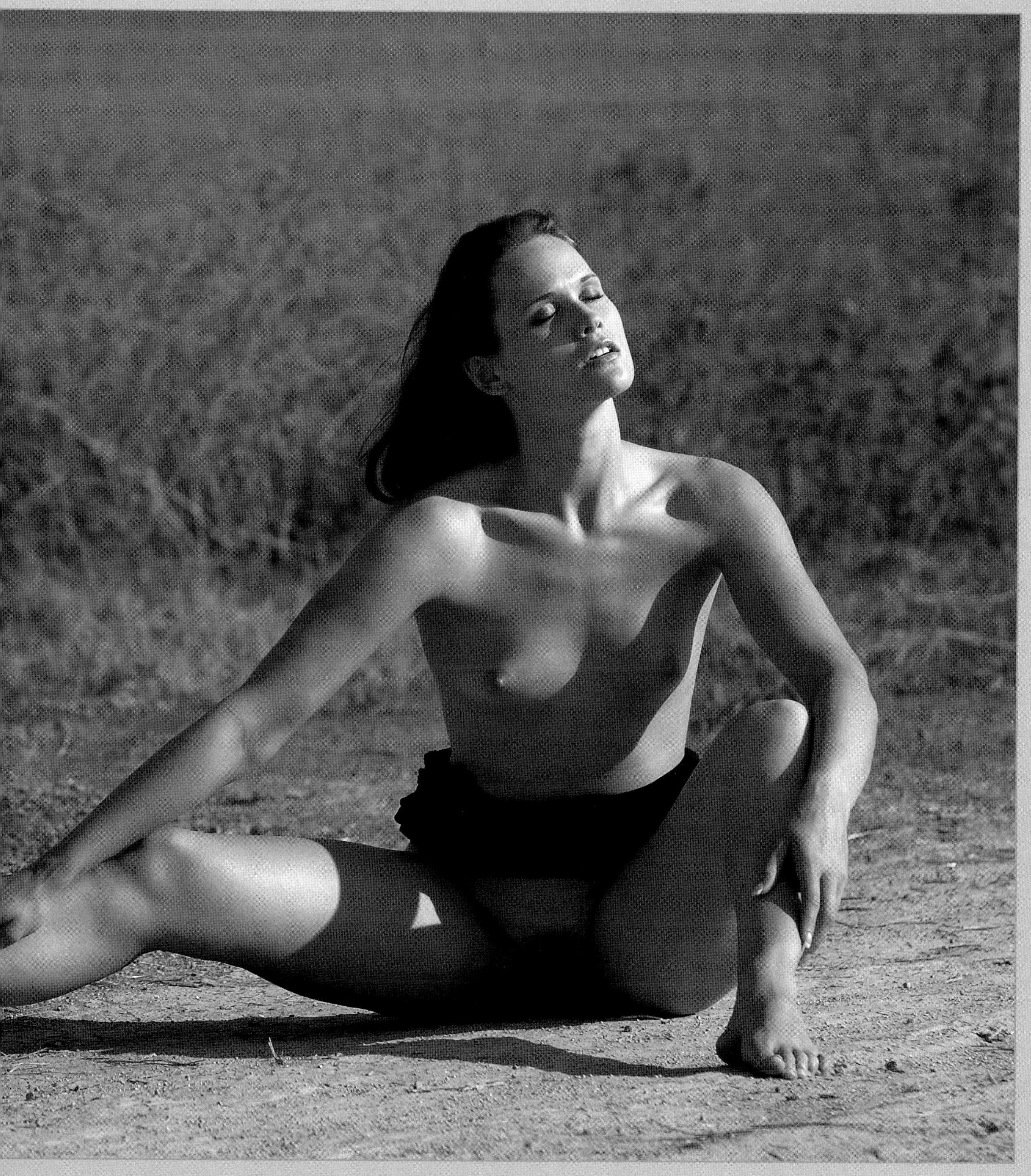

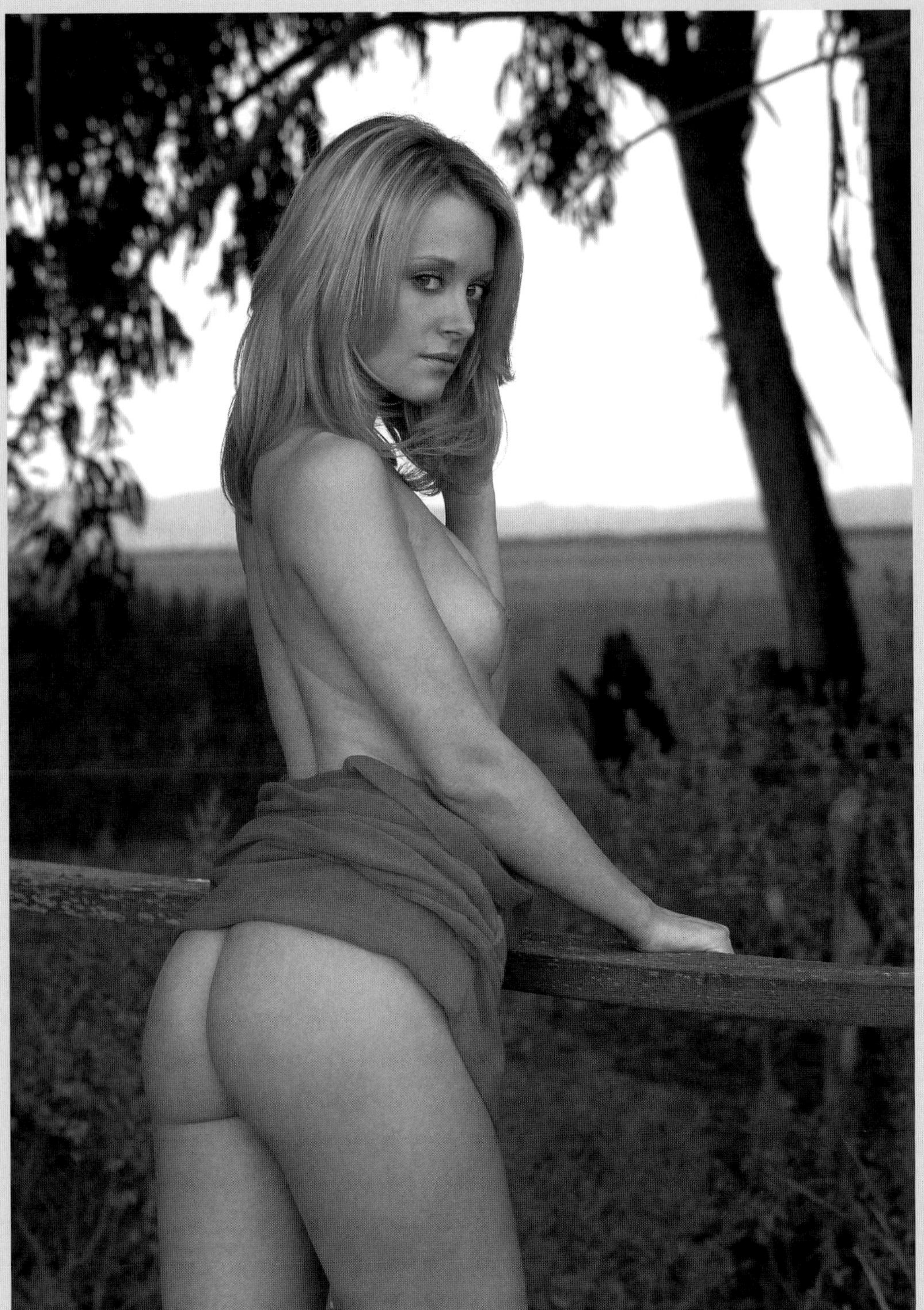

Setting

This image was shot in Sonoma during the late afternoon in a shaded area under a grove of eucalyptus trees. The sun was coming from the model's right. The model is leaning on an old, weathered board bridge, which made a good prop. It had nice texture, and gave the model a place to rest her hand. The angle balanced the strong horizon line in the background.

Voyeuristic Quality

The dress around the model's waist adds separation to the image and emphasizes her buttocks. Paired with the model's turned head and facial expression, it gives the image a voyeuristic quality.

Horizon Line

When you are shooting in an area with a clear, straight horizon line, be careful positioning the model. The horizon line should not dissect the model's body. Do not place it at the neck, eye, or waist. Also, shorten the depth of field so the horizon line is in soft focus.

Camera: Nikon D200

Lens: 70/300 VR

Shutter Speed: 125th Second

F-Stop: 8.0

Mode: Digital color conversion

Model: Jamie

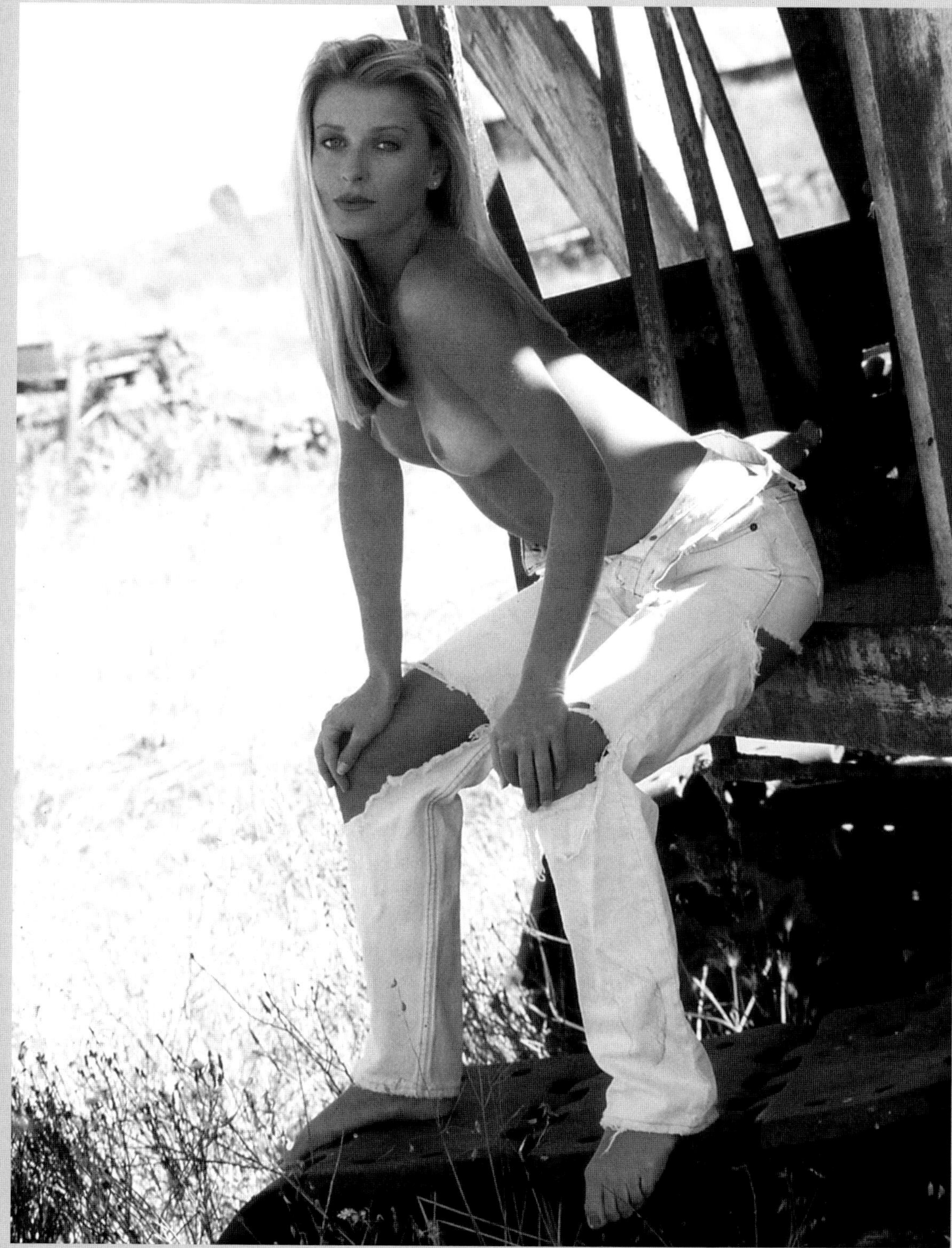

Camera:
Nikon FM

Lens: 80/200 mm

Mode: Kodak Ektachrome Film

Model: Karen

Location

This image was shot in the early, bright afternoon sunlight in Sonoma. The model sat on an old dragline. I chose the location for the great texture of the machinery and interesting angles. It also provided a hard surface contrast against the soft beauty of the model.

Clothing

The light-colored, ripped jeans are a nice accent in the photo. They contrast well with the model's tan skin and add some texture. They also add an area of white that helps balance out the lighter background and bring continuity across the entire image.

Exposure

While many areas of the photo work, I feel the background is overexposed and a little too light. My goal is always to make sure the exposure on the model is good, which is the case in this image.

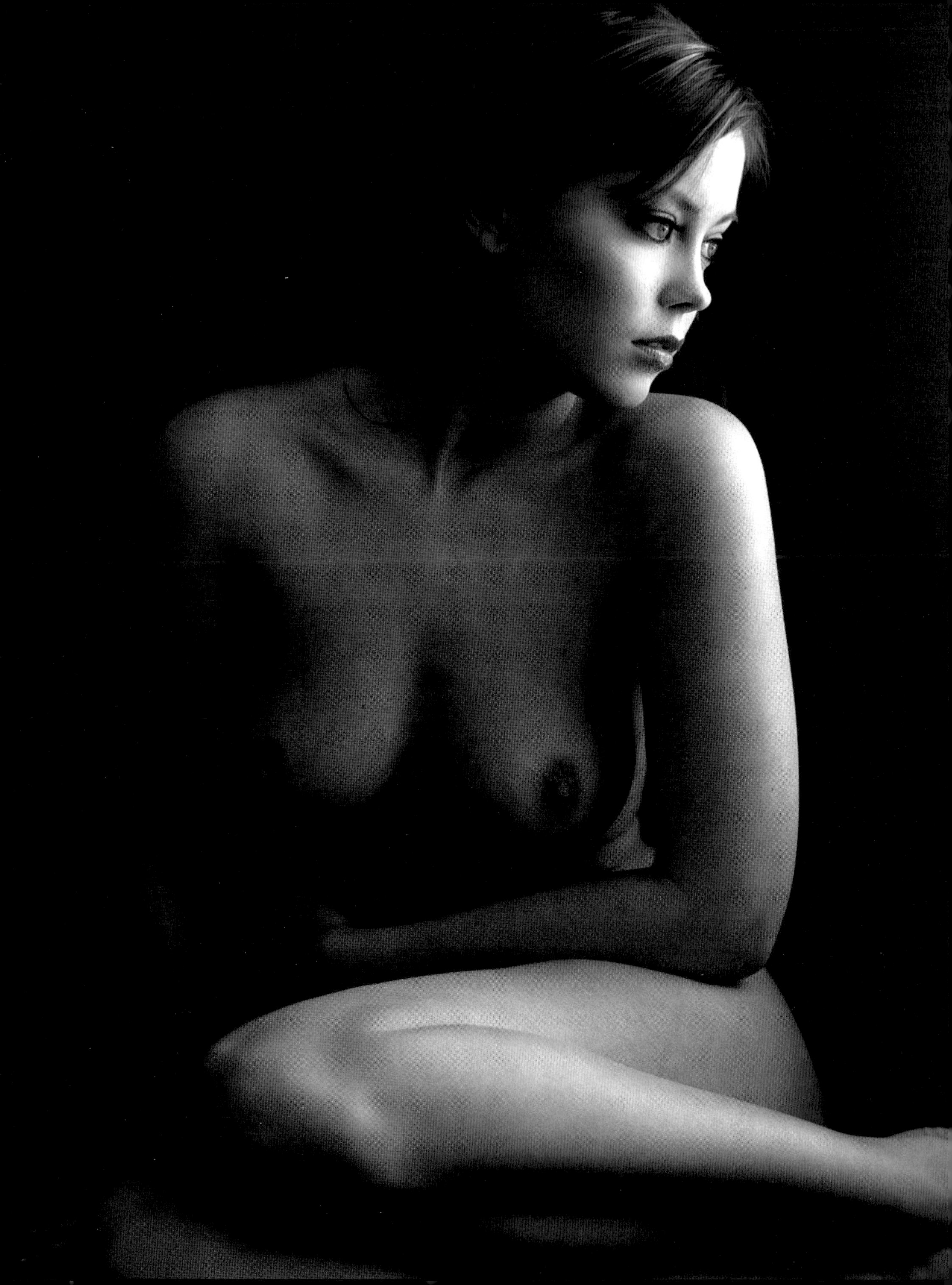

Light

This image was shot in my Novato studio in the mid-morning using only natural window light. I love the effect natural morning light has on the soft skin of the model. It highlights her face and creates very delicate shadows on the rest of her body.

Position

Positioning is the key to making an image like this work. You cannot adjust natural light to make it fall where you want, you have to move the model into the light. The model was positioned so her profile caught the most light, with softer light on the left side of her body.

Mood

In addition to the model's position, the pose helps set a tone for the entire composition. She has a serene expression on her face and is looking down and away from the camera. This gives the image a very peaceful, reflective feel.

Camera: Nikon D100

Lens: Tamron 28/75

Shutter Speed: 30th Second

F-Stop: 2.8

Mode: Digital color conversion

Model: Brooke

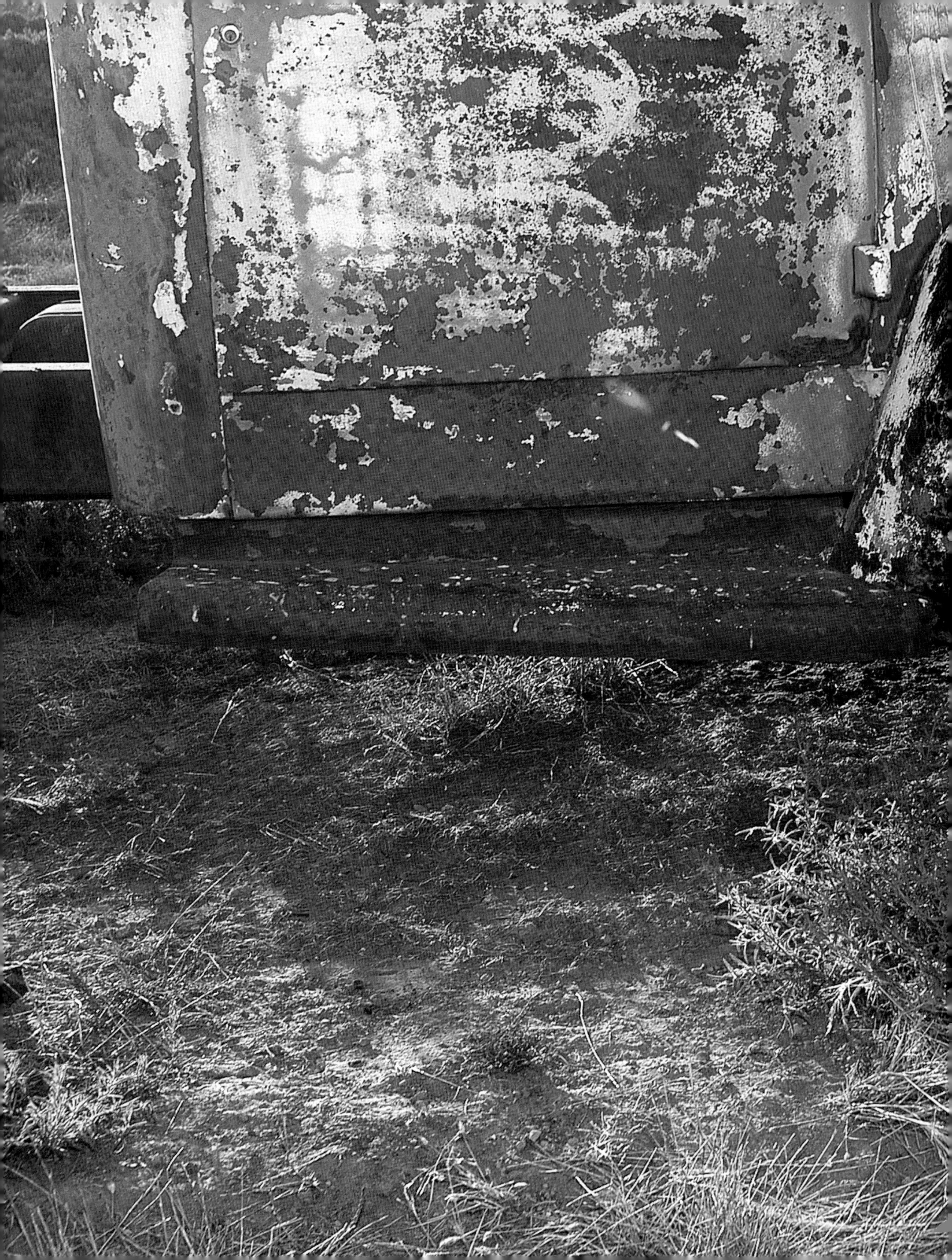

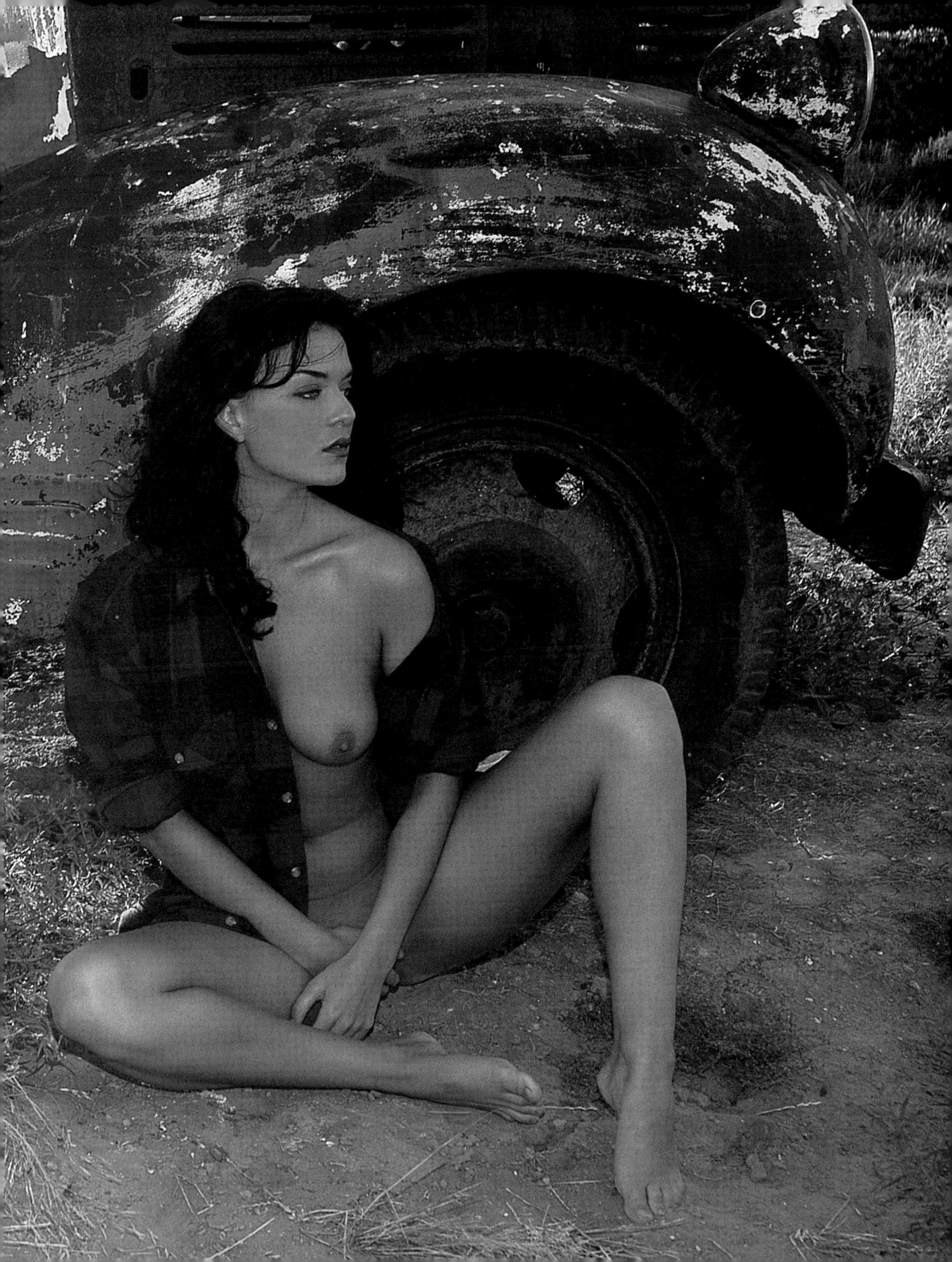

Masculinity

The double-spread image on the two preceding pages was shot in the late afternoon in Sonoma. I choose the location for the overwhelming masculine feeling. The broken-down truck was rather barren and rusted, and the ground was dusty with patches of rough grass. I felt this would provide excellent contrast with the soft femininity of the model. I also added an old red-and-black-checked work shirt to enhance the masculine theme and heighten the contrast.

Flash Fill

This image was flash filled to properly light the model. To set the flash, I took a light reading from her face and set the camera to that setting. I then set the flash to one stop lower to create a '-1' EV effect.

Camera: Nikon D100

Lens: Tamron 28/75

Shutter Speed: 125th Second

F-Stop: 5.6

Mode: Digital color conversion

Model: Betcee May

tip

The body language of the model often sets the tone of an image. Although a pose may be carefully crafted, if the model is loose and relaxed it can look natural. This image is a good example of that premise. Her hands were positioned to preserve some modesty, yet the image still retains the casual feel.

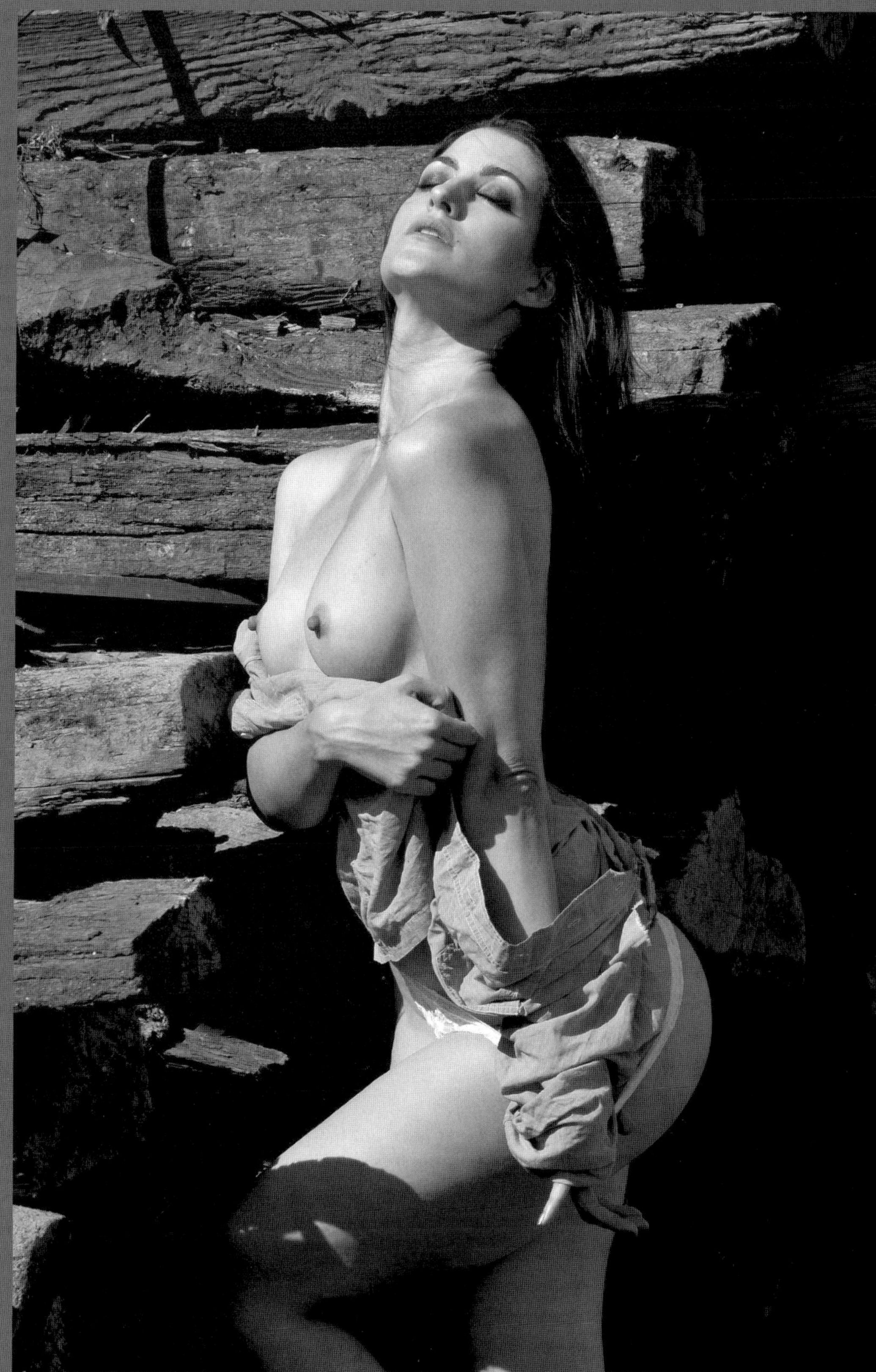

Background

This image was shot in Sonoma in front of a stack of old railroad ties. It provides interesting texture as well as a good shadow area to accent the line of the model's body.

Lighting

This image uses all natural light. It was taken during the late afternoon, with the sun coming from the west. This bathes the skin in warmth and also creates deep shadow areas.

S-Curve

This pose is particularly effective because it emphasizes the roundness and S-curve of the model's body. The bent leg accents the buttocks, while the arched back thrusts the breasts forward. This creates a very sensual, feminine pose.

Clothing

The shirt around the model's waist adds additional texture and separation to the image. This image, originally shot in color, is part of my "Blue Shirt Project" where different models are photographed wearing the same blue shirt all across the United States.

Camera: Nikon D300

Lens: Nikon 70/300 VR

Shutter Speed: 200th Second

F-Stop: 14.0

Mode: Digital color conversion

Model: Krystinna

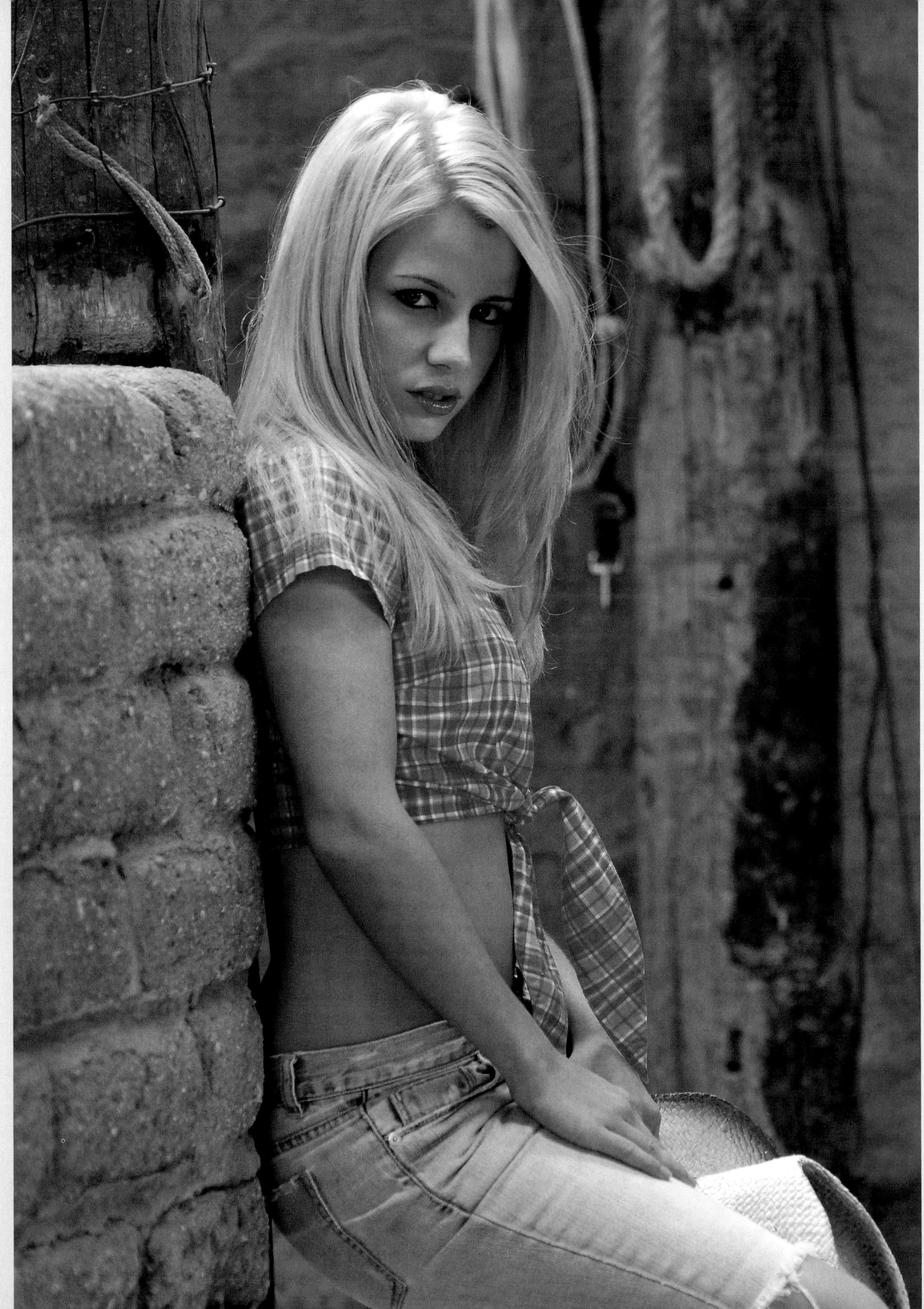

Setting

Shot in Sante Fe, New Mexico, this is an image where the location can be determined from the picture itself. All the elements work together to give the image a very Southwestern feel. This image was shot in a horse stable with sky lights, so no supplemental lighting was needed.

Props

Not only do the props define the location, they help define the pose. The textured wall was a good backdrop for the model to lean against. The cowboy hat gave the model something to hold in her hands. The clothes also add to the image. The shirt tied at the midriff paired with the ripped jeans is very sexy, complementing the sensual pose and facial expression.

Camera: Nikon D300

Lens: Nikon 70/300VR

Shutter Speed: 25th Second

F-Stop: 4.8

Mode: Digital color conversion

Model: Jaimie

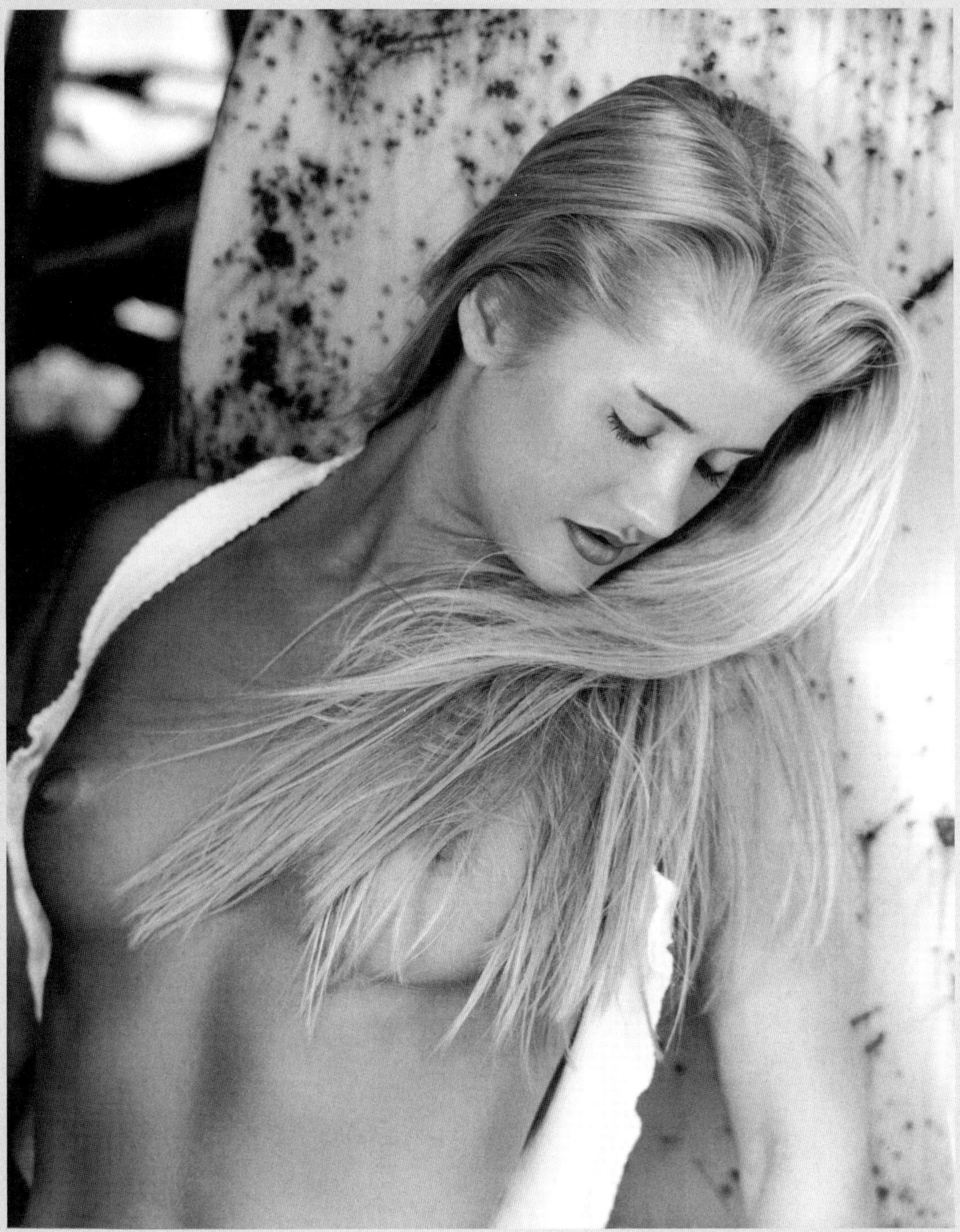

Camera: Hasselblad

Lens: 150 mm

Mode: Digital color conversion

Model: Kirsten

Head Shots

Head shots are a staple of glamour photography. These are often shot in a studio, but the examples on pages 88 and 89 show that effective head shots can also be taken outdoors with natural lighting. In the image above, the model posed against a rusted tank, which added contrast and texture to the background. Her hair was splayed across her breast and shoulder to add drama to the shot. The pose was very contemplative, almost demure, and accentuates the delicate structure of her face. The lighting was very even, flattering, and natural.

The example on page 89 is a stark opposite. The model is addressing the camera with a very sensual expression. The lighting was also natural, but I placed the model in a groove of trees to create a pattern of light on her face. The shadows add mystery and the entire image has an enticing aura of sexuality.

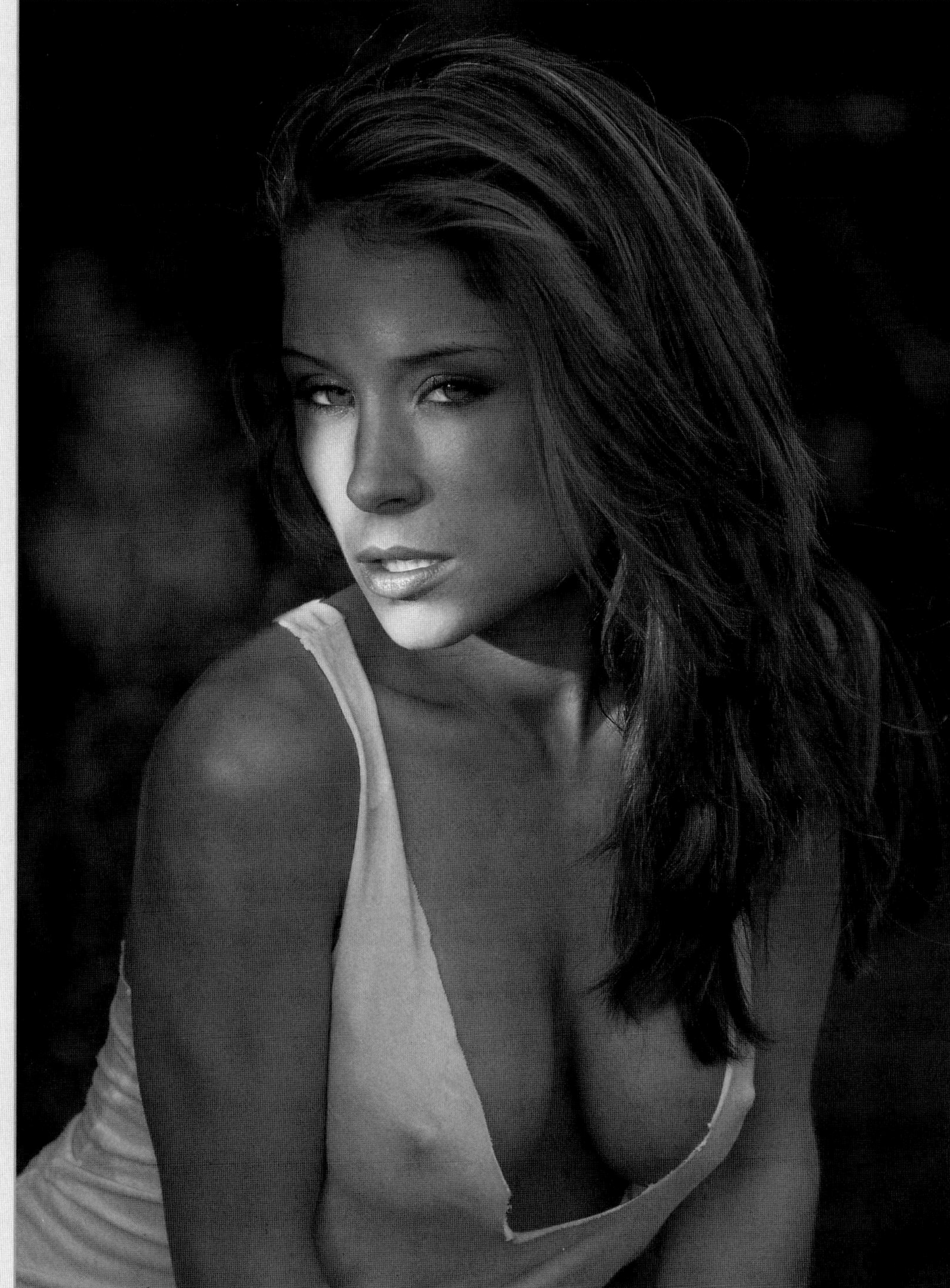

Camera: Nikon D200

Lens: 70/300 VR

Shutter Speed: 125th Second

F-Stop: 5.0

Mode: Digital color conversion

Model: Amanda

Creating Separation

Both these head shots have a common element: White clothing was used to create separation in the image. Be aware when you are shooting an image with a lot of similar tones. A white or black element may be needed to boost the contrast.

The model at left, although light-haired, had very tan skin. I added the unbuttoned white tank top to separate her from the background and create a white area in the image. This is particularly effective near her white shoulder and gave needed definition to her breast.

In the image above, the model's hair has many of the same gray tones as the background. Her white tank top brought needed lightness to the image. It also helped enhance and define the breasts. Although not overly revealing, the shirt does help accent the smoldering, sexual overtone of the image.

Overcast Weather

This image was shot at a workshop in Cody, Wyoming. The day was gloomy and overcast with drizzling rain. Working in these conditions can be challenging, but also an opportunity to get different types of shots than you would with bright sunlight, as evidenced in the flat, dark gray sky.

In order to get proper exposure, I took a light reading from the model's skin and used flash fill to light the image. Because the day was overcast, the background is mostly dark gray tones. Combined with the darkness of the vehicle, all of the elements made the model's fair skin really stand out.

Setting

This was a rare and unusual setting. The model is posing on an old 1937 Nash sedan. The pose is unique because it foreshortens the body. I widened the frame to show all of the empty windshield and most of the grill so it was clear she was laying on a car. I also tilted the camera slightly to add to the drama of the image.

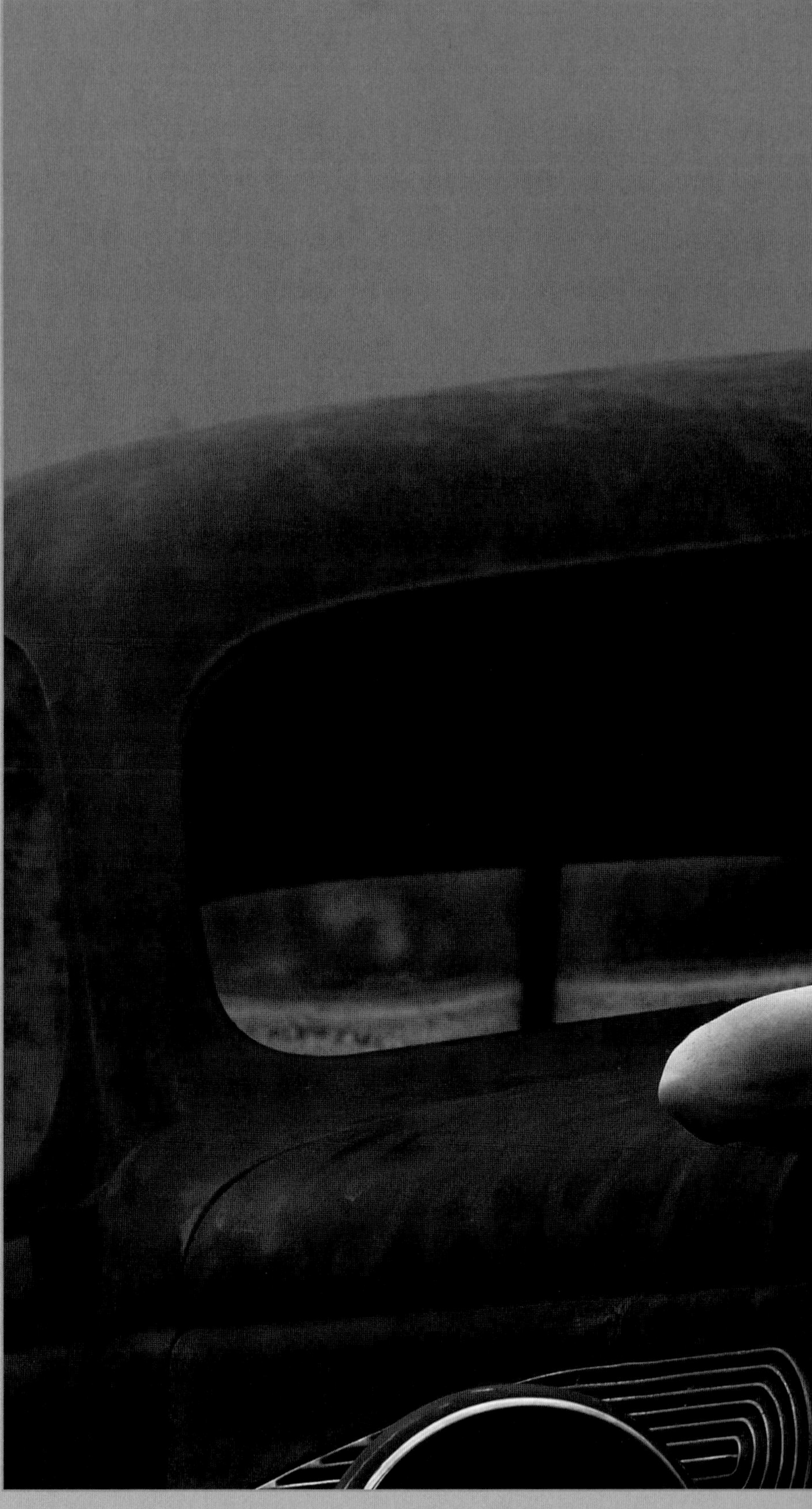

Camera: Nikon D200

Lens: 70/300VR

Shutter Speed: 200th Second

F-Stop: 7.1

Mode: Digital color conversion

Model: Elise

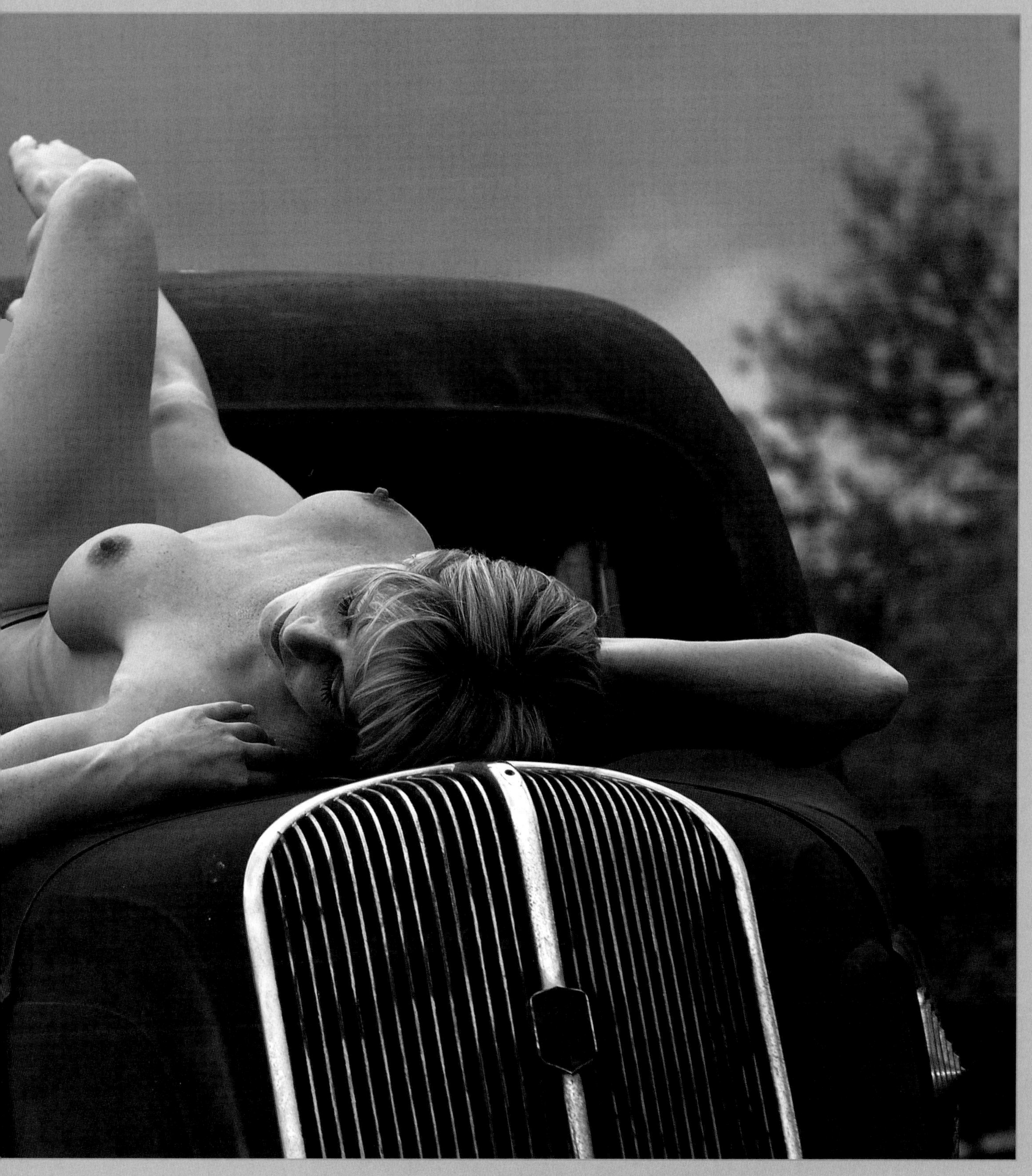

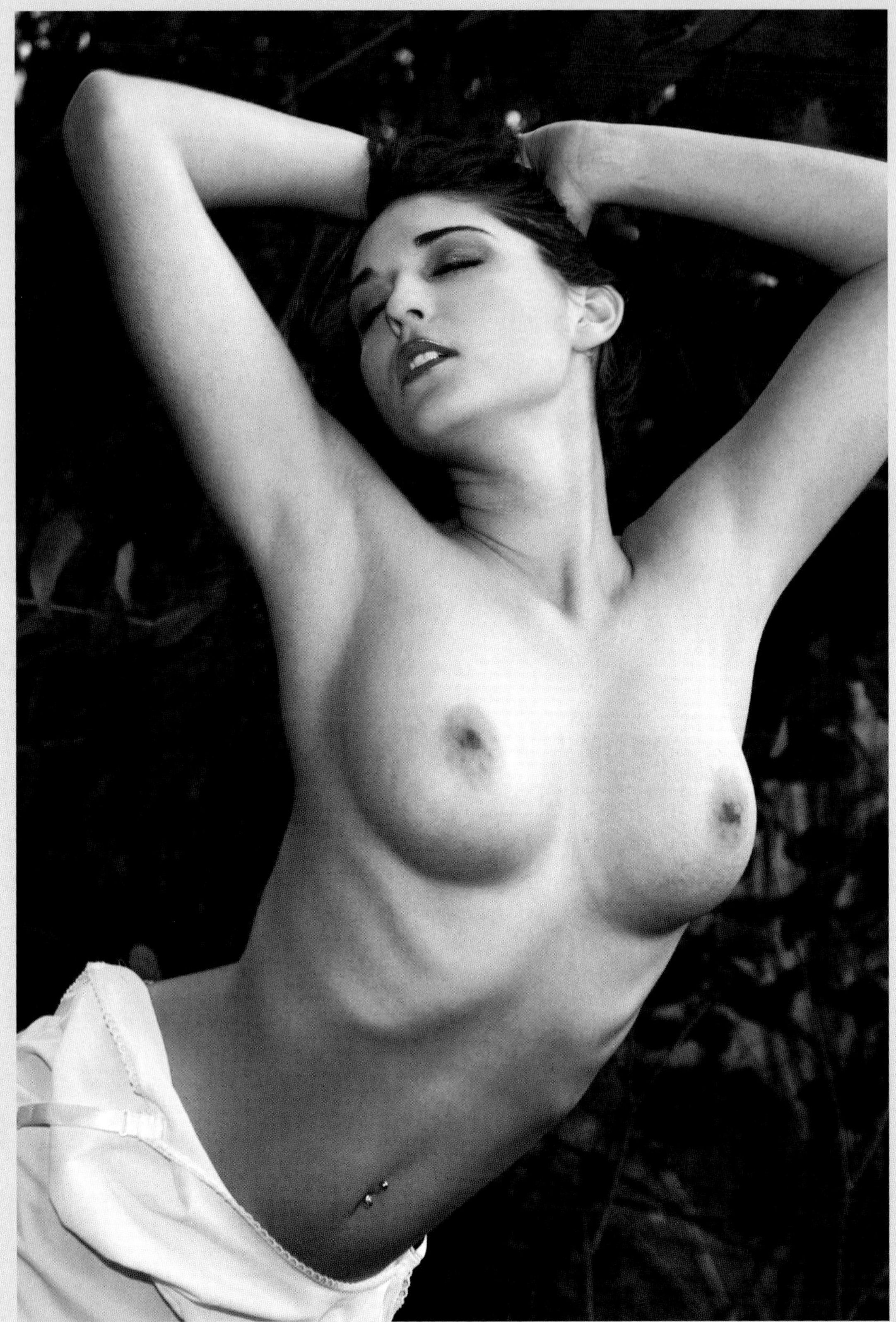

Contrast

This image was shot in the late afternoon in Sonoma. Although it was shot outdoors, the background is secondary. The dark foliage simply provides contrast and texture. The stark contrast is what makes this image so dramatic and effective. The dark hair of the model blends with the background while her body stands out in sharp relief.

Pose

The pose really makes this image work. The lifted arms created beautiful negative shapes and frame the model's head. The breasts are lifted and the line of the body is smooth and flowing. Although the angles are sharp, the image has a very sensual, delicate appeal.

Camera: Nikon D100

Lens: Tamron 28/75

Shutter Speed: 60th Second

F-Stop: 4.0

Mode: Digital color conversion

Model: Carlotta

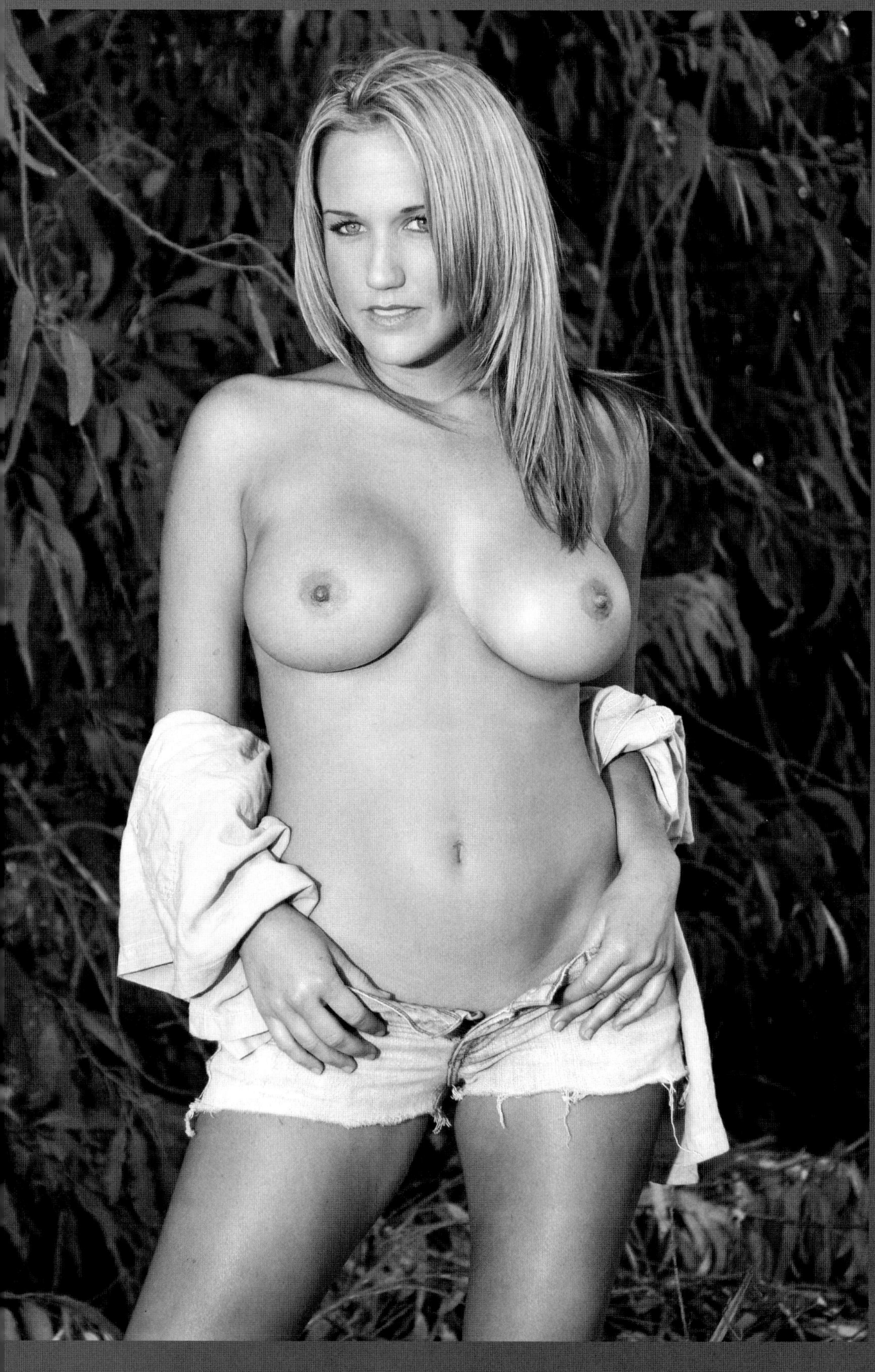

Blond

This location was chosen specifically to offset the light hair and skin of the model. She is positioned in front of a grove of eucalyptus trees, which had dark green leaves and even darker shadow areas. This created excellent separation for her hair. The leaves also added texture and pattern to the background.

Clothing

Light-colored, ripped, cut-off jean shorts are a great item of clothing in almost any shot. They are casual, yet extremely sexy. By undoing the top of the shorts, and pushing them slightly off her hips, the model added even more sensuality. Paired with the shirt on her arms, the clothing really frames and accentuates her body. It also adds to the voyeuristic quality of capturing a woman undressing.

Hips

Notice how the model has bent her leg, raising her left hip. This increases the femininity of the pose by adding a slight angle to her lower body.

Camera: Nikon D300

Lens: 70/300 VR

Shutter Speed: 125th Second

F-Stop: 5.6

Mode: Digital color conversion

Model: Sam

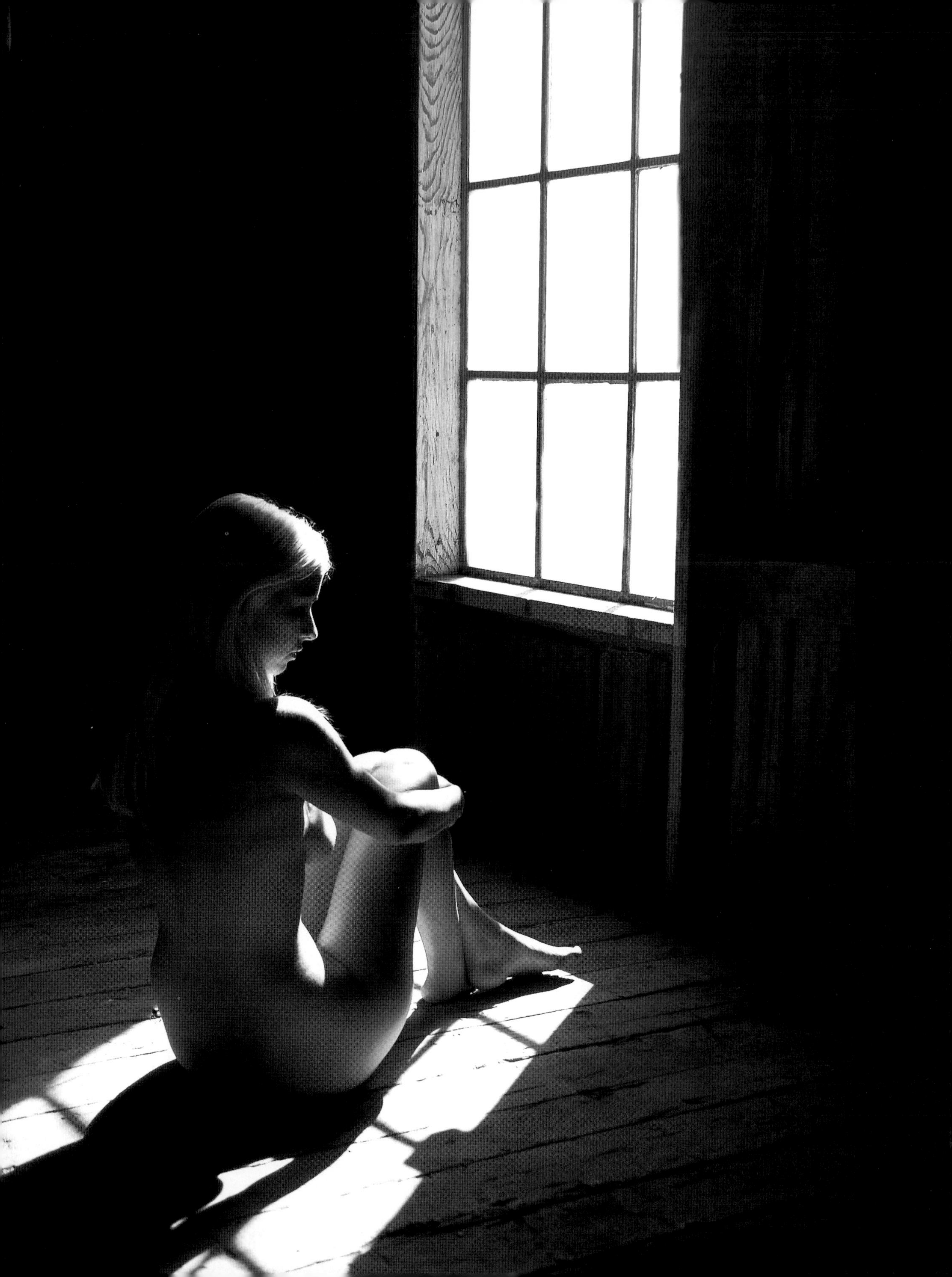

Light

This image was shot in St. Joseph, Missouri in a workshop. The light was coming through the mullioned window, creating a grid pattern on the floor. The model posed in a series of positions (you can see another example on page 117).

Pattern

This image is based on the patterns of light, with the model casting her own shadow on the floor. I widened the frame to capture the window as well as the model. I wanted a very still, simple black and while image showing the bright simplicity of the lighting and the silhouette of the model's body. I had her turn her head slightly into the light and look down to capture her profile and top of her head.

Mood

The mood of the image is simple, serene, and reflective. To maintain and enforce the simplicity and starkness of the image, I removed a few elements in Adobe Photoshop® that I found distracting. For example, there was a electrical outlet on the wall that looked out of place. I also brightened the window so nothing in the background would distract from the bright white light. Because of the amazing contrast in this image, this photo works much better in black and white than in color. The color distracts from the beautiful simplicity of the elements.

Camera: Nikon D200

Lens: 24/120 VR

Shutter Speed: 200th Second

F-Stop: 6.3

Mode: Digital color conversion

Model: Danielle

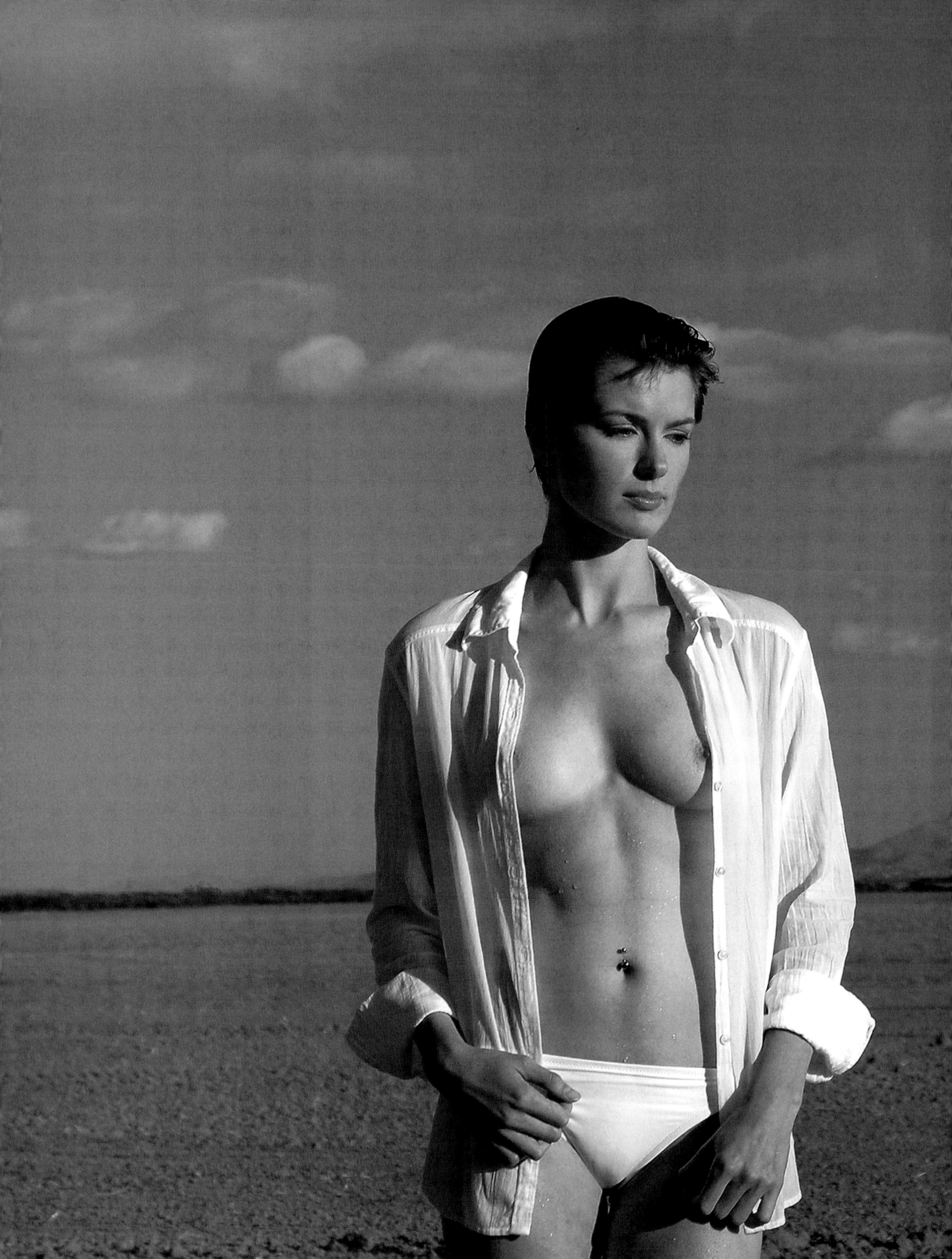

Space

All images have a foreground and a background. The model is typically in the foreground and is the focus of the image. In the double-spread image on the two preceding pages, I wanted to create an image that visually described the vastness of the open landscape, while still maintaining the focus on the model. This produced a stark illustration of foreground and background. Shooting horizontally really showed the openness of the area and let me capture more of the clouds. This image is very brilliant in color as the sky is a rich blue and contrasts with the browns of the earth. However, reducing it to shades of gray pulls more focus to the model and enhances the feeling of barren space.

Fashion

This image has more a fashion photography feel than typical outdoor glamour photography. The feminine pose contrasts with the model's wet, slicked back hair and white shirt. Although her breasts are partially exposed, it feels more natural than sensual.

Camera: Nikon D200

Lens: Nikon 24/120VR

Shutter Speed: 250th Second

F-Stop: 8.0

Mode: Digital color conversion

Model: Katya

hint

I shot this image using a polarizing filter to make the clouds stand out, reduce glare, and increase contrast. I shot using the pre-programmed "auto" setting. This lets the camera do the work because the camera will compensate for exposure loss. If you are not familiar with a filter or unsure exactly how to use it, this will help.

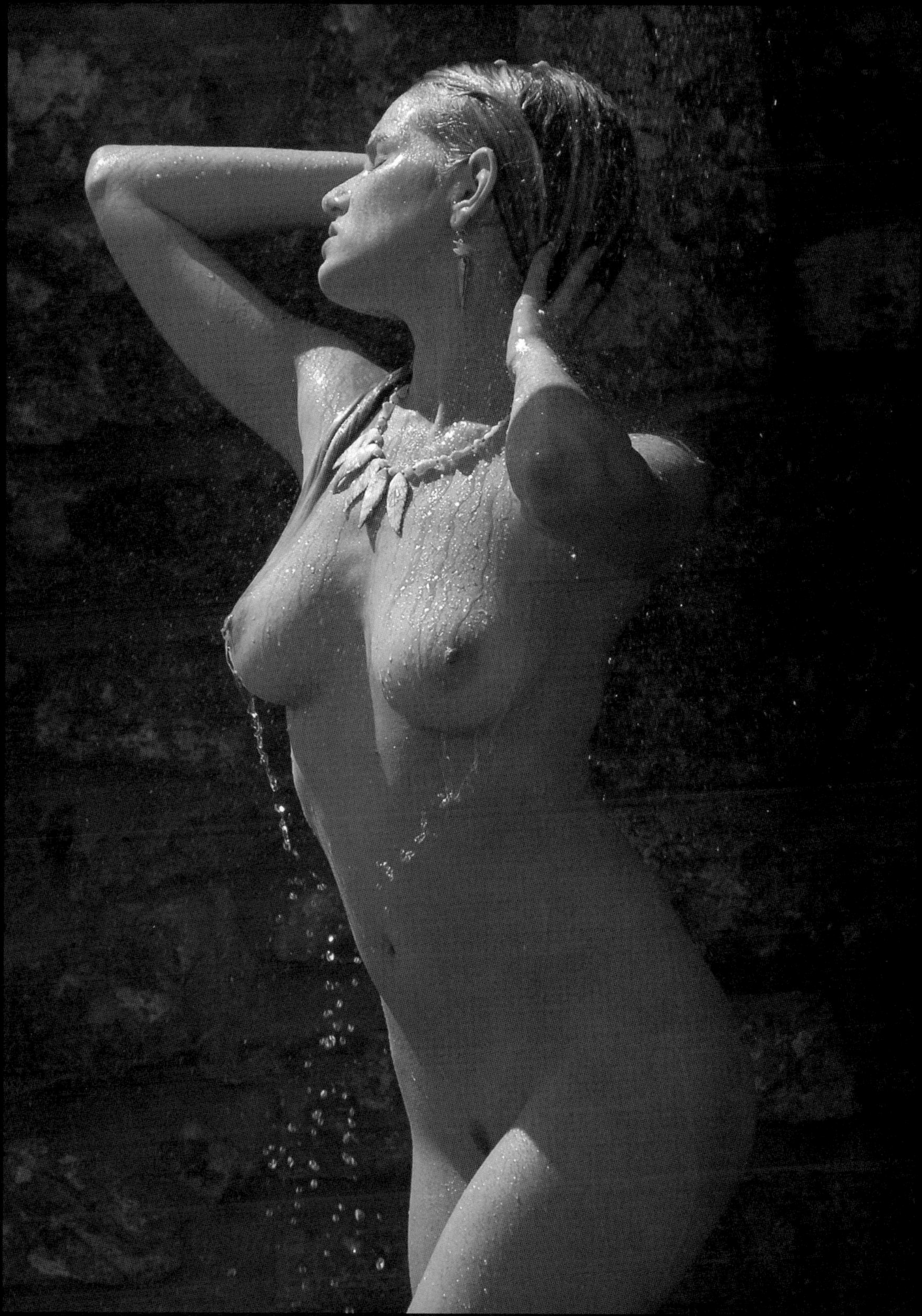

Camera: Nikon D200

Lens: 24/120VR

Shutter Speed: 1000th Second

F-Stop: 5.6

Mode: Digital color conversion

Model: Liz

Water

Water adds an instant element of sensuality in glamour photography. In this image, the model was standing in an outdoor shower, facing the late afternoon light. The light was ideal to capture the falling water and highlight the upper body of the model.

Pose

The model created a series of poses working in the water. This pose is very natural and sensual with the arched back and raised arms. I was able to capture the play of the water on her body.

Props

Always be open to the model's ideas and suggestions. In this image, the model brought the necklace and wanted to wear it in the shower. It catches the light well, breaks up the neckline, and adds a nice shadow to her chest.

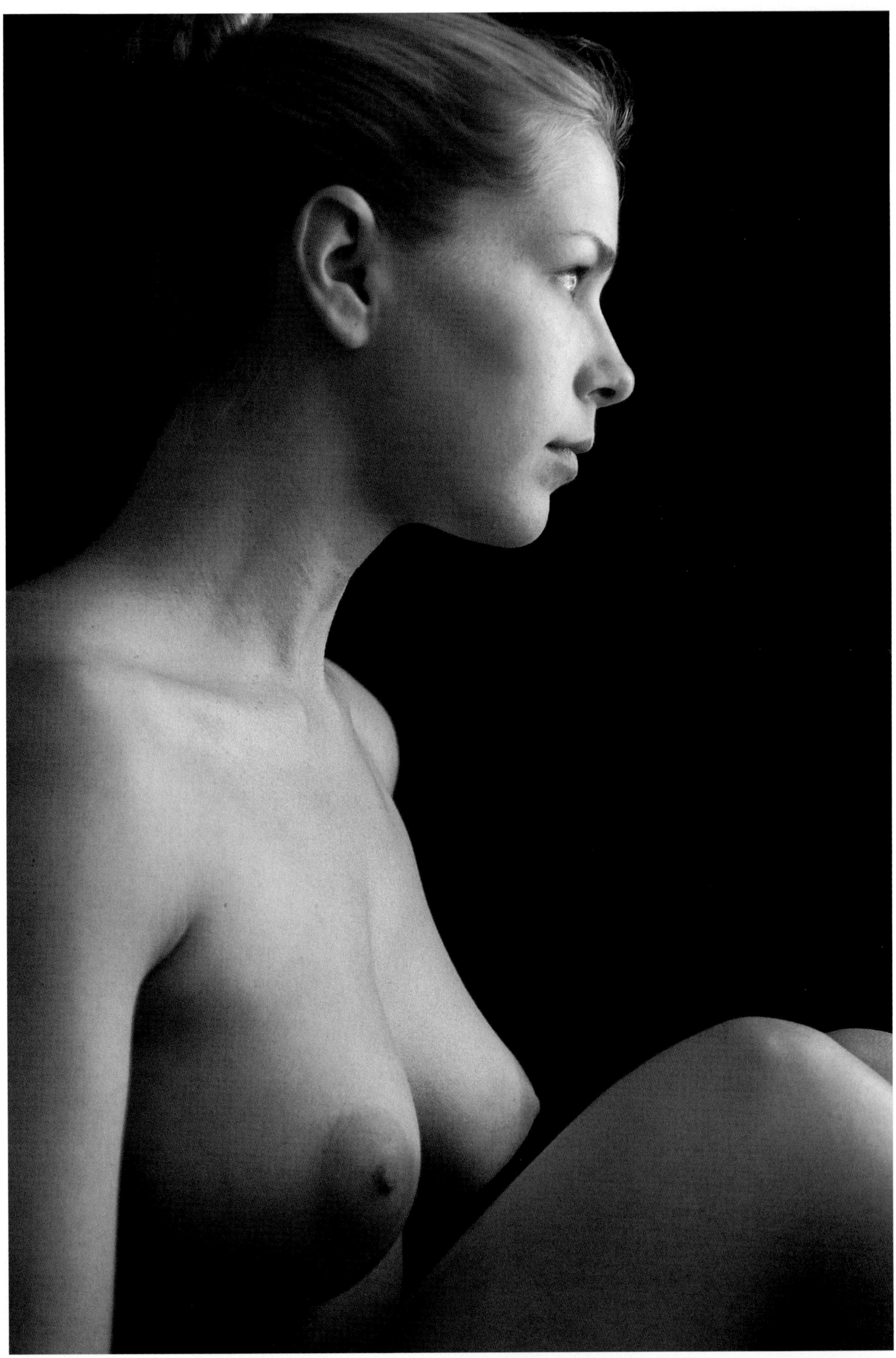

Simplicity

This image was shot in my Novato studio, using natural window light and a black velveteen backdrop. The goal was to capture the pure essence of the female form as simply as possible. I wanted to create a strong image with definite areas of black and a cleanly defined profile. This image could also be cropped and used as a head shot.

Natural Beauty

The model was the key to this image. She has a lovely profile, defined cheekbones, and a long, graceful neck. Her strong facial structure is highlighted by pulling her hair back into a bun. I like to shoot images that play to the strength of the model and classic beauty always lends itself to simplicity and clean lines.

Camera: Nikon D100

Lens: Tamron 28/75

Shutter Speed: 130th Second

F-Stop: 2.8

Mode: Digital color conversion

Model: Sarah

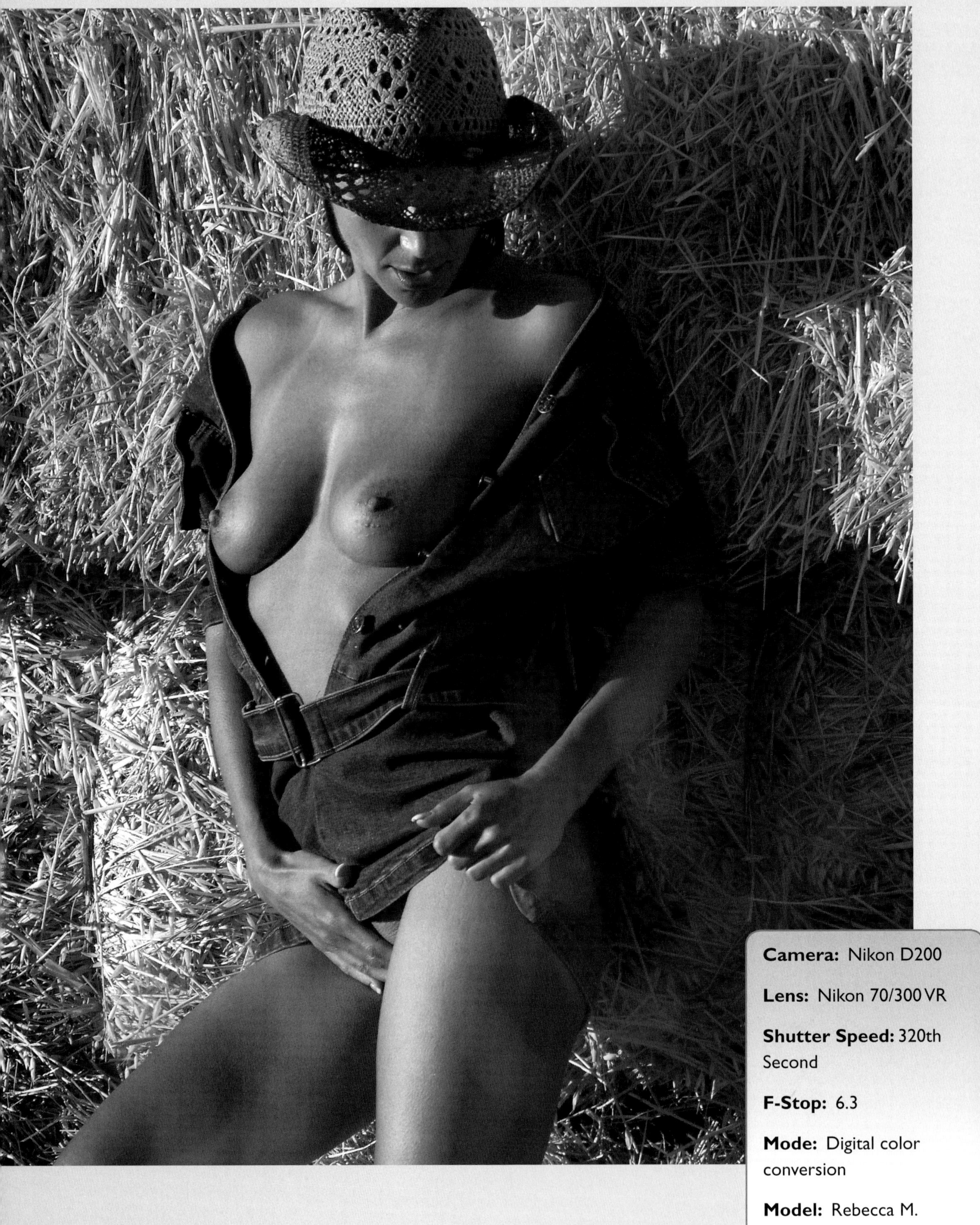

Camera: Nikon D200

Lens: Nikon 70/300 VR

Shutter Speed: 320th Second

F-Stop: 6.3

Mode: Digital color conversion

Model: Rebecca M.

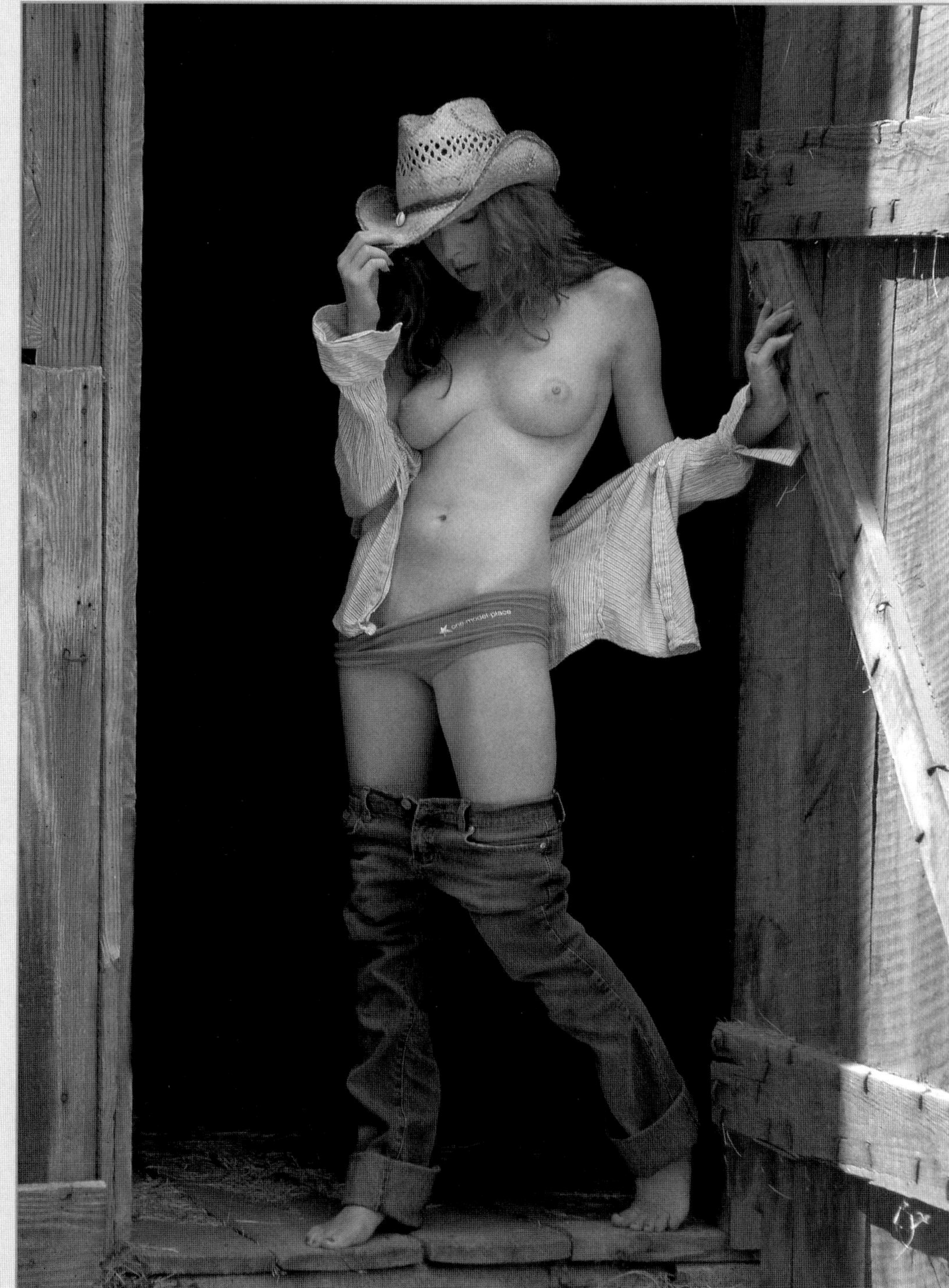

Camera: Nikon D200

Lens: 24/120 VL

Shutter Speed: 125th Second

F-Stop: 5.3

Mode: Digital color conversion

Model: Amanda R.

Hats

The images on pages 102 and 103 are examples of models wearing a cowboy hat as a prop. Hats can be a great prop to set the tone of an image or give a model something to hold in her hands. Worn correctly, a hat will create an aura of mystery and allure. However, you need to be careful with a hat as it can shade a model's face too much. I prefer to have the model looking down, rather than into the camera when wearing a hat.

In the image at left, the hat almost totally conceals the model's face. It also helps create the theme of the image, adding another layer of texture to the hay in the background. It also has a very defined pattern, adding more shadows and interest to the image.

In the image above, the hat is an extra element that works with the clothing and adds complexity to the image. This was taken at a work shop in Chester, South Carolina. The model is framed in the door of an old barn. The weathered boards have good texture and the doorway provides a strong horizontal frame for the model. The hat adds a light area of contrast for the model's hair, creating needed separation from the darker background.

Interaction

This image was shot in my Novato studio using early morning window light and flash fill. Created as a series of glamour nudes, this image captured the model's interaction with the camera. The model is an expert at posing and facial expressions. Without using any props or backgrounds, the image conveys a feeling of sensual aggressiveness.

I shot this horizontally in order to capture more of the model's body and introduce a little soft contrast to balance the dark shadow on the side of the model's face. This could also be cropped and used solely as a head shot, giving an entirely different feeling to the image.

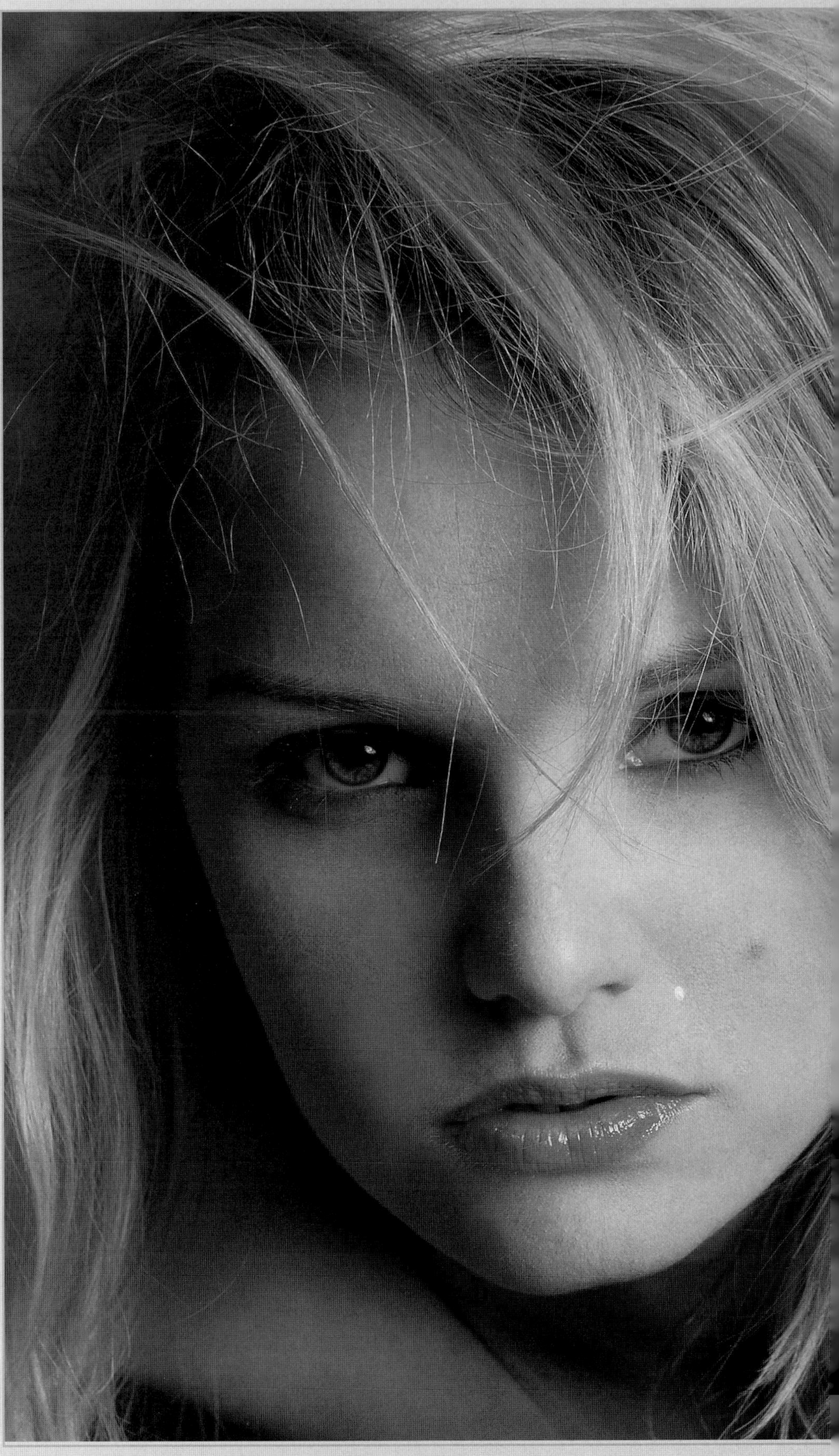

Imperfections

While this model is an incredible beauty, her slight imperfections really make the image intriguing. Her hair is tousled and unstyled. This gives the image voyeuristic appeal, as if a gorgeous woman has been caught just waking up. Encourage models to try something a little different in the studio. Even the act of applying lipstick can created a sensual image if captured just right.

Camera: Nikon D200

Lens: 70/300 VR

Shutter Speed: 125th Second

F-Stop: 10.0

Mode: Digital color conversion

Model: Liz

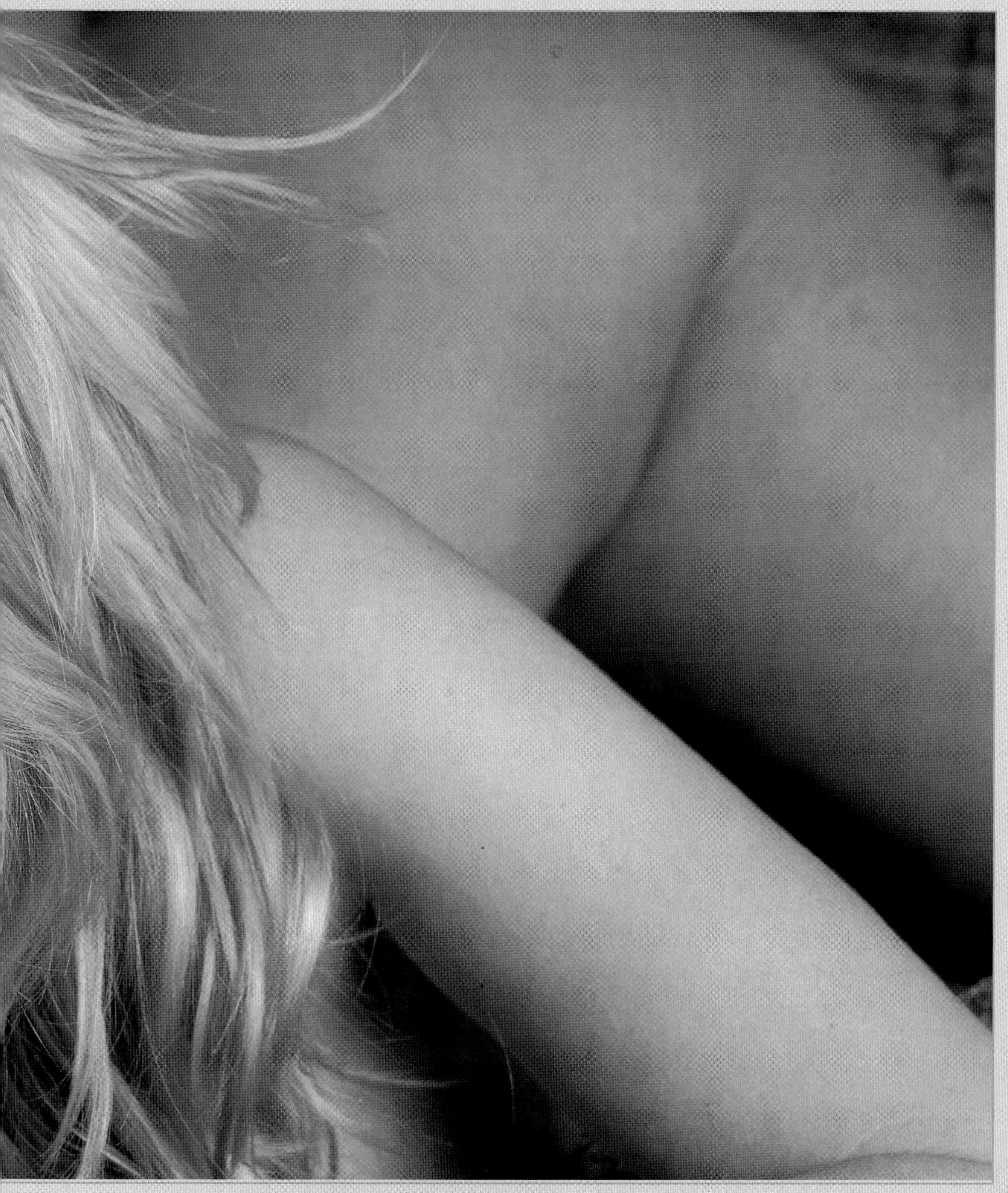

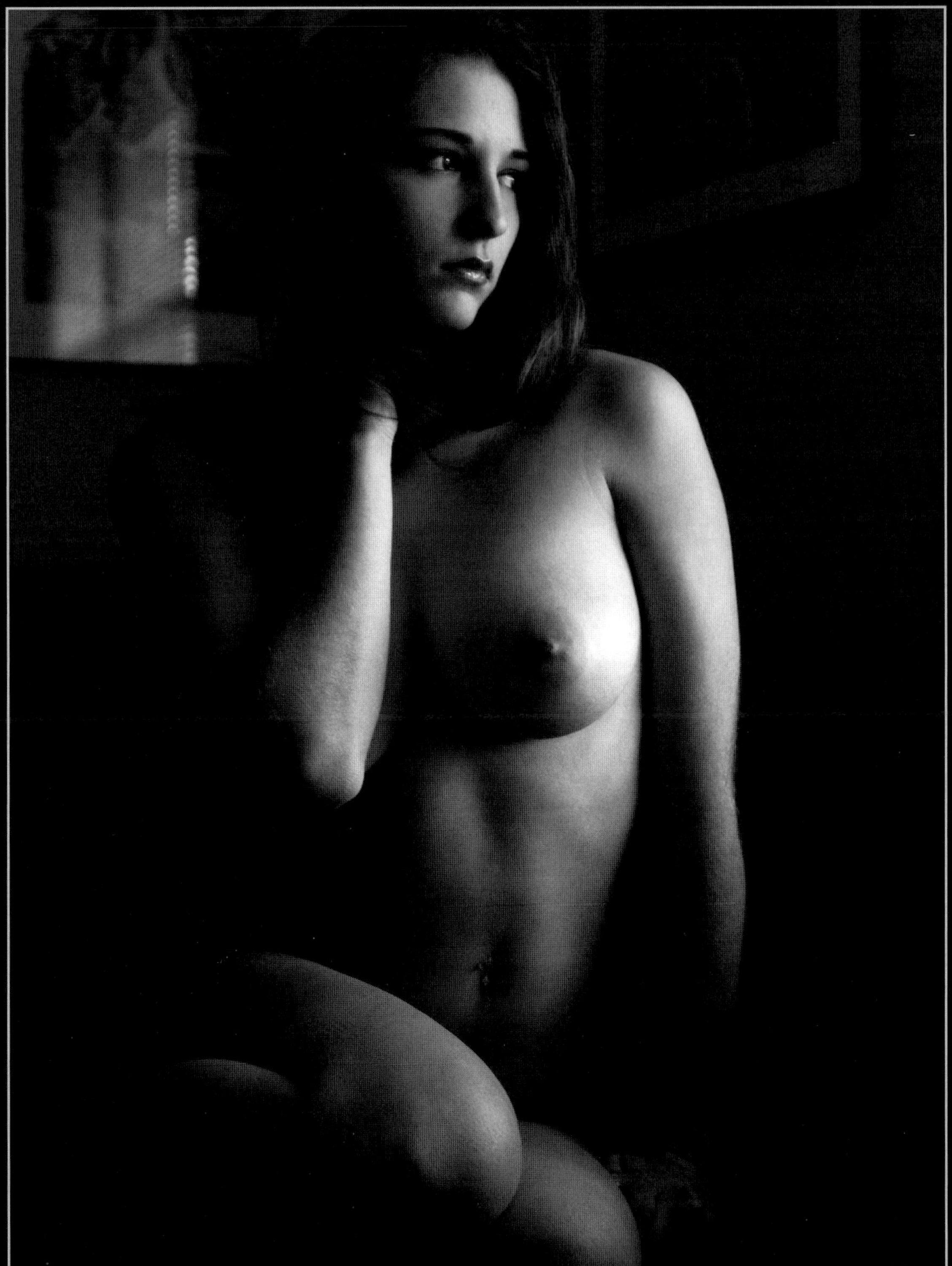

Camera: Nikon D100

Lens: Tamron 28/75

Shutter Speed: 60th Second

F-Stop: 2.8

Mode: Digital color conversion

Model: Carlotta

Window Light

This image was shot in my Novato studio using natural window light. The window lets in beautiful, strong eastern light in the morning. I enjoy working with natural light as it softens the skin and creates rich shadows. However, I have found that the window light can get too strong. To diffuse and soften it, I use parachute material or another sheer fabric when needed.

Pose

The pose really makes this image work. The lifted arm creates a clean line connecting the model's head and body. By turning her head toward the window, her face is still illuminated, yet with a dark shadow area that blends with her dark hair. The pose is relaxed, feminine, and reflective — making this image more of an artistic nude than a glamour nude.

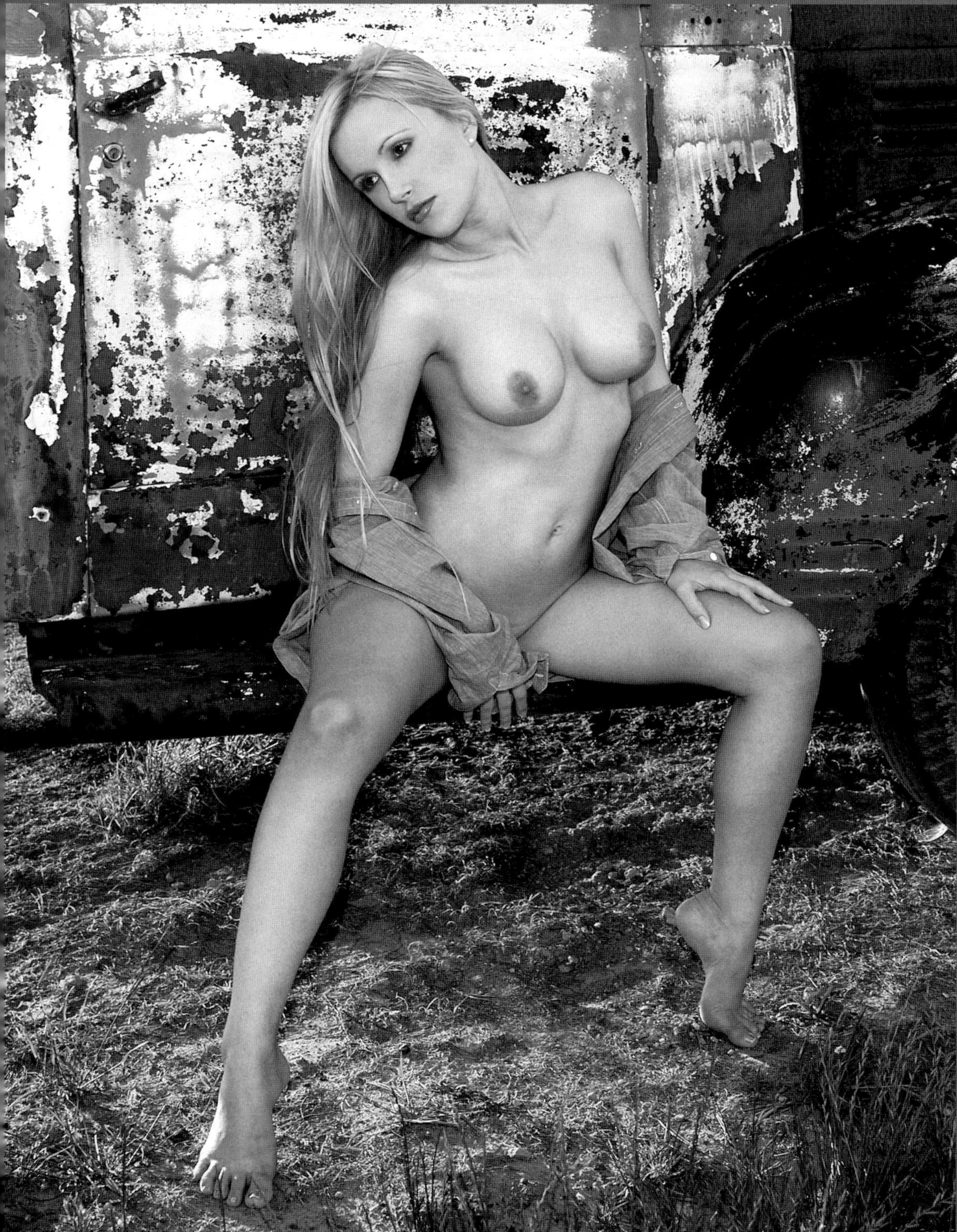

Camera: Nikon D100

Lens: Tamron 28/75

Shutter Speed: 125th Second

F-Stop: 5.6

Mode: Digital color conversion

Model: Tavia

Lighting

This image is unique because of the unusual lighting situation. The model was positioned on an old truck with the late afternoon sun behind the truck. The sun was very strong and shining brightly underneath the truck. This illuminated the ground, which created separation and detail in the foreground. I used flash fill to properly light the model.

Pose

The pose is sensual, dramatic, and very angular. The model lifted her heels to accent the muscles in her legs. Her left shoulder is lifted and her head sharply turned, creating good flow. She swept her hair behind her shoulder to highlight the graceful line of her neck. The shirt was used only as an accent; this pose would have been just as effective without it.

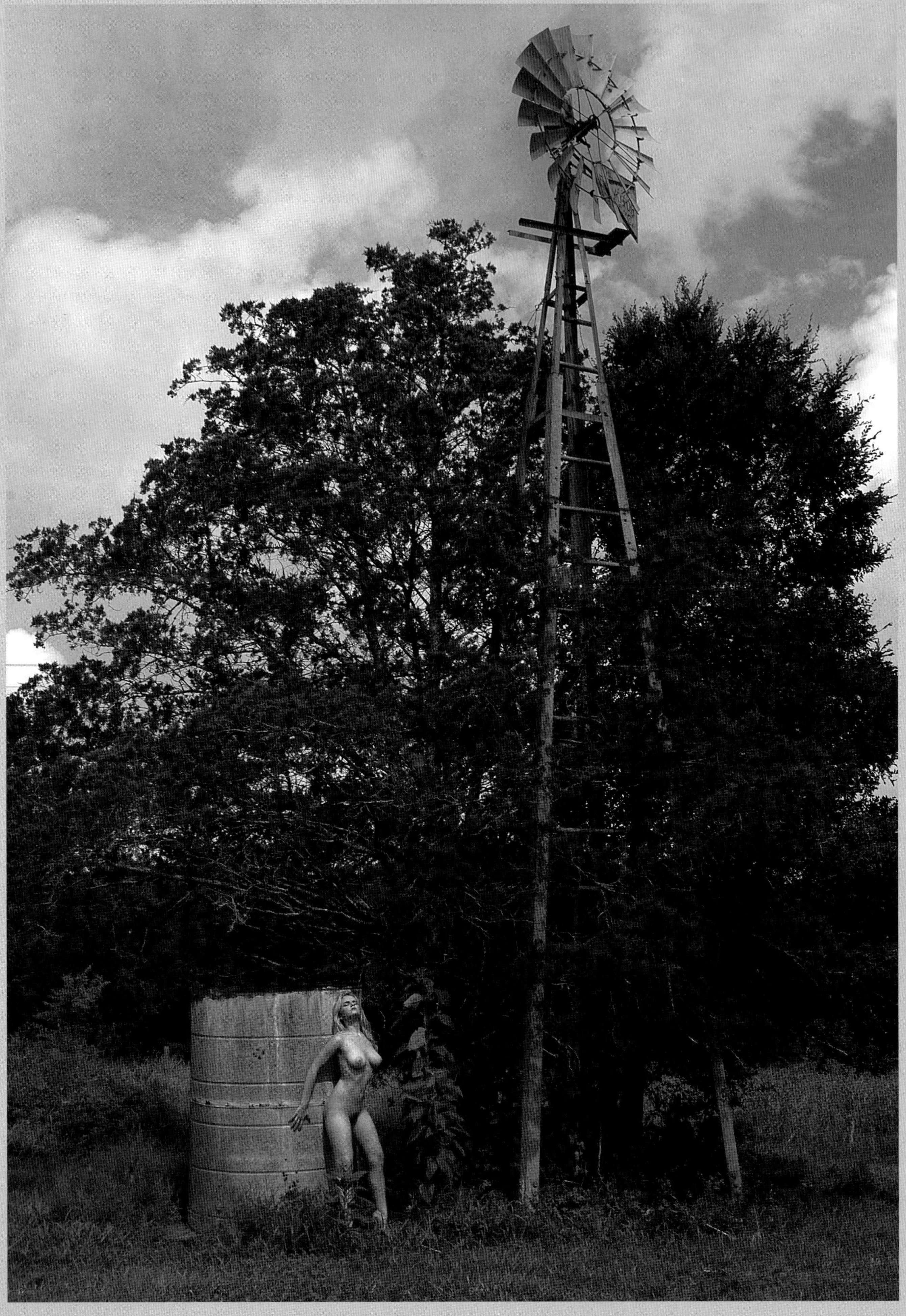

Landscape

This image was shot during a workshop in Texas. The model is leaning against a water tank near a windmill. I had her stand against the tank to give the model a sense of proportion within the landscape.

Nature

I enjoy creating images where the model is not the sole focus, but an unexpected element complementing the beauty of nature. In this image, the model's fair skin helps her stand out against the darker tank. The light catches her chest and fair skin. Many natural elements lend to the strength of this image. The sky was a deep, rich blue with fluffy white clouds, which gave great contrast. The trees provided a lot of background texture but stop below the top of the windmill, which allows the windmill to stand out in stark relief against the sky.

Camera: Nikon D100

Lens: Tamron 28/75

Shutter Speed: 500th Second

F-Stop: 8.0

Mode: Digital color conversion

Model: Liz

hint

When shooting outdoor glamour photography, step back and survey the entire location. You may find an opportunity to create an unusual photograph of the entire landscape, integrating the model into the natural setting. You will need to shoot at quite a distance from the model for a an image like this, so communicate your vision of the shot with her in advance. You may not be able to direct the model from behind the lens.

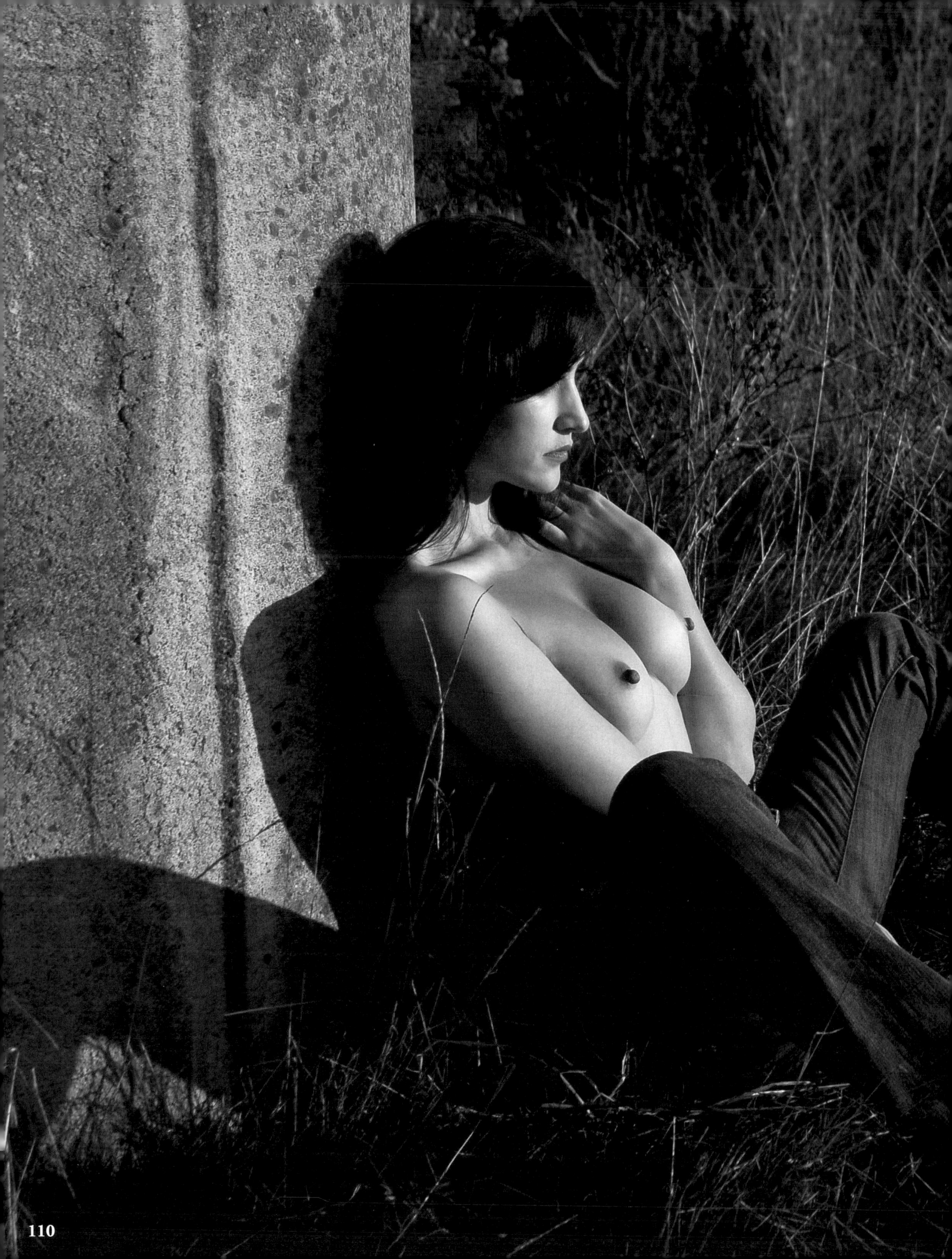

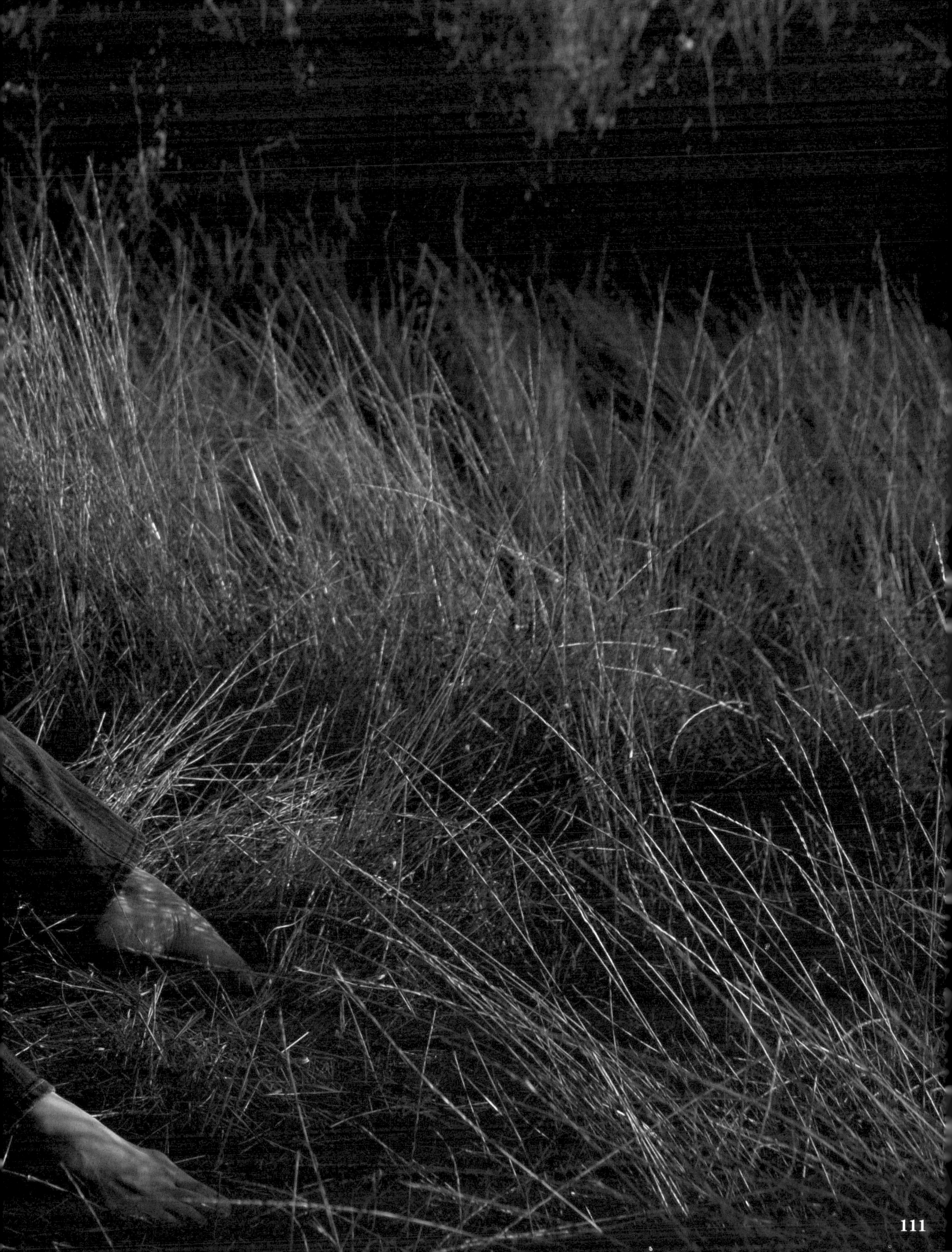

Contrast

The double-spread image on the two preceding pages was shot in the late afternoon, with natural light. The model was facing west, looking at the setting sun. I choose this location for the intense contrasts. The model had very fair skin, which played well against her dark hair and dark jeans. Her dark shadow contrasted well with the lighter concrete wall. The grasses were very textured with deep shadow areas.

Variations

I shot a similar image and had the model take off the dark jeans. However, the jeans add an additional texture and dark area to the photo. They blend well with the grass, which really showcases the model's profile and upper body. Whenever possible, I like to shoot a number of variations of a scene, just changing props or clothing.

Camera: Nikon D300

Lens: 24/120VR

Shutter Speed: 1000th Second

F-Stop: 5.6

Mode: Digital color conversion

Model: Shteena

hint

When shooting outdoor glamour photography in a strong lighting situation such as this, take your meter reading facing the light source. If the meter faces the camera, the reading will be incorrect.

Camera: Nikon D200

Lens: 28/75 Tamron

Shutter Speed: 60th Second

F-Stop: 2.8

Mode: Digital color conversion

Model: Tiana

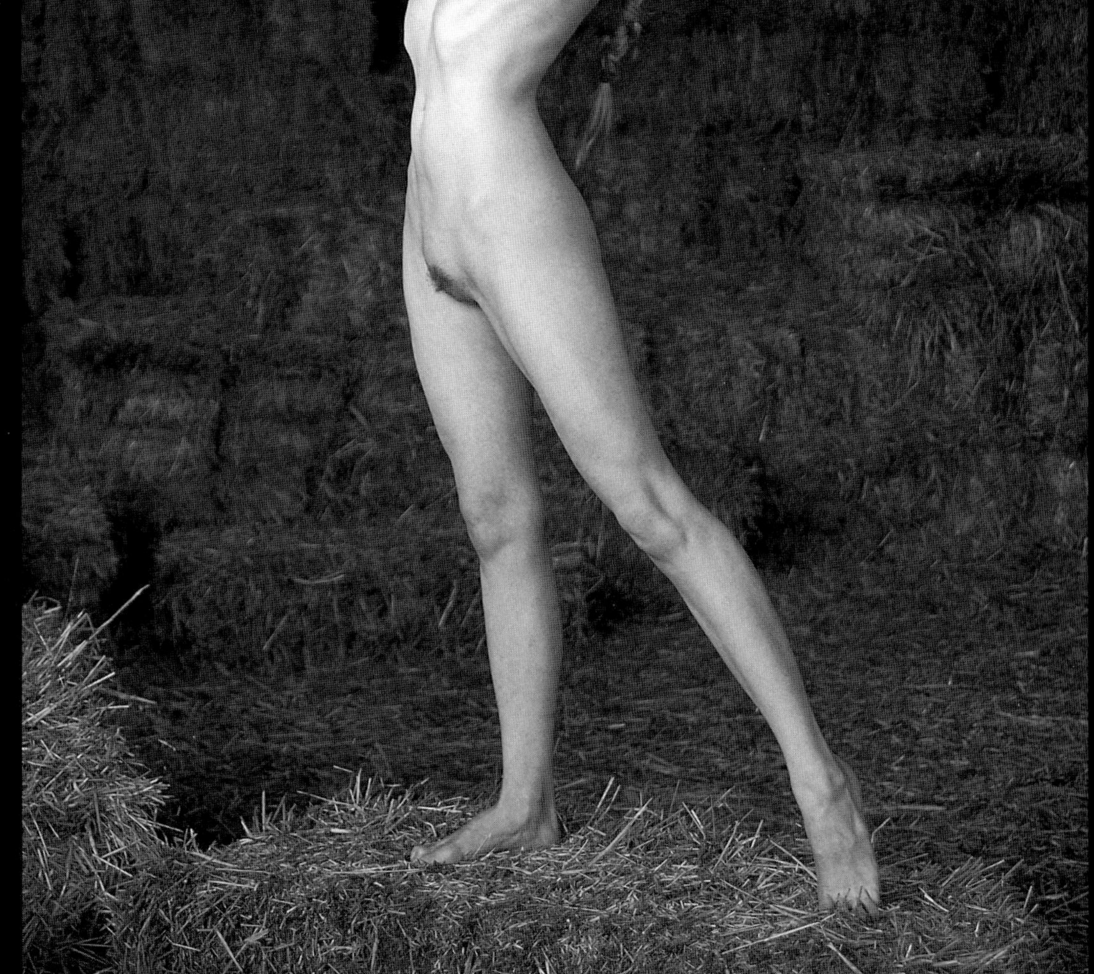

Location

This image was shot in Sonoma in an old barn. Old barns are great structures for glamour photography. They are often constructed of weathered boards or have exposed beams that have great texture and make good backgrounds. In this case, the barn was filled with hay, another excellent source of texture. With the late afternoon sun streaming in, the light created a dark gradational background, which really made the model stand out.

Pose

The drama and strength of this pose contrasts well with the softness of the background. By arching her back and lifting her arms, the model created a very fluid, graceful pose. Stretching her leg back and pointing her toes accentuated the lines of her body. The soft, even lighting makes her entire body glow and separate well from the rest of the interior.

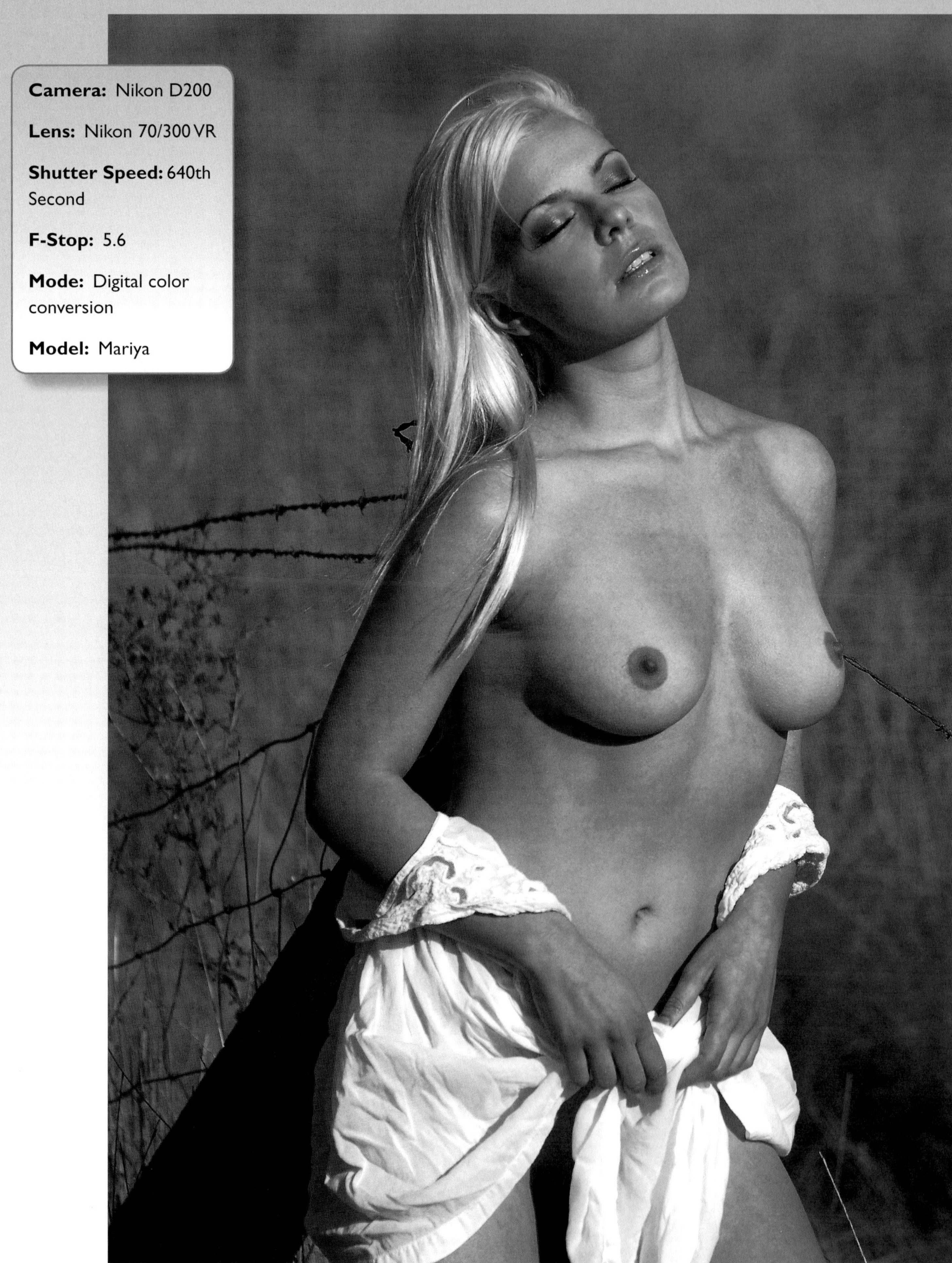

Camera: Nikon D200

Lens: Nikon 70/300 VR

Shutter Speed: 640th Second

F-Stop: 5.6

Mode: Digital color conversion

Model: Mariya

Fences & Bridges

The images on pages 114 and 115 both feature models in front of a rail. In outdoor glamour photography, a fence can be a great prop. It gives the model something to lean against and will provide a contrasting angle for her body. In the image at left, the model is leaning against the wooden post of a barbed wire fence. The barbed wire adds an interesting texture to the background and is a great juxtaposition against the model's smooth, soft skin.

In the image at right, the model is standing on wooden bridge, leaning on the top rail. Not only does the wood have great grain, it adds dimension to the photo with multiple angles.

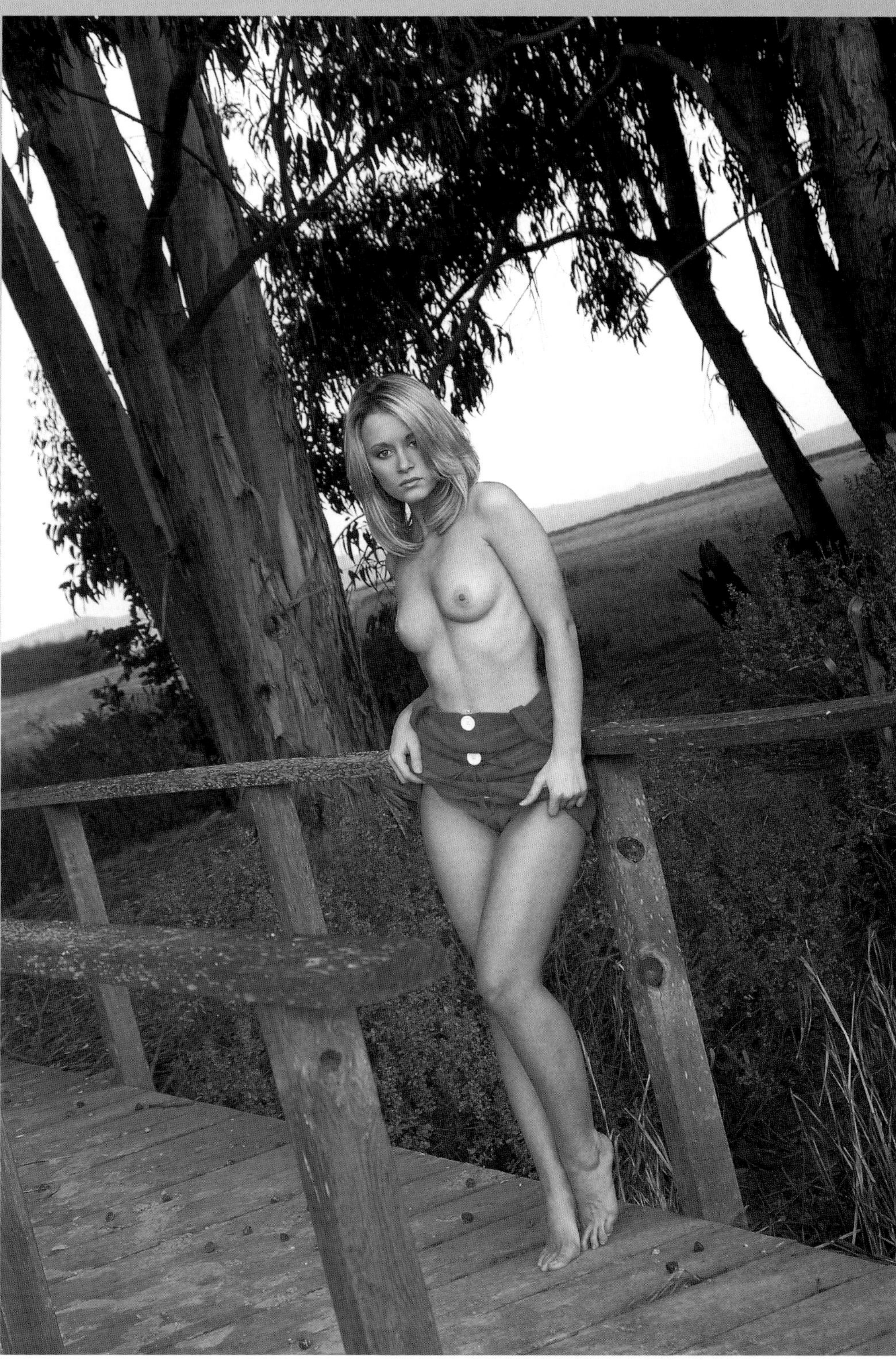

Hands & Clothing

Both of these models also have clothing at their waists. In the image at right, the white jacket adds a needed area of lightness and separation, as well as lending a measure of modesty to the image. In the image at left, the opposite is true. The dress is a darker gray tone that creates a darker area of separation against the model's lighter skin. The clothing also de-emphasizes the model's hips and can serve as an accent to the legs.

When working with clothing as an accent (where the model is holding it more so than wearing it) be sure to pay close attention to the model's hands. You do not want the model tightly clutching the fabric. The hands should be relaxed and lightly holding the clothing, not gripping it. Improper hands can change the entire complexion of the image, making the hands look claw-like, or making the model seem fearful.

Camera: Nikon D200

Lens: Nikon 24/120VR

Shutter Speed: 60th Second

F-Stop: 8.0

Mode: Digital color conversion

Model: Jamie

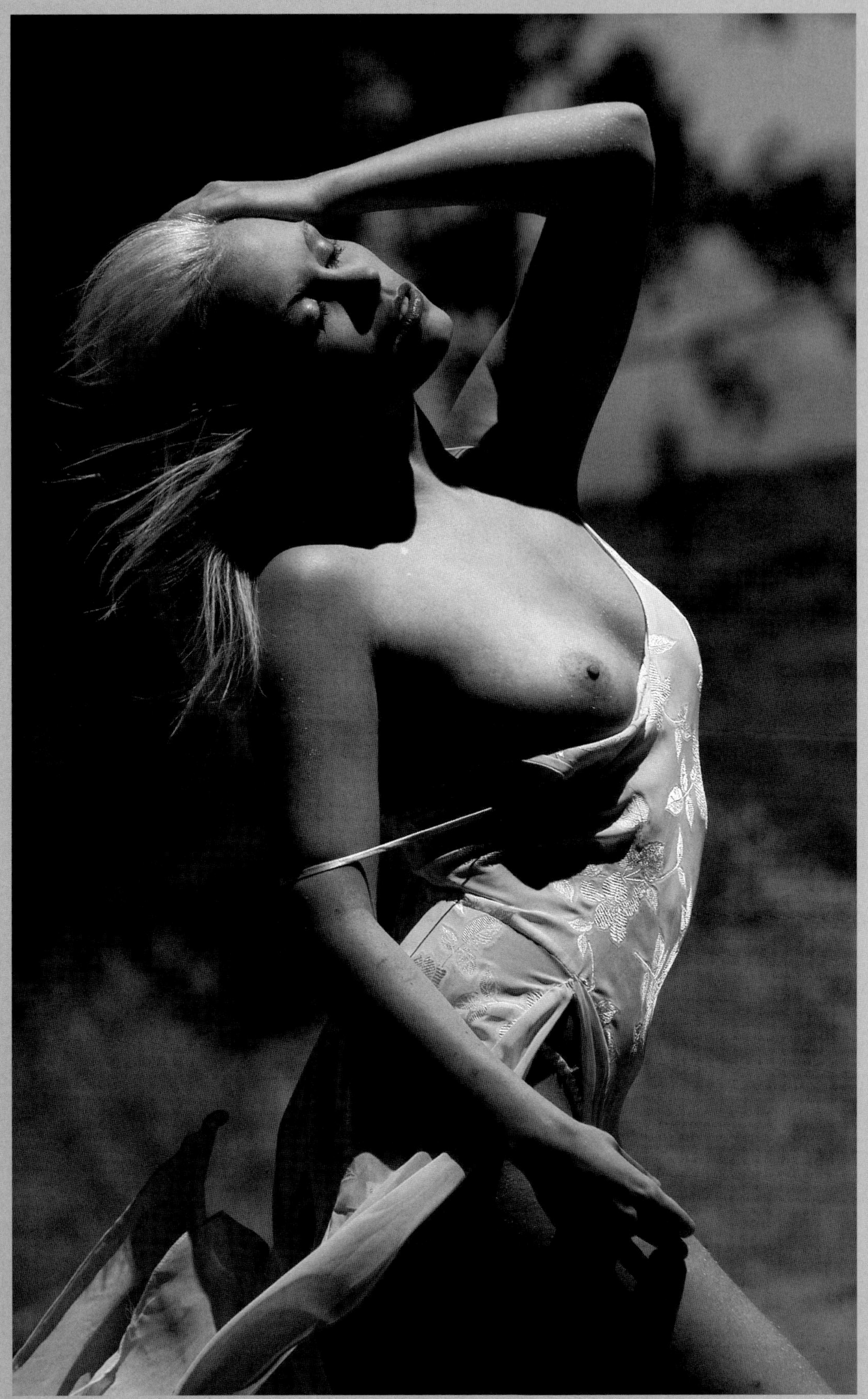

Drama

Shot in Sonoma in the mid afternoon, this image is an excellent example of how to work in a natural setting with bright sunlight. The sun created very intense shadows, so I asked the model to create a more dramatic pose to take advantage of the sun. Her head is tilted up to fully light her face and her eyes are closed to avoid squinting.

Wind

I like to take advantage of wind when possible. In this image, I placed the model in a more open area so her hair and skirt would be blown back, creating a sense of movement. Her pose helped accentuate the movement; with her head back and her body arched, the wind naturally and gently caught her just right.

Separation

When positioning a light-haired model outdoors, look for dark background area so the hair separates well.

Camera: Nikon D100

Lens: Nikon 70/300VR

Shutter Speed: 1600th Second

F-Stop: 9.0

Mode: Digital color conversion

Model: Sarah K.

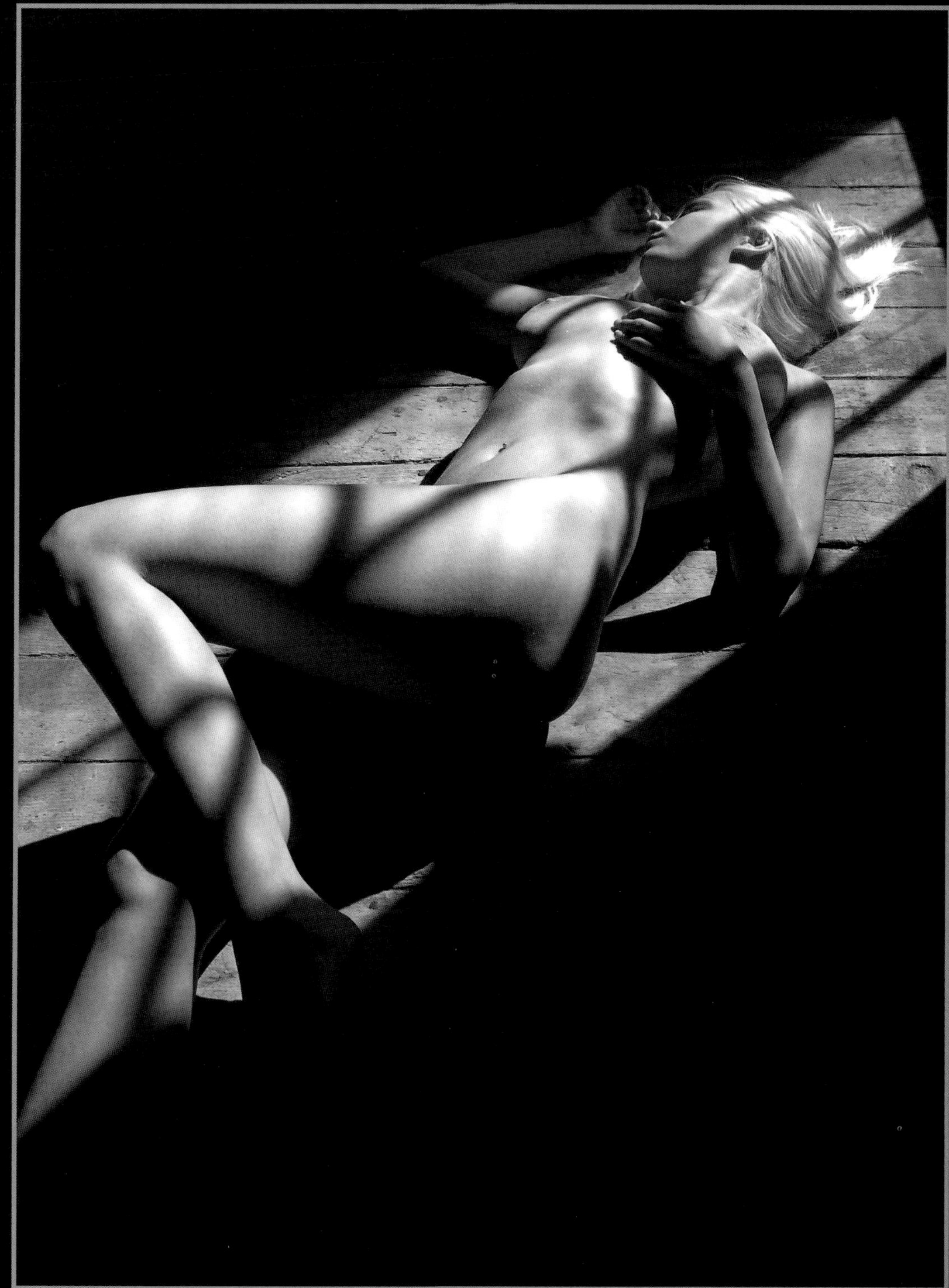

Camera: Nikon D200

Lens: Nikon 24-120VR

Shutter Speed: 500th Second

F-Stop: 6.3

Mode: Digital color conversion

Model: Danielle

Window Light

Shot at a workshop in St. Joseph, Missouri, this image is part of a series taking advantage of window light. The model was in a rustic building in front of a window. She tried many different positions including sitting, standing, and reclining to capture the play of light and shadows on her body. When shooting in a situation like this, be very aware of how shadow patterns hit the body. The shadow patterns shouldn't interfere with the face, especially the eyeline and nose.

Angles

The variety of angles in this image add interest and vitality to the composition. The sunlight causes the shadows to fall diagonally. By bending the arms and legs and twisting the hips slightly, the model creates additional angles that enhance the overall effect. This gives an abstract, artistic quality to the photo.

Studio

This image was shot in my Novato studio using strobe lighting. The goal was to create a black and white image that was a study of stark contrasts with very black blacks and white whites. I didn't want the feeling of the image to be stark, however, I wanted it to be intimate and casual.

Feeling

To achieve the casual feeling, we added some rumpled elements. The white fabric on the bed is wrinkled, which adds some nice shadow areas and texture. The model has tousled hair, partly covering one eye, giving her a more playful look.

Camera: Nikon D100

Lens: 28/75

Shutter Speed: 125th Second

F-Stop: 6.3

Mode: Digital color conversion

Model: Jennifer

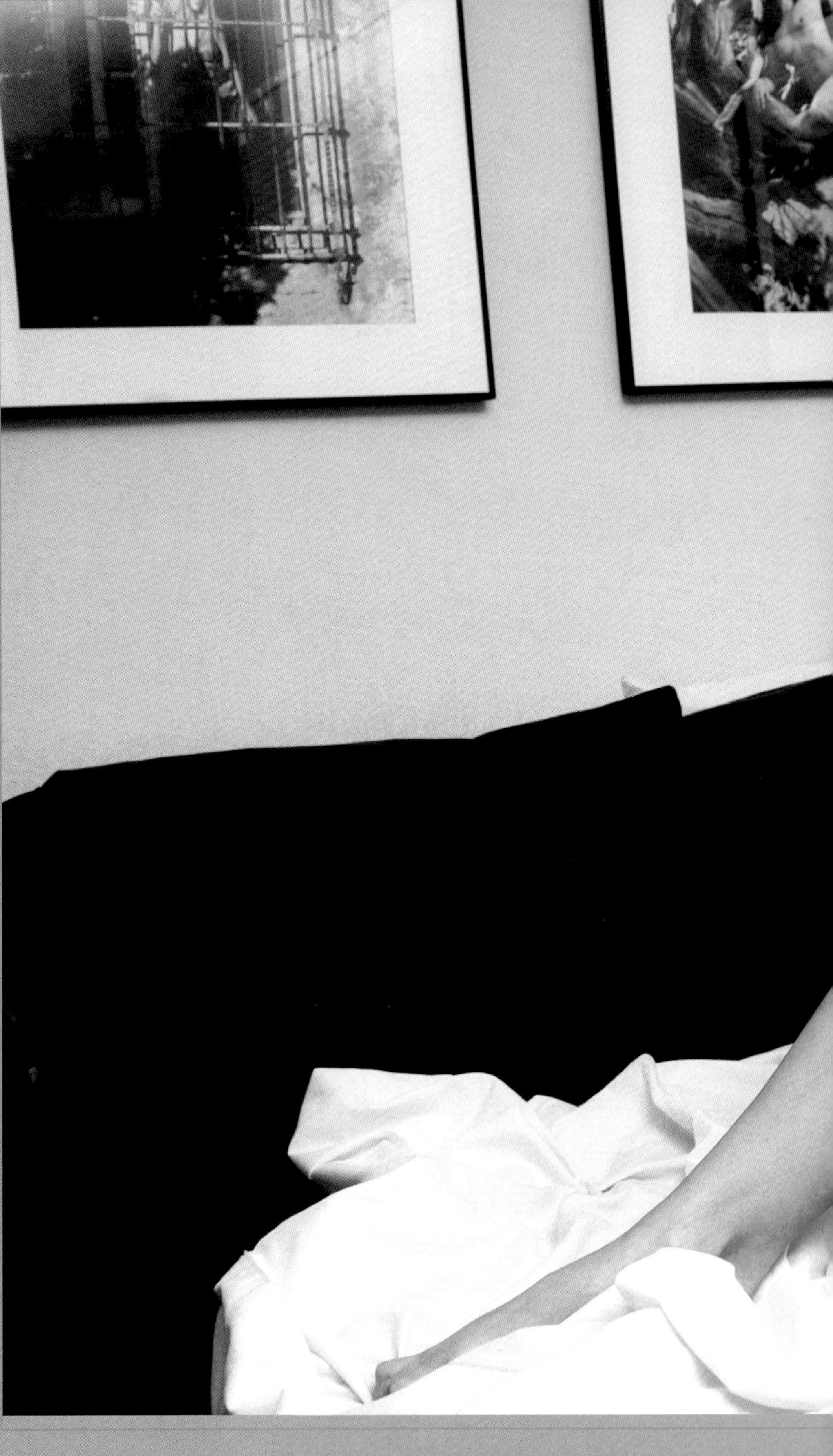

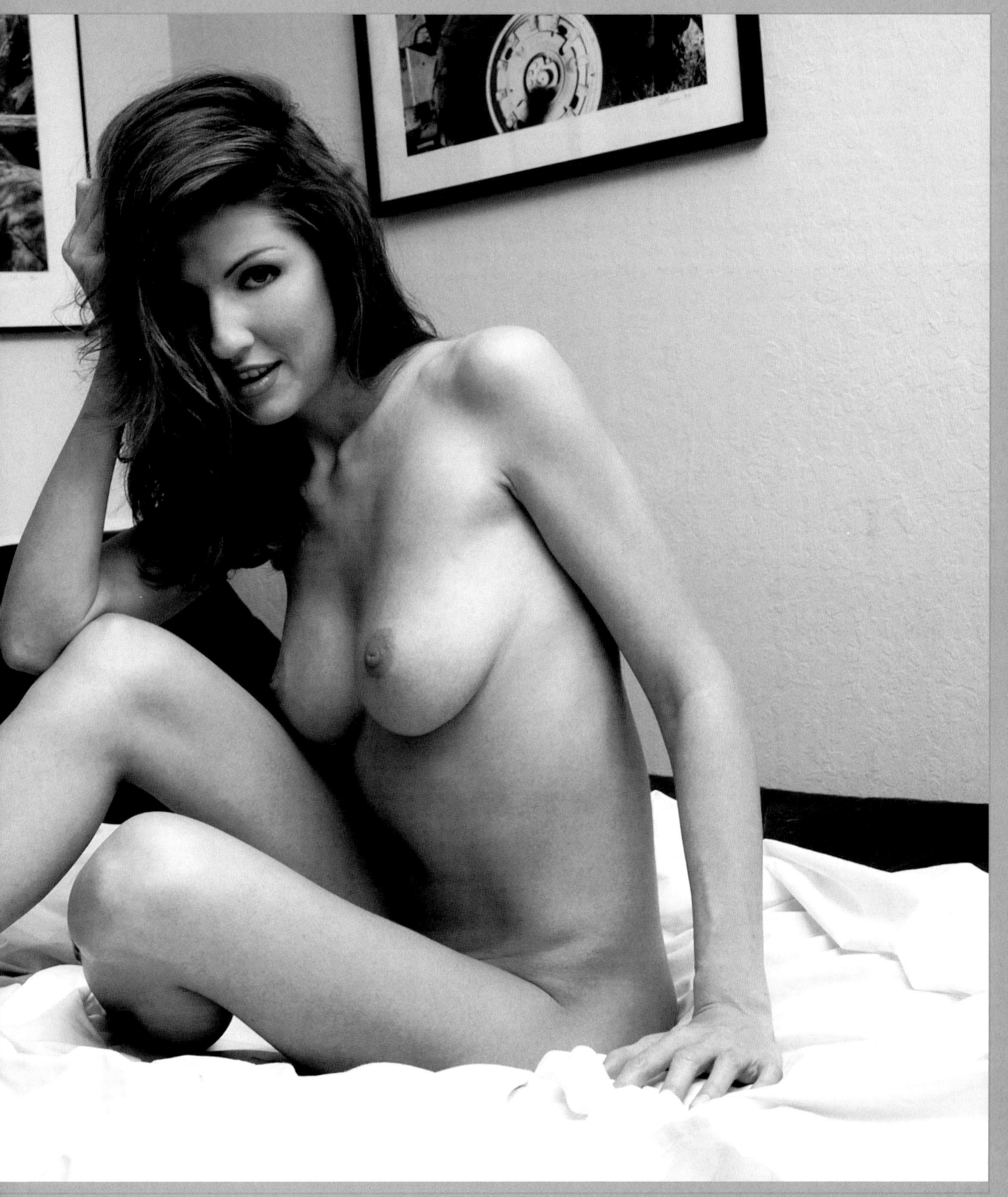

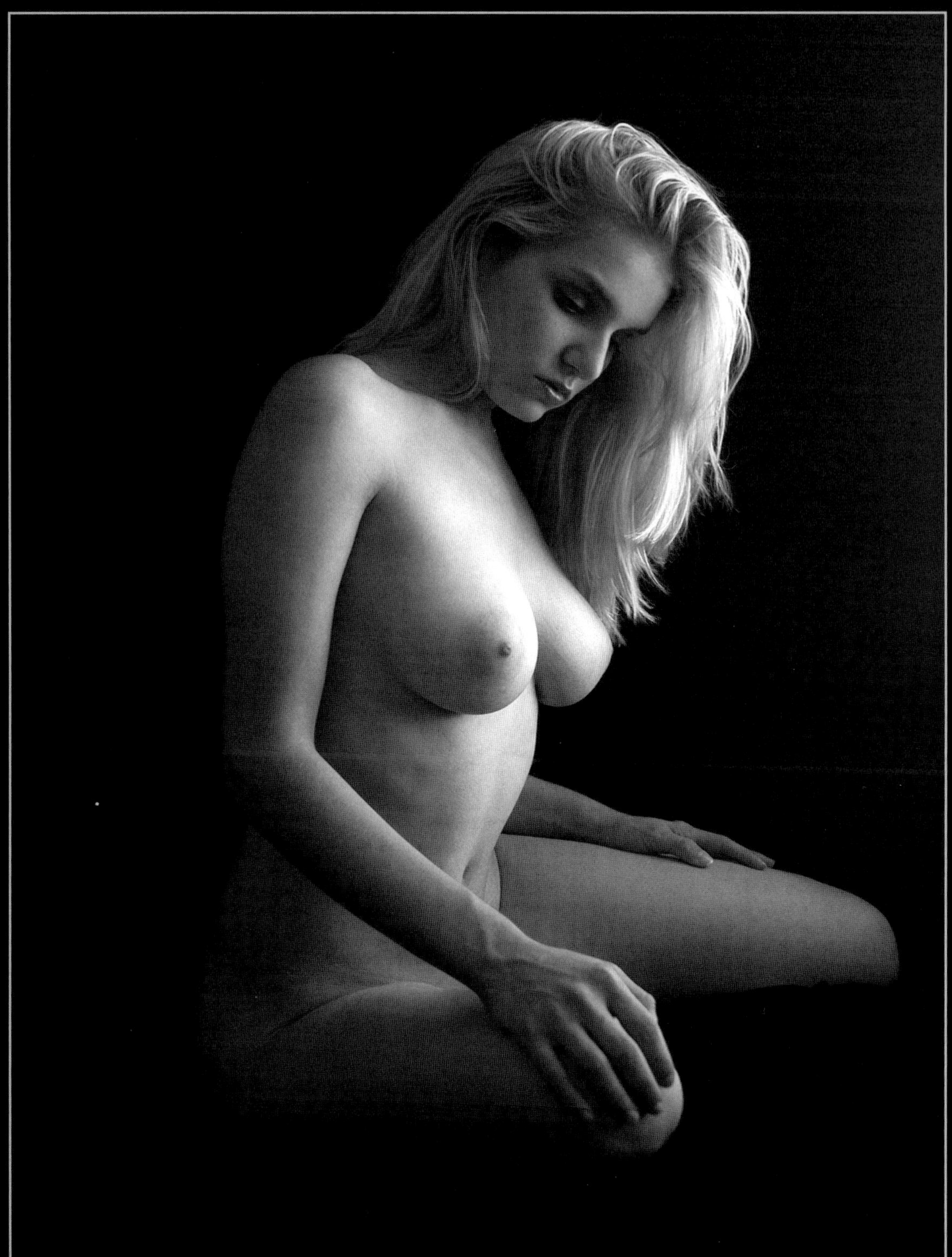

Camera: Nikon D100

Lens: Tamron 28/75

Shutter Speed: 30th Second

F-Stop: 2.8

Mode: Digital color conversion

Model: Liz

Simplicity

This image was shot in my Novato studio with natural window light. I used a tripod with an electronic release to capture this simple, elegant, and dramatic nude. A black velvet backdrop lends depth and richness to the solid background. The light is very soft and gently highlights the model's blond hair, giving the image good separation.

Pose

The pose is very casual and natural. By looking down and turning her head, the model creates a slight shadow on her profile under her hair. This helps give definition to her shoulder and breast.

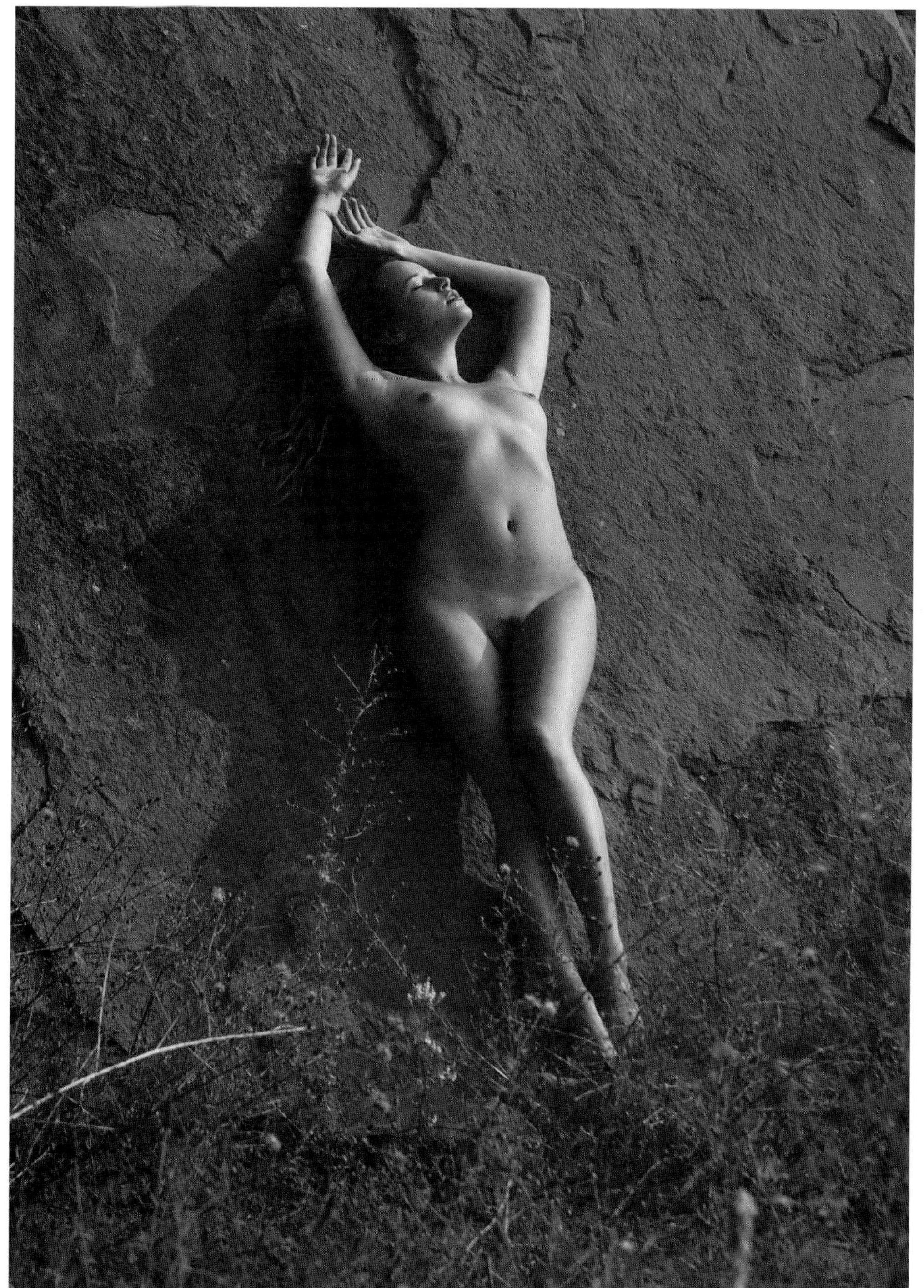

Perspective

This image was shot during a workshop in Roscoe, New York. I chose the location for the background texture of the bluestone rock in the quarry. The uneven, pitted surface provided great contrast with the model's skin.

The large slab of bluestone and foliage in the foreground also created an interesting perspective for this photo. Because the model's feet are camouflaged behind the brush, the viewer cannot immediately tell how this image was shot. It looks as if it could have been taken from above with the model lying flat on the ground. It was actually shot straight on, while the model was leaning against the stone and stretching her arms overhead.

Pose & Cropping

The pose lends to the perspective. The model looks very comfortable and relaxed, as if she is laying down. The uneven hands and bent leg also add an air of sensuality to the image.

The cropping continues to add to the mysterious perspective. The bluestone slab was very large so I was able to fill the frame with it. There are no other trees or visual clues in the background.

Conversion

Camera: Nikon D300

Lens: 24/120VR

Shutter Speed: 250th Second

F-Stop: 9.0

Mode: Digital color conversion

Model: Julie

This image was originally shot digitally in color. It works well in color, but I wanted to convert it to black and white as the composition is very strong. This image was rather difficult to convert. There are a lot of dark, subtle gray tones in the stone. Since these areas add texture to the image and define the background, I did not want them to be a solid black or muddy. Also, the model's shadow needed to separate from the background. I used a combination of Photoshop plug-ins from Nik software (**www.niksoftware.com**) to enhance all the features of the image. I used Silver Efex Pro™ to convert the image to black and white. This let me select areas of contrast and brightness to keep the background definition. Then I used Sharpener Pro 3.0™ to sharpen the image.

Setting

This image is another example of complimenting the beauty of nature with the beauty of the female form. Shot in Paradise, California, the waterfall, rock formation, and pond created an idyllic setting for a glamour photo.

Contrast

This image was originally shot in color, but converts very well to black and white because of the striking contrast. The dark rock formations set off the model's light skin. The falling water creates another light area. The pose and angles of the model's body mirror the movement of the water.

Direction

The model had to swim across the pond to get to the rocks. The roaring waterfall was also very loud. It was very hard to direct her from behind the camera. We discussed the shot in depth in advance, such as where I wanted her to sit and the types of poses I wanted to see.

Camera: Nikon D100

Lens: Nikon 70-300VR

Shutter Speed: 50th Second

F-Stop: 4.5

Mode: Digital color conversion

Model: Sarah

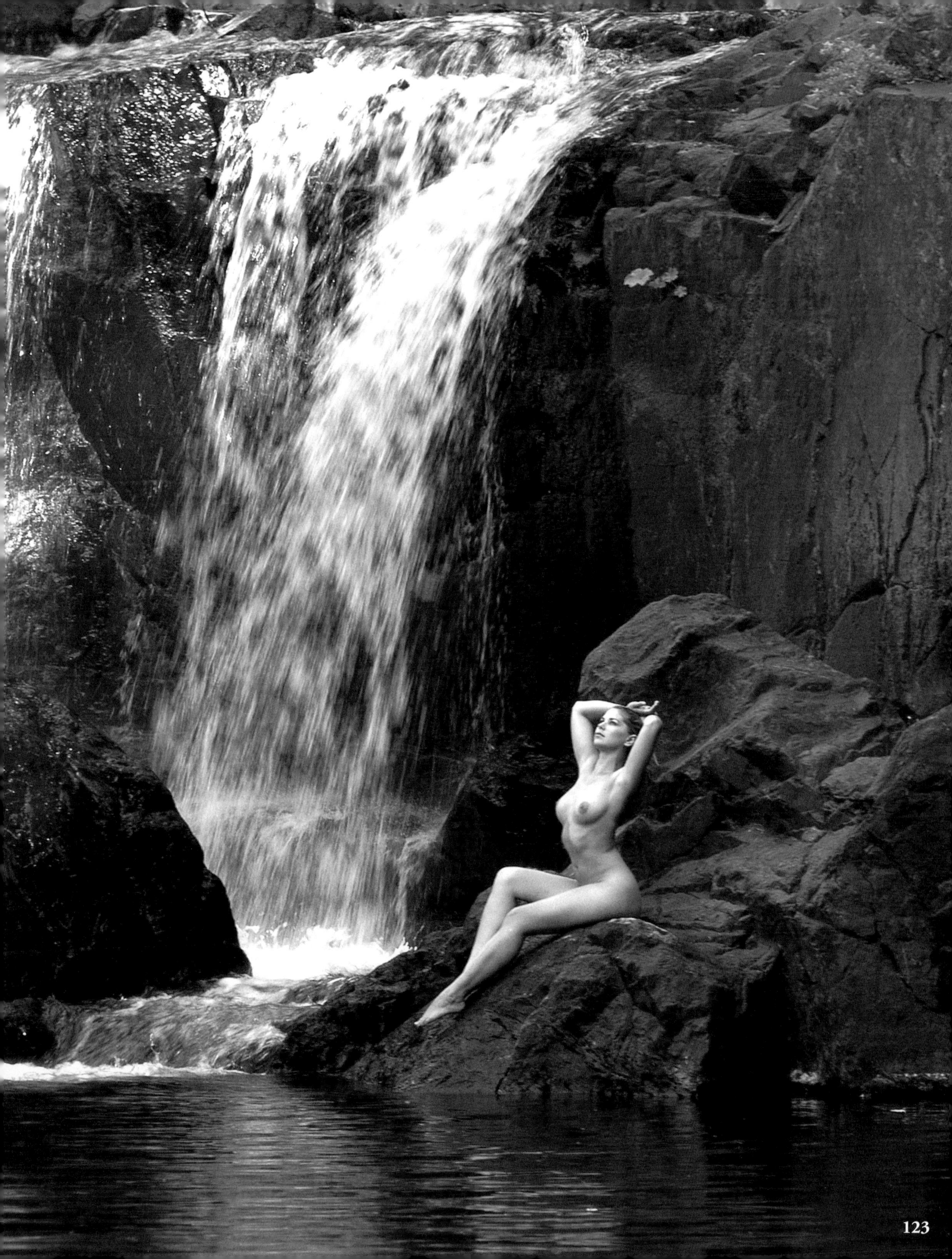

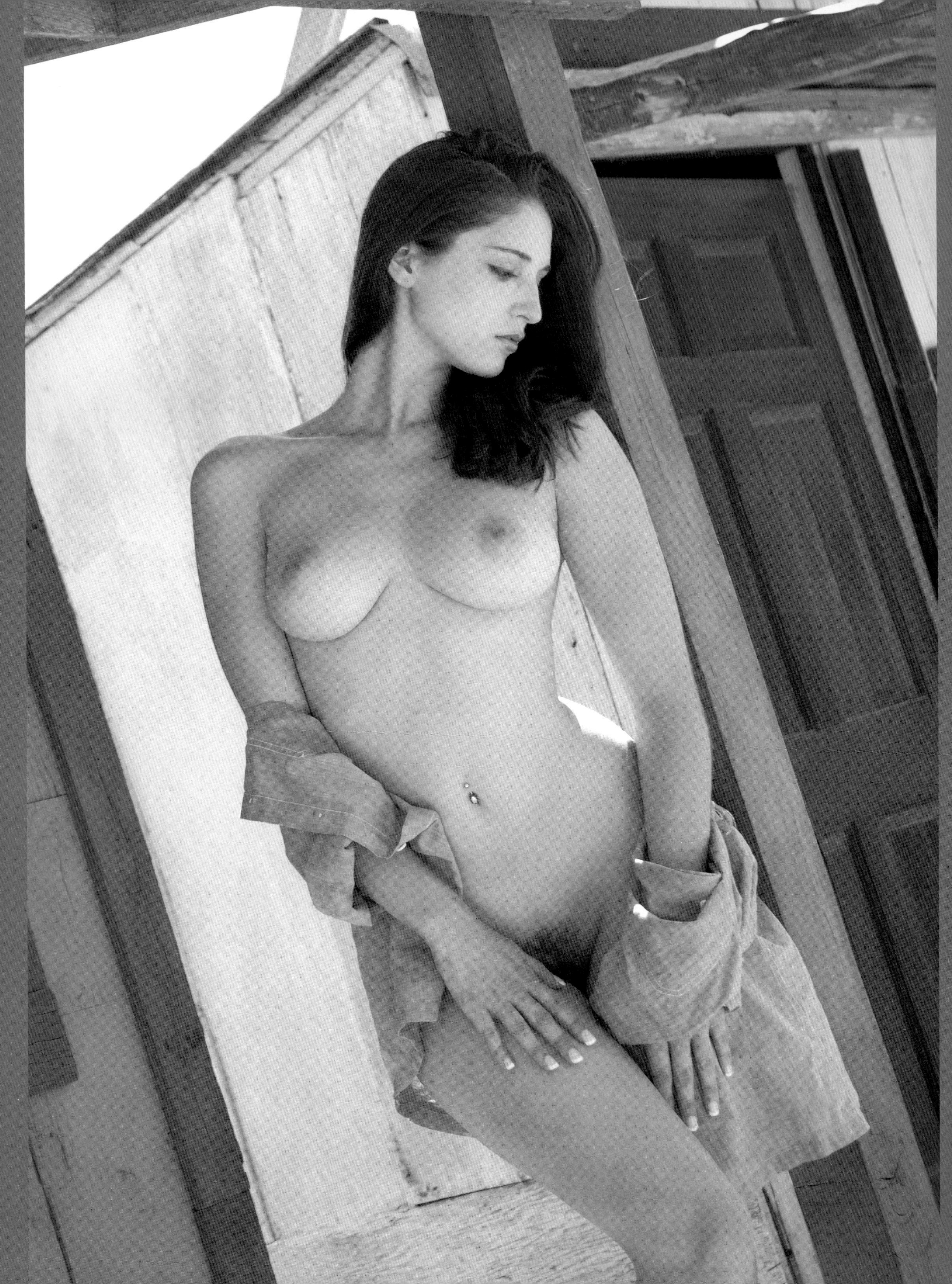

Location

This image was shot at a workshop in Tucson, Arizona in mid afternoon with natural lighting. The lighting was very even from top to bottom with few deep shadow areas. The angles of the door and wood posts are interesting. Otherwise the background is not as strong as I prefer. It does have a lot of contrast, but I like more depth and texture. I tilted the camera slightly to add some interesting facets to the angles.

Pose

The pose is what really makes this an effective image. It is very feminine with soft, beautiful angles. The bent legs helps accent the hips. The arms are natural and make the shirt work as an accent, adding an additional layer of texture. By turning her head, the model lets her hair frame her face, which showcases her beautiful profile.

Camera: Nikon D200

Lens: Nikon 24/120 VR

Shutter Speed: 125th Second

F-Stop: 5.6

Mode: Digital color conversion

Model: Carlotta

hint *The model's fingernails also play an important role in glamour photography. I prefer a French manicure, like the model in this image, as it is very soft and natural. When converting color images to black and white, red nail polish will typically convert as a dark gray tone.*

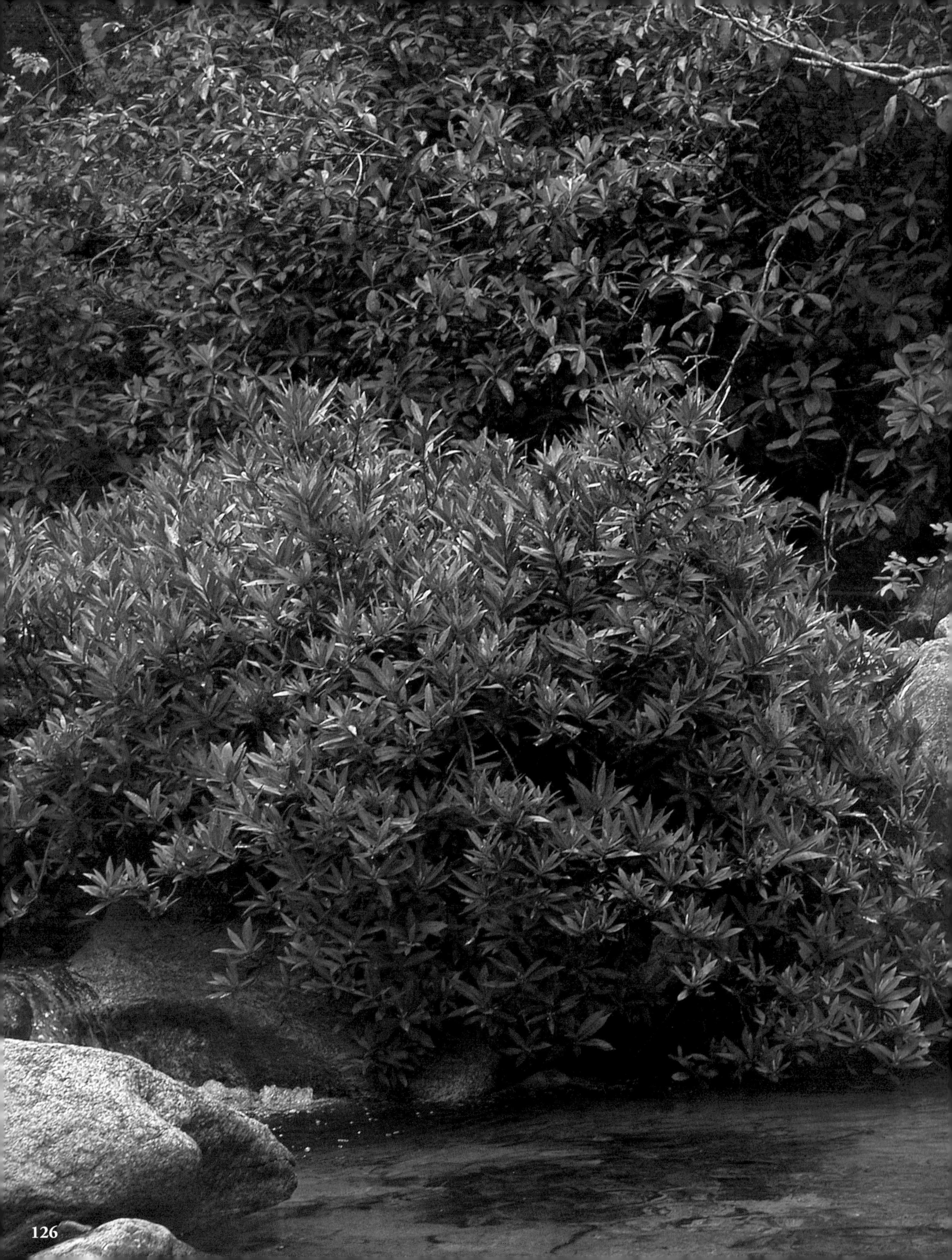

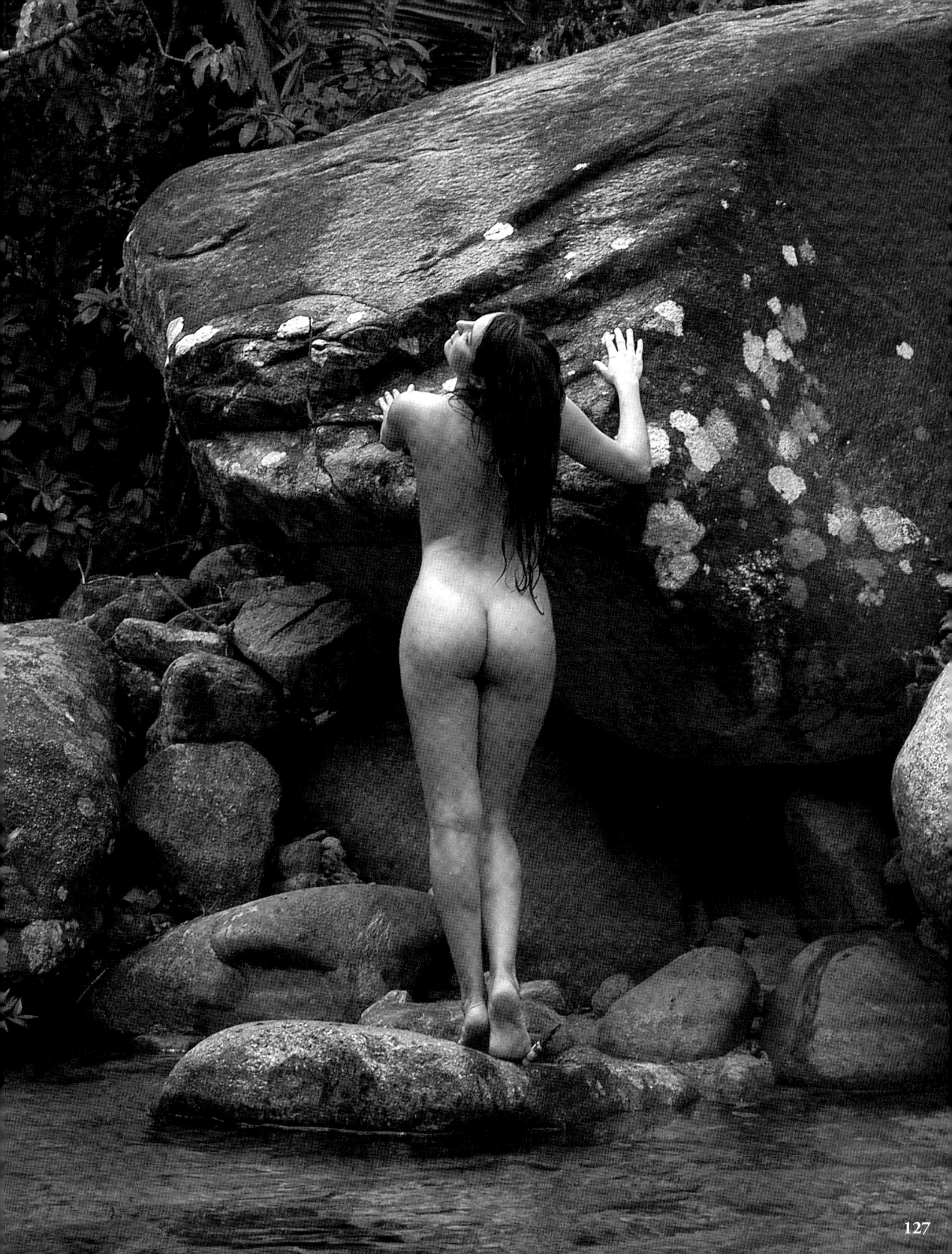

Texture

One of the most important factors in shooting outdoor black and white glamour photography is the juxtaposition of multiple layers of texture within an image. The double-spread photo on the two preceding pages is an excellent example of how to take advantage of texture and contrast in nature. The wide cropping of the image allowed me to include the foliage and water. The lichen on the stone at right adds another layer of texture. The model's fair, smooth skin against the darker, rough surface helps make the image work.

Composition

This image was shot in Puerto Vallarta, Mexico. By placing the model across the water, there is a feel of isolation that gives the image a voyeuristic quality. The horizontal shot places her to the left side of the composition, drawing the eye toward her. Posing with her back to the camera creates the sensation that she is deep in thought, that the camera has captured a private moment.

Pose

The focal point of this image is female sensuality. With her head titled back, the sun naturally lights her face. The slight bend to her right legs creates a slight shadow and helps give an artistic quality to the image.

Camera: Nikon D100

Lens: Tamron 28/75

Shutter Speed: 320th Second

F-Stop: 6.3

Mode: Digital color conversion

Model: Elizabeth

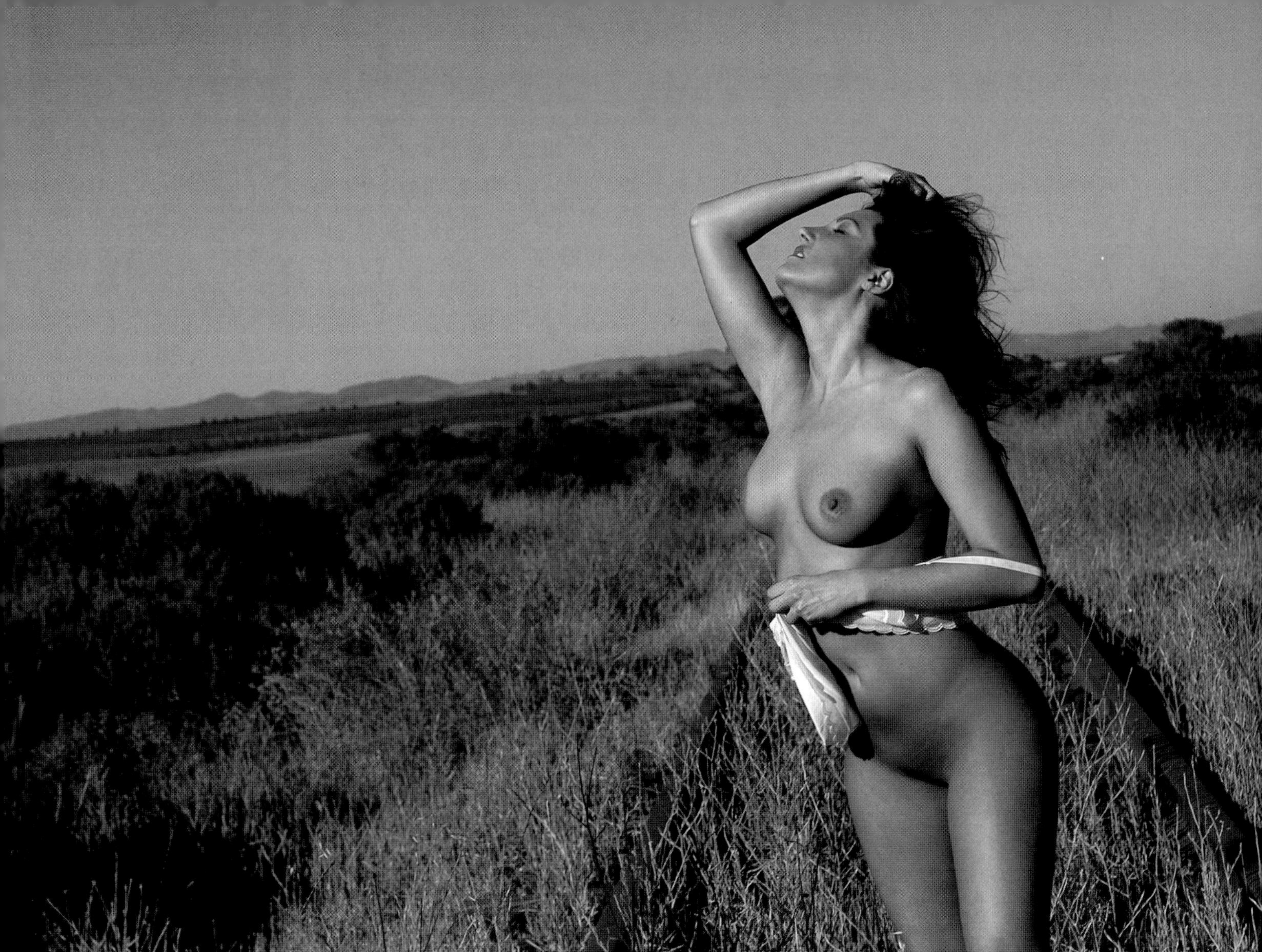

Pose

This image was shot in Sonoma in the early evening. The sinking sun casts strong shadows on the landscape and the model. I had the model lift her head so the sun would fill her face without casting shadows under her eyes.

Landscape

This image is another example of shooting horizontally in order to capture more of the landscape and set the tone of an image. The low brush provided good texture for the foreground. The photo has a lot of depth, which gives the image the feeling of wide open space. The model is positioned between overgrown railroad tracks that recede to the horizon, further underlying the vastness of the area.

Horizon Line

When shooting in an area with a clearly defined horizon line, watch where the horizon intersects the model. The model's head should be completely above the horizon to be framed in the sky. I prefer not to have the model split in half by the horizon. For example, I like to have the top third of her body at or above the horizon line.

The horizon might not always be completely straight. In this image it angles down, which I feel adds interest and movement. However, you can easily straighten a horizon line in Adobe Photoshop®, so don't let an imperfect horizon line stop you from choosing an otherwise excellent location.

Camera: Nikon D100

Lens: Tamron 28/75

Shutter Speed: 2000th Second

F-Stop: 5.6

Mode: Digital color conversion

Model: Elizabeth

Setting

This image is an example of outdoor glamour photography in a much more urban-looking area than I often use. It was shot in the Marin Headlands, within old military bunkers. I chose the location for the textures in the background. This included the graffiti, which was yellow, turquoise, and white. (You can see another photo taken during this session in my *Outdoor Glamour Photography: The Complete Digital Guide to Taking Successful Outdoor Glamour Photographs* book). Converting the image to black and white added a whole new feeling to the image. With the background colors muted to subtle shades of gray, the directional sunlight became much more vivid. The sunlight lit the model face and chest and created a beautiful shadow pattern on the stairs. The focal point of the image shifted more to the light and the model in black and white.

Pose

The model created this pose, essentially balancing on her arm and toes, and arching toward the light. Try new creating unique poses by asking the model to "do something different" and then fine tune her pose as needed paying close attention to the hands, angles and lighting patterns.

Camera: Nikon D200

Lens: Nikon 24/120VR

Shutter Speed: 250th Second

F-Stop: 8.0

Mode: Digital color conversion

Model: Stephanie

tip

*Color seems integral to some images, such as this photo. It had very strong colors in the graffiti, and this can be difficult to visualize in black and white. Try converting it and the results may be very unexpected. I like using the Nik Silver Efex Pro™ (***www.niksoftware.com***) plug-in in Adobe Photoshop. It has some excellent presets that can quickly change the exposure or tone an image.*

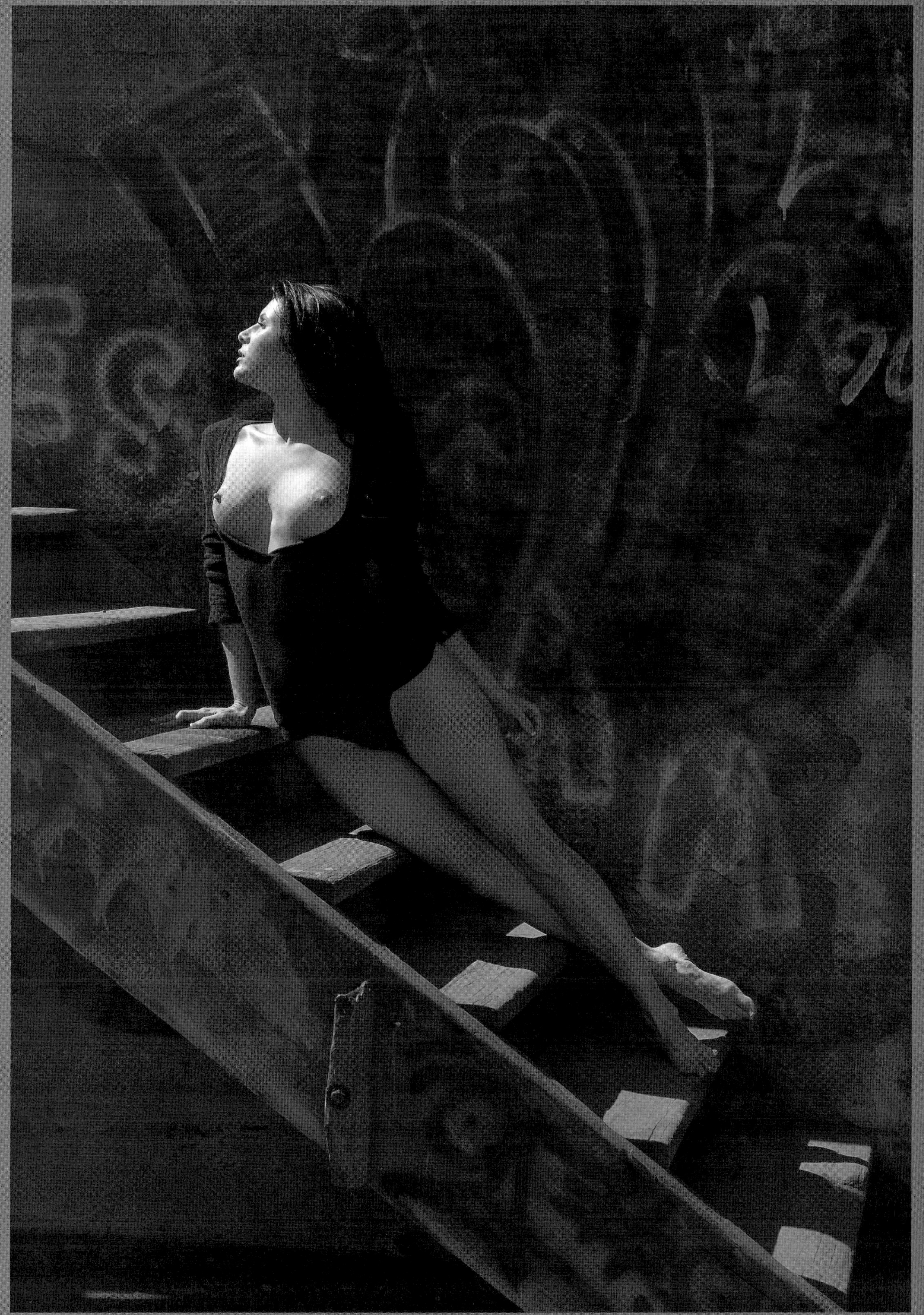

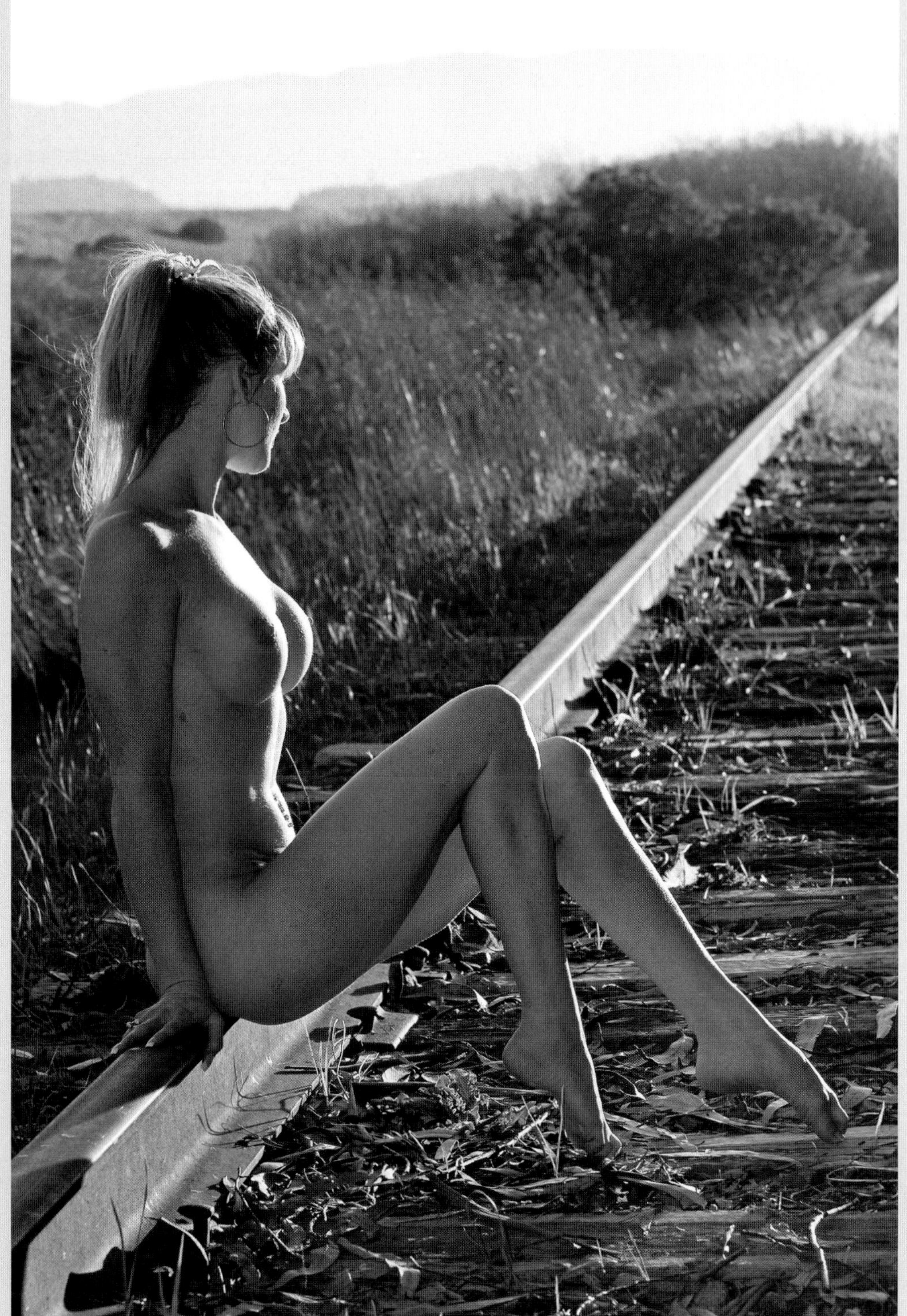

Camera: Nikon D200

Lens: Nikon 24/120VR

Shutter Speed: 125th Second

F-Stop: 7.1

Mode: Digital color conversion

Model: Elise

Seated Poses

The images on pages 132 and 133 are examples of seated poses in outdoor glamour photography. There are some common factors required to make seated poses look good.

First, weight distribution is key. It is helpful if the model can lean against something, such as the beam at right. No matter how thin or beautifully proportioned a woman is, putting all of her weight on her bottom will cause it to expand in width.

Second, point the toes. By rasing the foot even slightly, the leg muscles will flex and tighten, making the legs look longer and leaner. High heel shoes will also do this, but I prefer bare feet becuase it is much more natural.

Balance

In the image at left, the model has balanced almost all her weight on her hands. This is a much more dramatic image. Although the setting is peaceful, we feel as if the model is waiting for something. This is reinforced by the railroads tracks receding into the distance and the lighting. The setting sun rims the model's face and the edge of her body. It makes the viewer wonder what the model is looking at.

Relaxation

The image on page 133 has a much more relaxed feeling. Shot in the early morning with northern light, the lighting is very even with a much gentler shadow. The model has raised her feet enough to accent the legs, but still gives a feeling of relaxation. Her expression is also very contemplative in this implied nude.

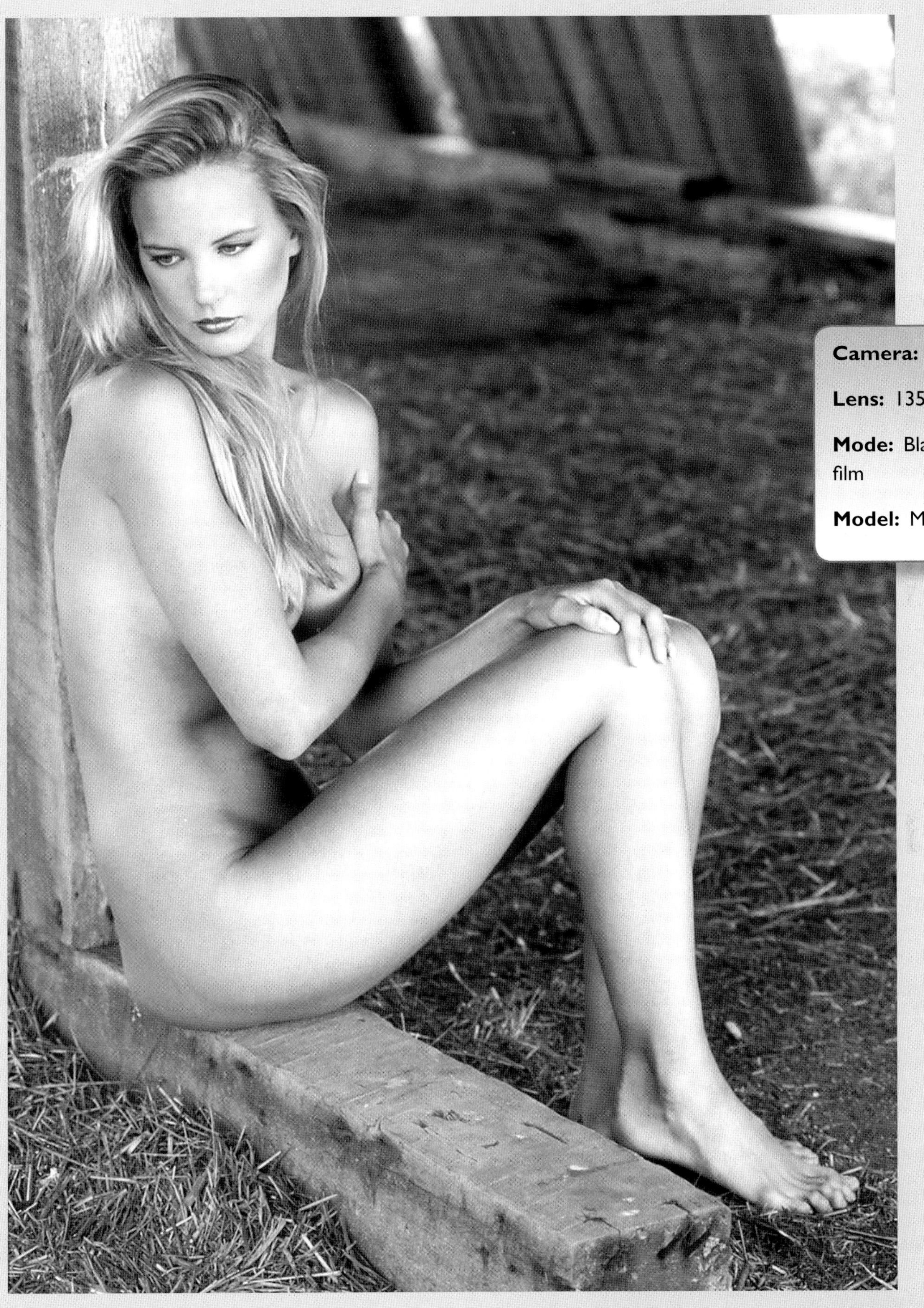

Camera: Pentax

Lens: 135 mm

Mode: Black and white film

Model: Michelle

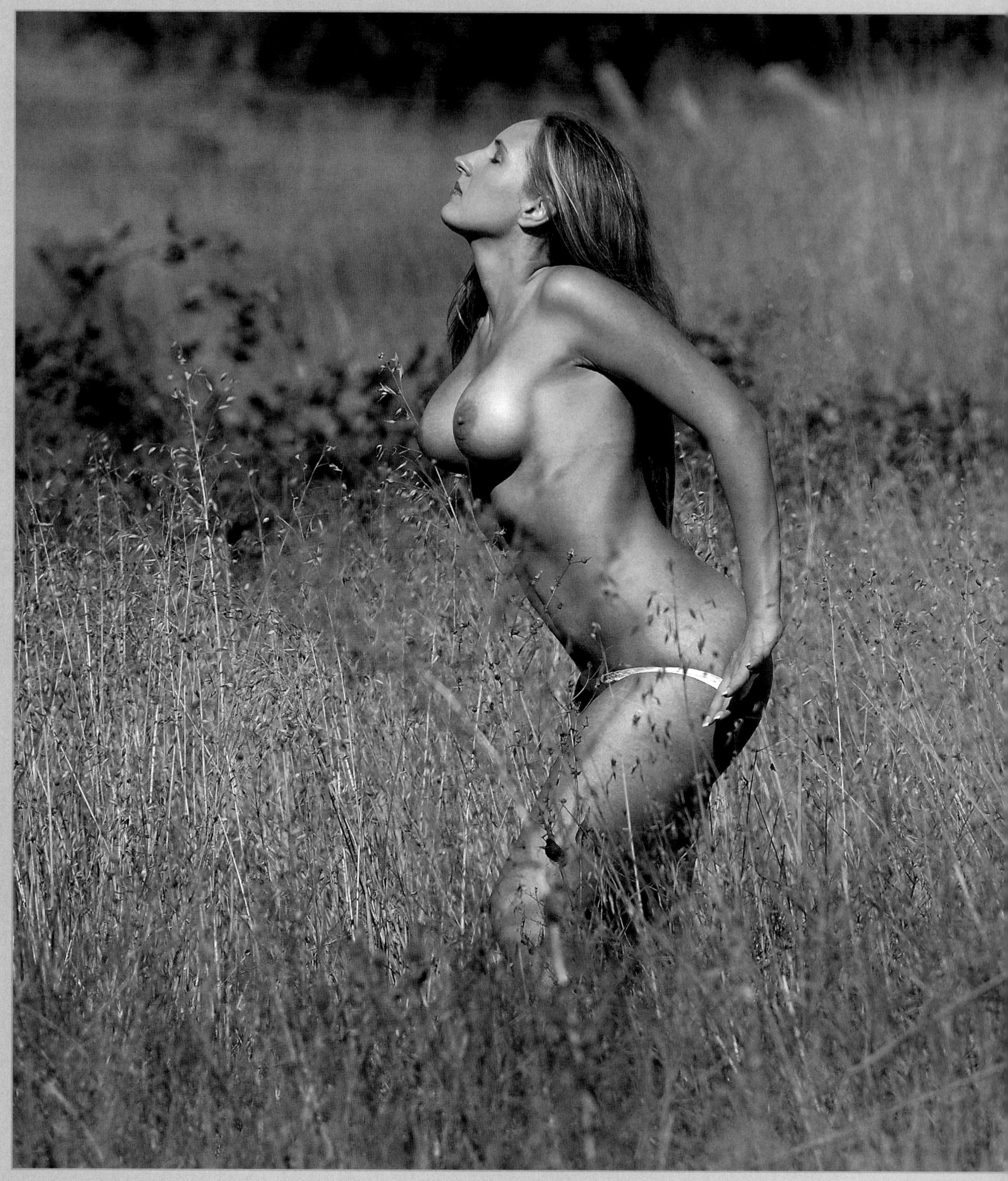

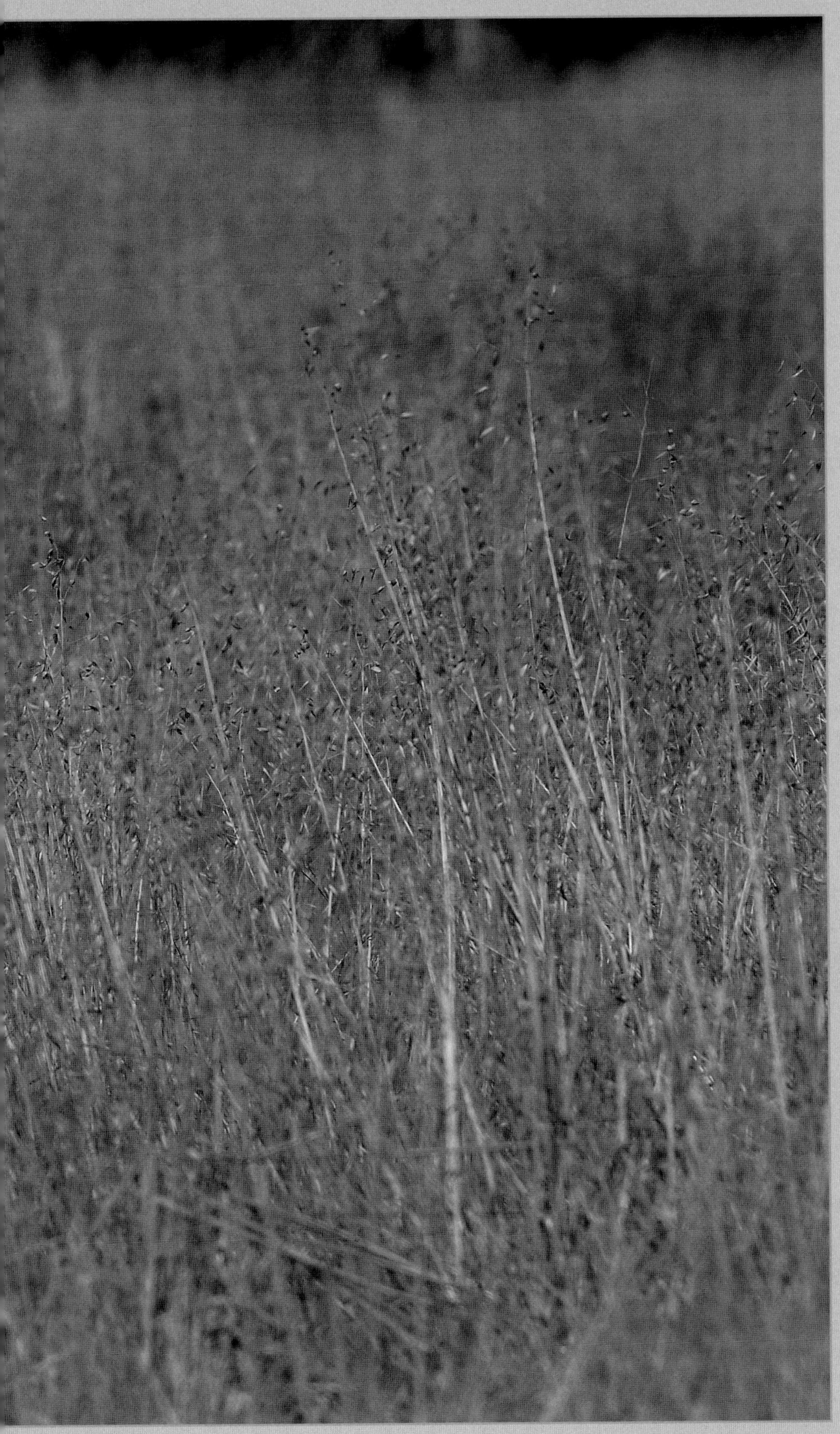

Texture

This image was shot in the late afternoon in natural sunlight. The sun was behind the camera. Originally shot in color, the wide variety of textures are what make this image work in black and white. The abundant grasses create beautiful details in the foreground and recede into shadow patterns in the background. The variety of gray tones in the textures add interest to the image.

Contrast

In addition to the contrasting tones, the smooth skin of the model really contrasts against the background. This makes the model stand out. The deep areas of shadow under her breasts and on her back also add definition to the image.

Clothing

The model has small white panties, which may not be immediately noticeable to the viewer but define the image. They give the model something to do with her hands and help emphasize the bend in the legs.

Camera: Nikon D200

Lens: 70/300 VR

Shutter Speed: 500th Second

F-Stop: 7.1

Mode: Digital color conversion

Model: Jordanna

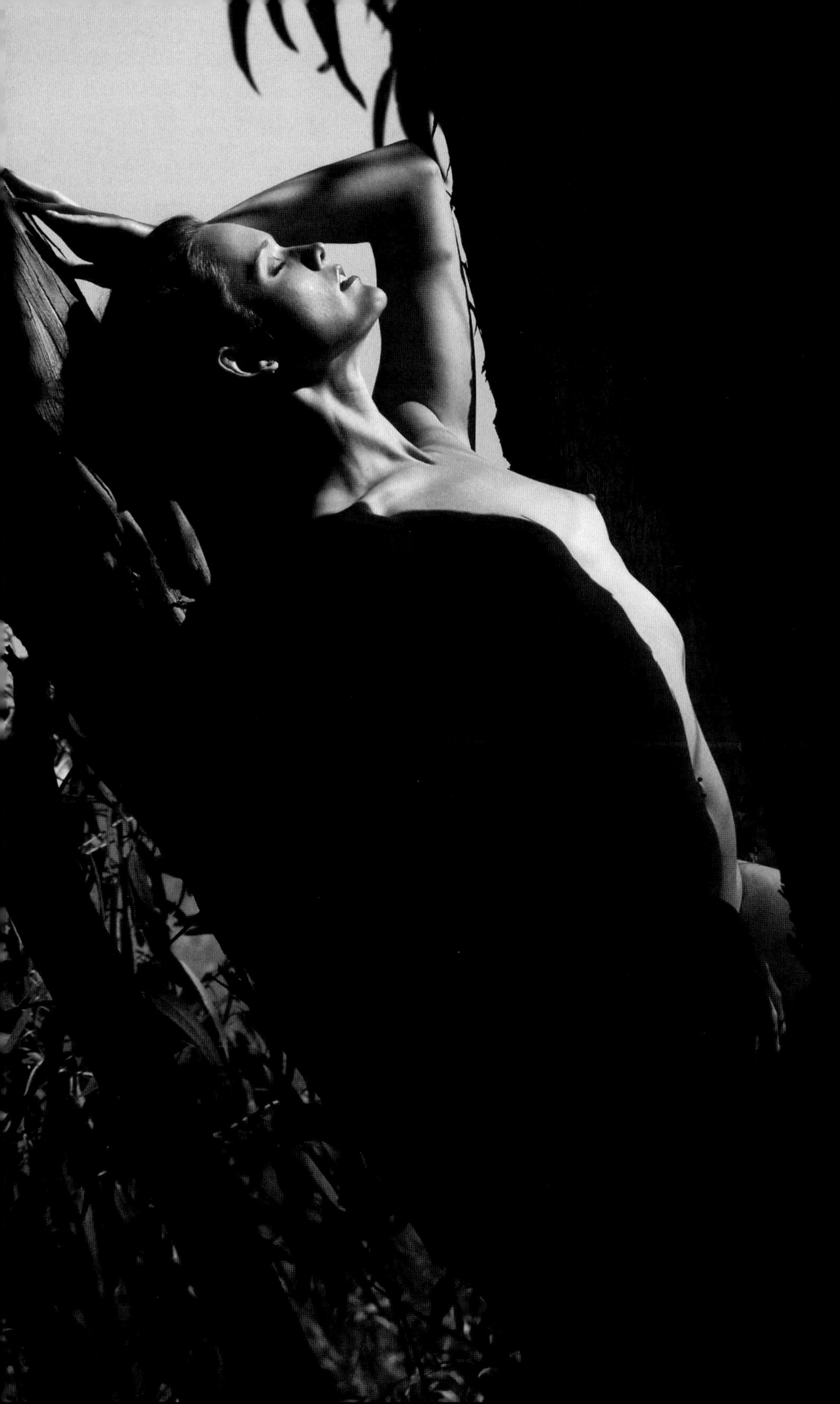

Black and white

Areas of high contrast often make highly effective black and white images. This is fairly easy to do in a studio but here is an example of creating rich contrast outdoors. Bright sunlight and deep shadows are the most important elements. In this image, the sun was coming between the eucalyptus trees so I positioned the model in the light.

Pose

It is important to create a pose suitable for the lighting situation. Since the light was dramatic, I asked the model to create a more dramatic pose. Her raised head allowed the sun to light her face fully while her raised arm creates another interesting angle.

Camera: Nikon D200

Lens: 24/120 VR

Shutter Speed: 500th Second

F-Stop: 6.3

Mode: Digital color conversion

Model: Rebecca

Creating Contrast

This image was shot in Sonoma in the late afternoon. I choose the tree for the beautiful texture of the bark. However, there wasn't enough natural contrast to create an effective black and white photo. The sheer black top added a solid area of contrast for the image. It creates a needed focal point. Black works well in this situation because the bark was fairly light.

Fabric

Look for fabrics that interact with the light or the model. Silky, reflective fabric work well. Soft sheer fabric is another good choice. Note the texture the sheer fabric adds to the model's torso.

Cropping

I like the tight cropping of this image. However, the model's finger is cut off on her left hand; I could have pulled back slight to avoid that.

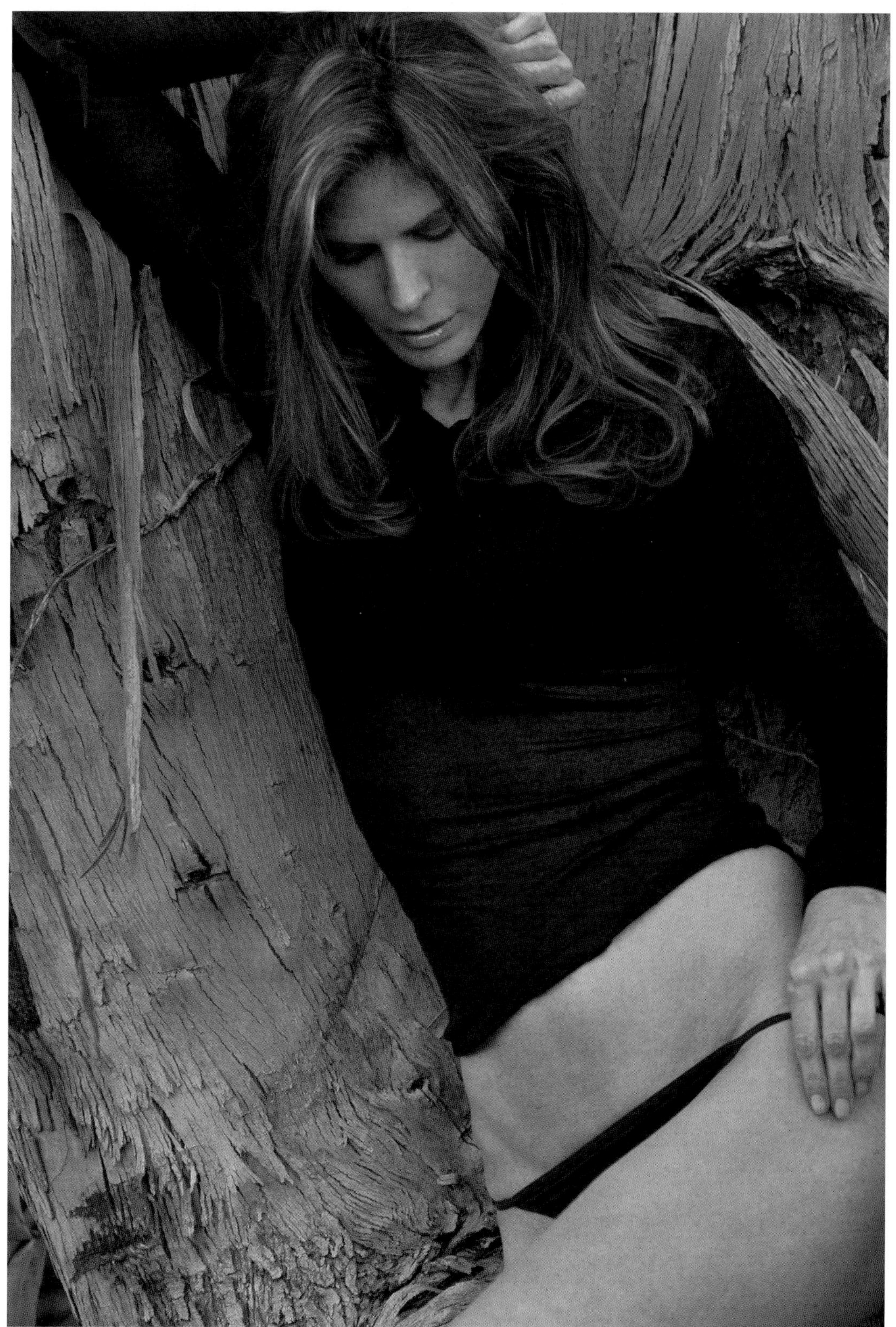

Camera: Nikon D300

Lens: Nikon 70/300VR

Shutter Speed: 125th Second

F-Stop: 7.1

Mode: Digital color conversion

Model: Franceska

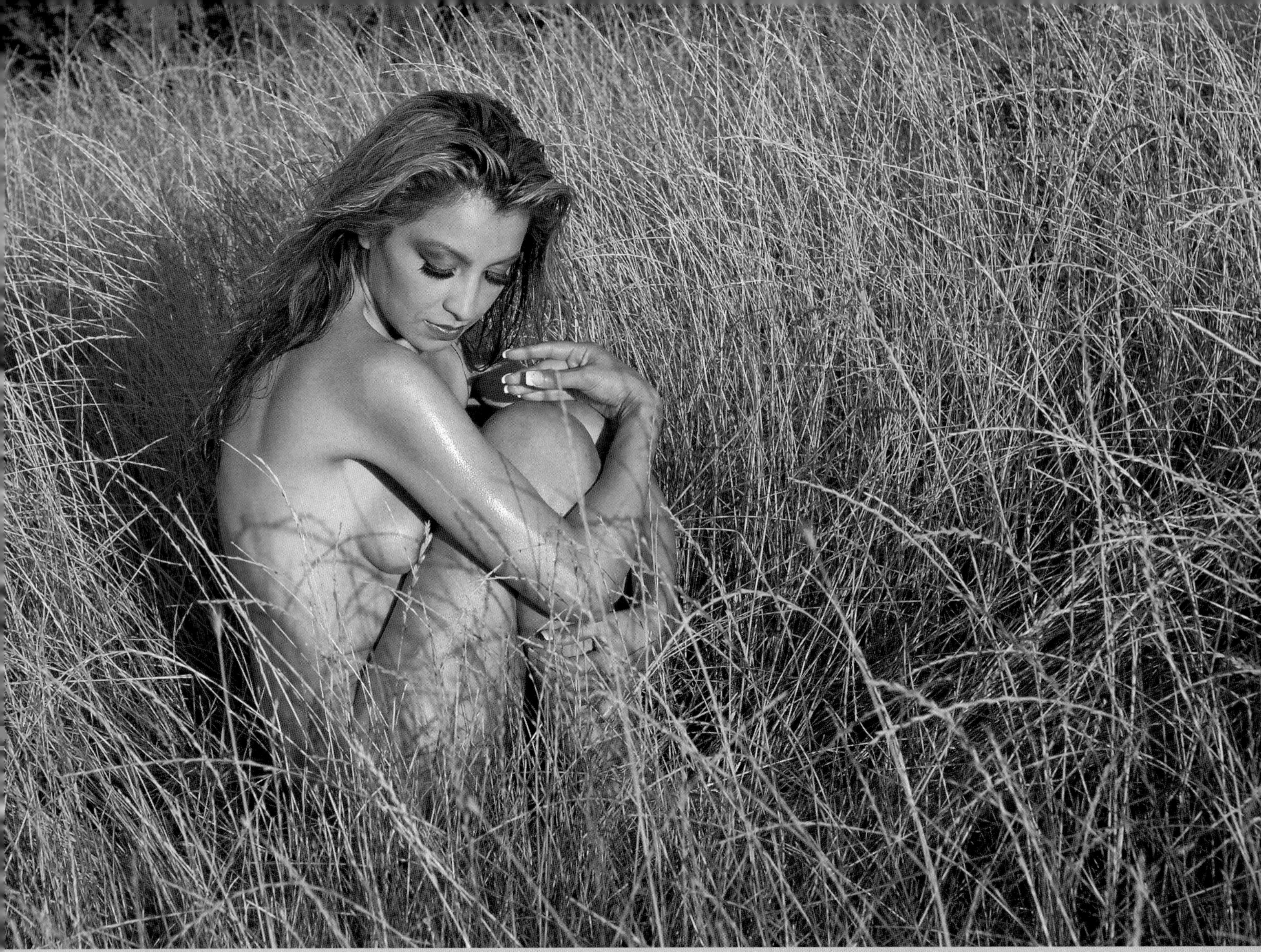

Framing

I chose this location for the abundance of natural texture. The tall grasses work well with this seated pose, framing the model. It has texture, depth and motion but in a very simple, natural setting.

Pose

The pose is very soft and introspective. She is looking down as if lost in thought. The one part of the pose I do not like is her right hand. The angle of the wrist is too severe.

Water

The model had honey blond hair very close in color to the grasses. In order to change the tone, I had her wet her hair. This darkens her hair and increases the contrast. She also rubbed a little water on her skin. This makes it glisten naturally.

Camera: Nikon D200

Lens: Tamron 28/75

Shutter Speed: 250th Second

F-Stop: 9.0

Mode: Digital color conversion

Model: Giselle

Location

This image was shot in the late afternoon in Sonoma. The model posed on an old wooden bridge in the late afternoon sunlight. The light is very dramatic and creates interesting shadow patterns.

Jewelry

The necklace adds another area of interest to the photo. The beads are multifaceted so it caught the light well, creating many tones. The light was also very solid on the chest area, so the necklace adds some color there and breaks up the torso.

Cropping

The original version of this photo was shot as a horizontal image and encompasses the model's right leg. I typically avoid cutting off appendages when shooting, so the cropping was done in Photoshop to create a vertical image.

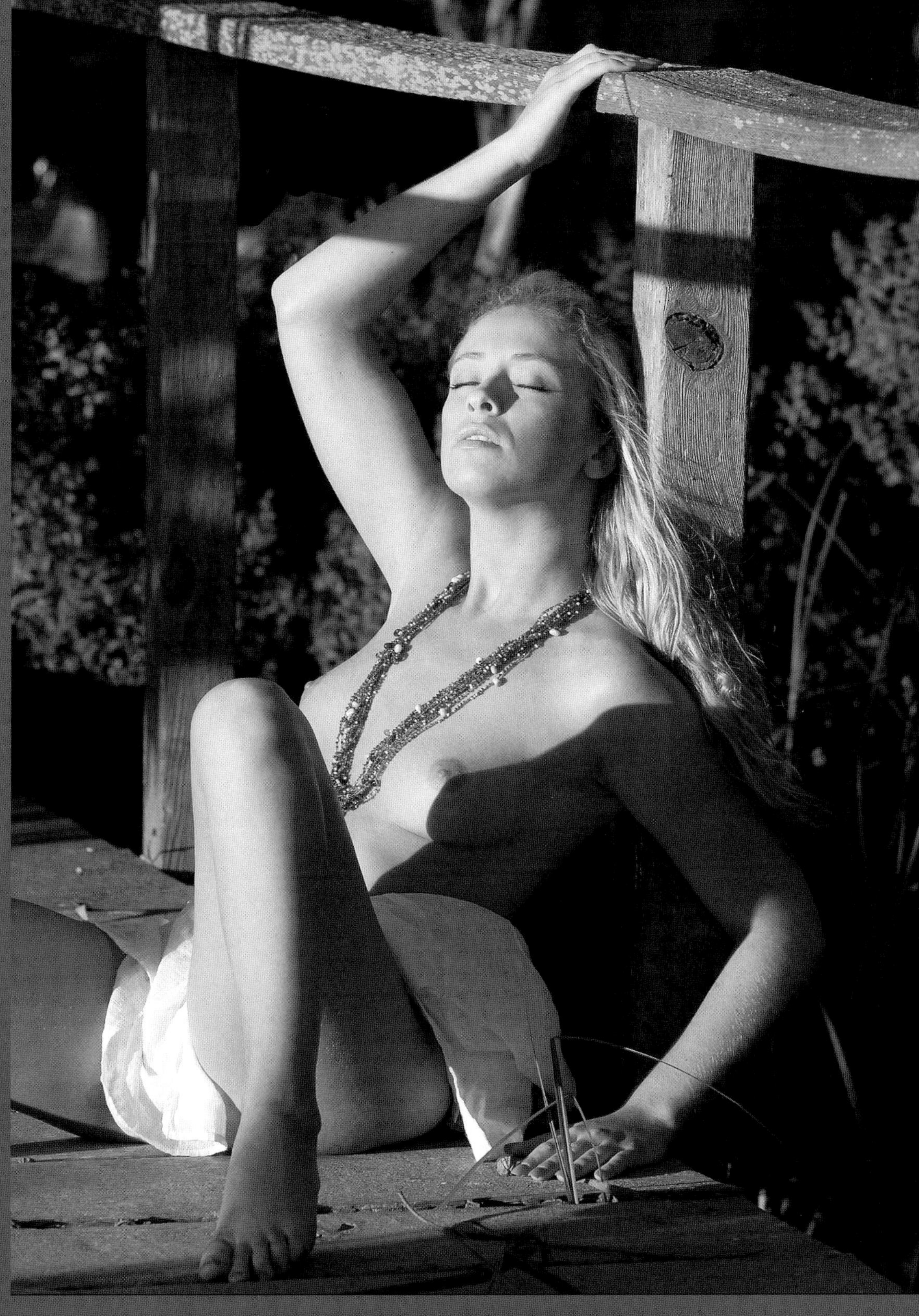

Camera: Nikon D200

Lens: Nikon 70/300 VR

Shutter Speed: 250th Second

F-Stop: 8.0

Mode: Digital color conversion

Model: Cristal

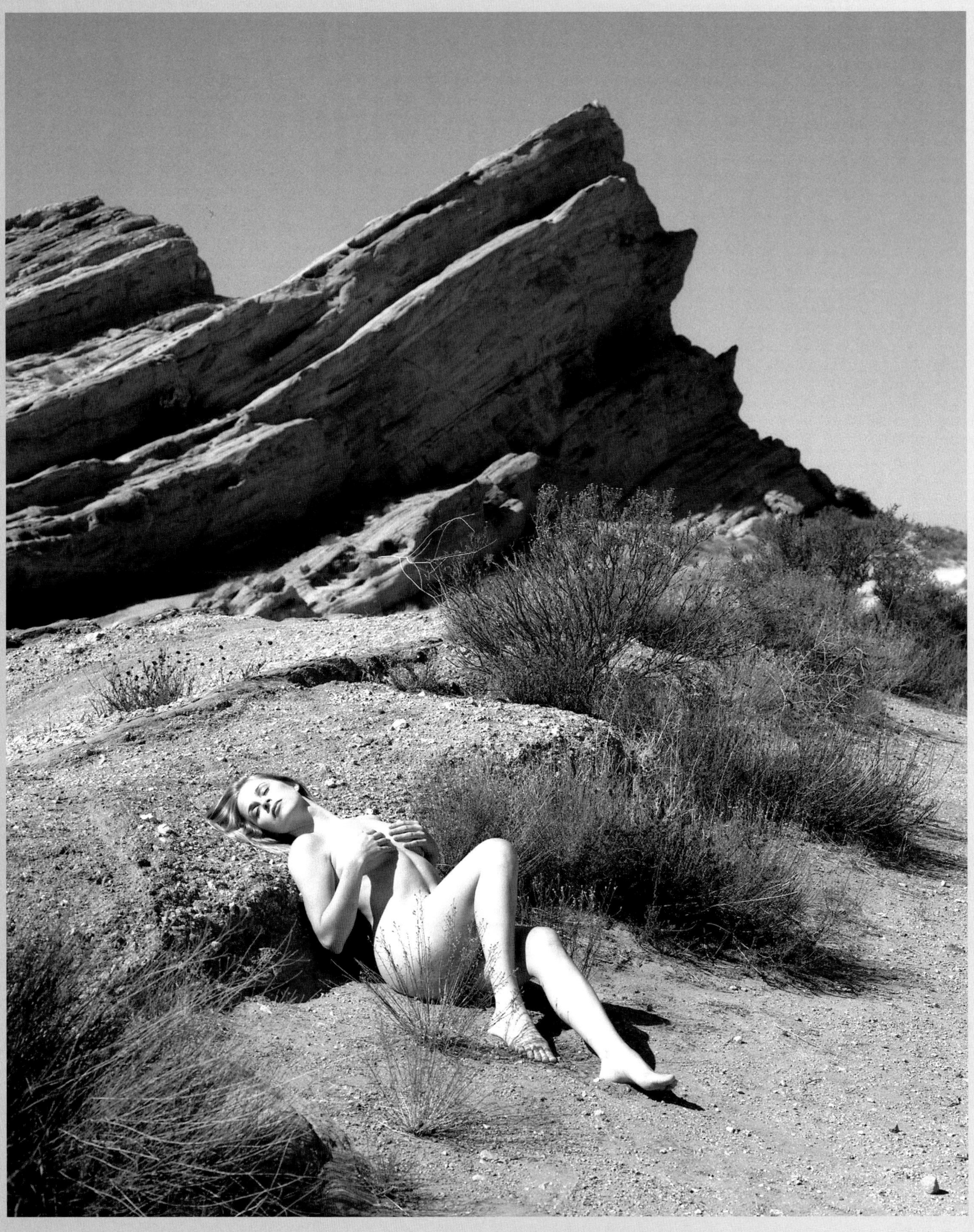

Angles

This image was shot in Southern California at Vasquez Rocks, a popular location for movies and television. This image was created to parallel the angles of nature and the angles of the female form. I liked the jutting rock formation in the background because of the striations of the stone and the interesting perspective. It also created a strong dark area which contrasted well with the model's lighter skin. The sand in the foreground lends more even tones to the image, while the dark grasses provide another area of darkness for continuity.

Pose

The pose was created to highlight the surroundings. The model is reclining but her torso is elevated to mirror the angle of the rocks. Her bent legs create shadows for definition, as well as another sharp angle in the image.

Camera: Pentax 67

Lens: 135 mm

F-Stop: 16.0

Mode: Black and white film

Model: Teresa

hint

Look for natural areas with strong structures and create a pose that mirrors the structure. The composition will be very harmonious.

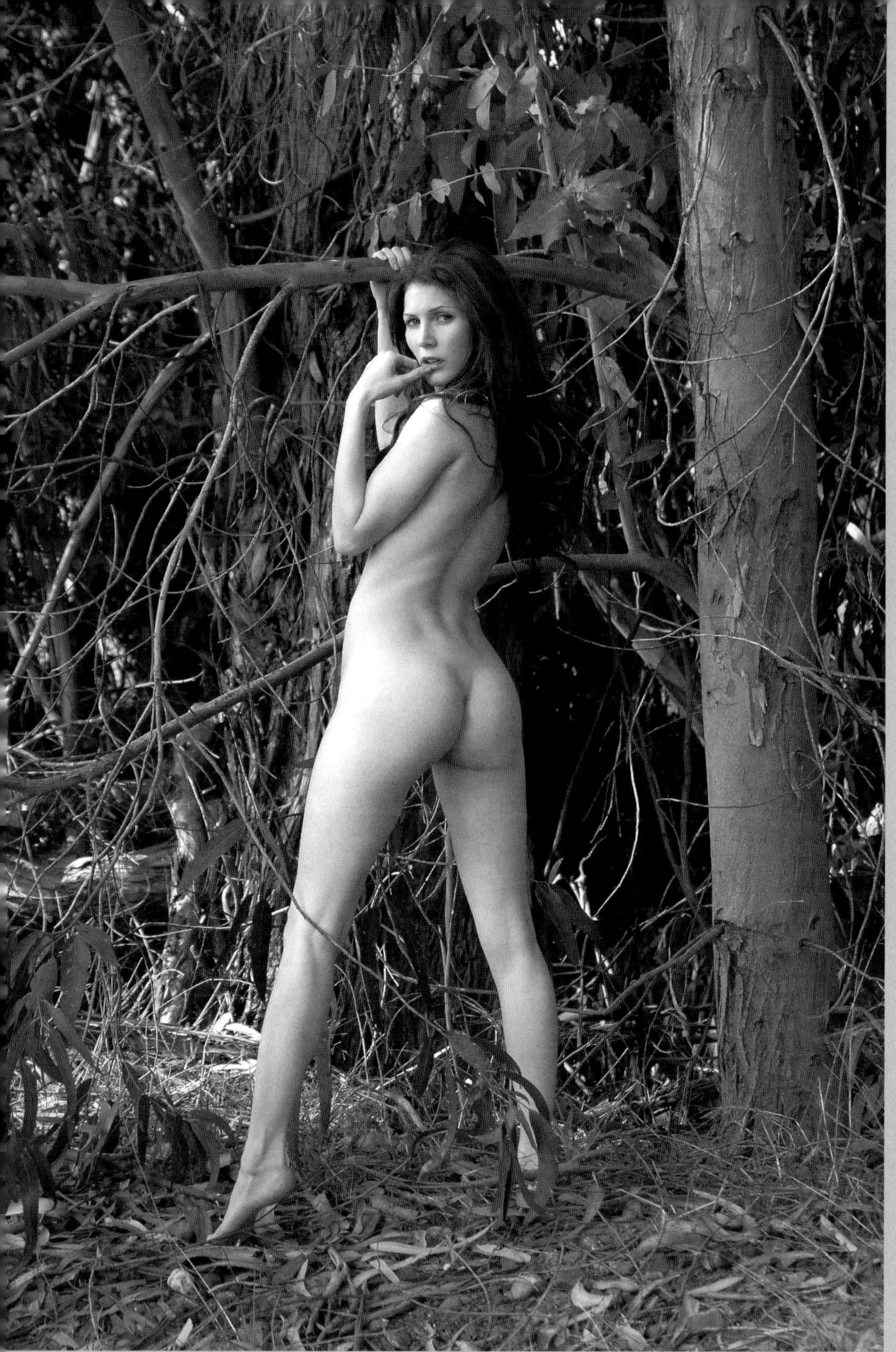

Setting

This image, shot in Sonoma County, shows the model in a groove of trees. The location provided a lot of texture in the bark, leaves, and other foliage. It also provided excellent contrast for the model. The darker shadows and leaves set off her fair skin.

Expression

The model's pose and expression work well together. She is turning as if captured before doing something and her expression is very quizzical, giving the image a somewhat candid feel. The tree limb was a good prop as it gave the model something to hold onto and helped her balance as she turned.

The end

When shooting a nude standing image from behind, have the model pose on the balls of her feet. This not only elongates the leg, it also lifts the buttocks.

Camera: Nikon D200

Lens: Nikon 24/120

Shutter Speed: 125th Second

F-Stop: 5.6

Mode: Digital color conversion

Model: Stephanie

Bill Lemon Workshops

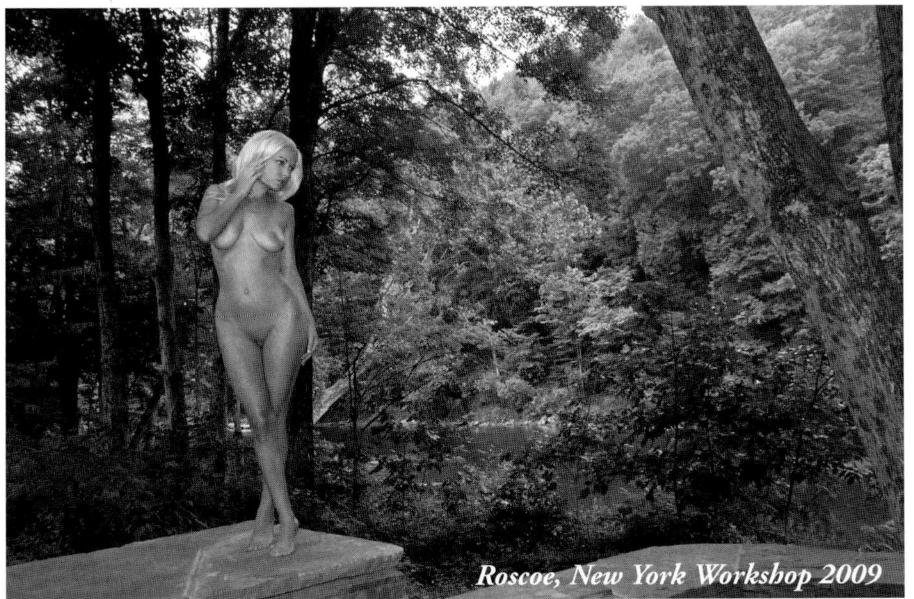

Roscoe, New York Workshop 2009

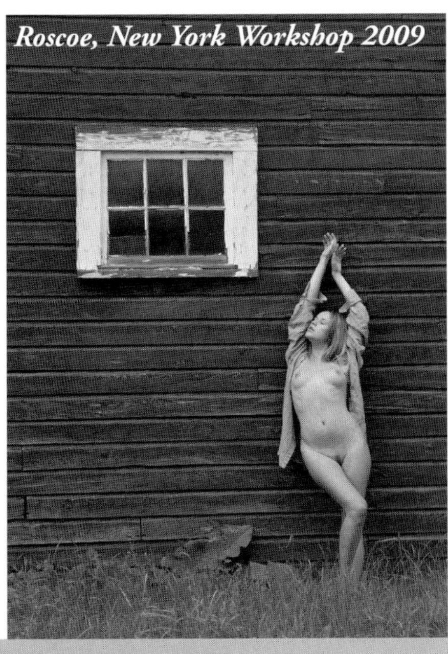

Roscoe, New York Workshop 2009

I've been conducting photography workshops since 1992, first in northern California and then around the country. I've tried different formats, and in 2004 my friend Spencer Colquhoun and I came up with the format that I use today.

I accept eight photographers and bring five professional models. The workshop consists of five shooting sessions, two in the morning and three in the afternoon. During this time, I take four photographers and one model and teach for an hour. The other four photographers and four models go shoot in individual model/photographer groups for an hour. We rotate this shooting schedule both days so that each photographer gets to shoot one-on-one with all the models. This arrangement has worked extremely well and my workshops sell out quite fast each year.

I also work in various scenic locations across the United States. Photographers and models alike enjoy working with the varied landscapes. The help of property owners around the country has made this possible. The images on this page were taken at recent workshops.

You can find the dates and locations of upcoming workshops online at:

- **www.billlemon.com**
- **www.billlemonworkshops.com**

I hope to see you at one of them.

— *Bill Lemon*

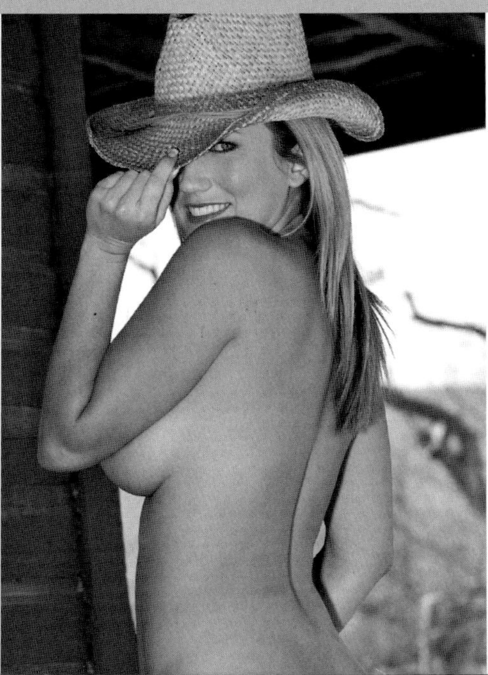

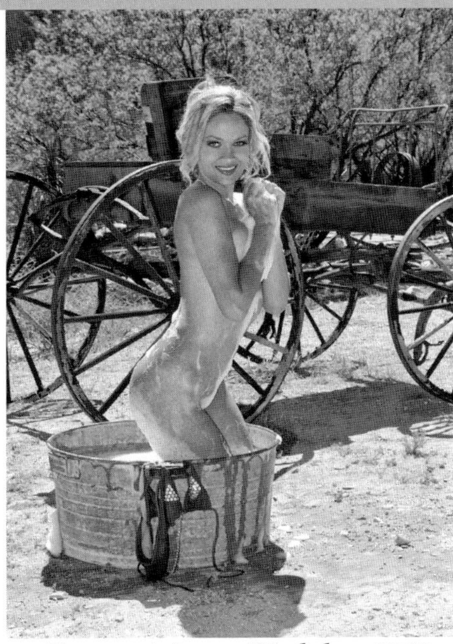

Tucson, Arizona Workshop 2009

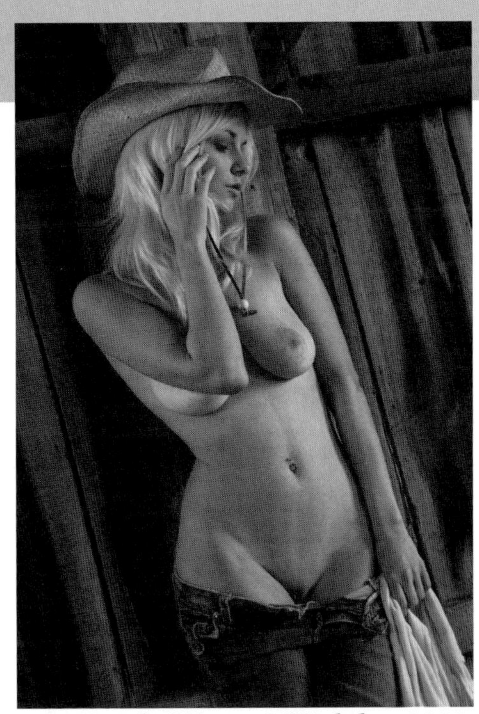

St. Joseph, Missouri Workshop 2008

Index